T0339834

Global Imbalances, Financial Crises, and Central Bank Policies

Global Imbalances, Financial Crises, and Central Bank Policies

Andreas Steiner

University of Osnabrück and Ifo Institute Munich, Germany

AMSTERDAM • BOSTON • HEIDELBERG • LONDON • NEW YORK
OXFORD • PARIS • SAN DIEGO • SAN FRANCISCO • SINGAPORE
SYDNEY • TOKYO
Academic Press is an imprint of Elsevier

Academic Press is an imprint of Elsevier
125 London Wall, London EC2Y 5AS, United Kingdom
525 B Street, Suite 1800, San Diego, CA 92101-4495, United States
50 Hampshire Street, 5th Floor, Cambridge, MA 02139, United States
The Boulevard, Langford Lane, Kidlington, Oxford OX5 1GB, United Kingdom

Copyright © 2016 Elsevier Inc. All rights reserved

No part of this publication may be reproduced or transmitted in any form or by any means, electronic or
mechanical, including photocopying, recording, or any information storage and retrieval system, without
permission in writing from the publisher. Details on how to seek permission, further information about the
Publisher's permissions policies and our arrangements with organizations such as the Copyright Clearance
Center and the Copyright Licensing Agency, can be found at our website: www.elsevier.com/permissions.

This book and the individual contributions contained in it are protected under copyright by the Publisher
(other than as may be noted herein).

Notices

Knowledge and best practice in this field are constantly changing. As new research and experience
broaden our understanding, changes in research methods, professional practices, or medical treatment may
become necessary.

Practitioners and researchers must always rely on their own experience and knowledge in evaluating and
using any information, methods, compounds, or experiments described herein. In using such information
or methods they should be mindful of their own safety and the safety of others, including parties for whom
they have a professional responsibility.

To the fullest extent of the law, neither the Publisher nor the authors, contributors, or editors, assume any
liability for any injury and/or damage to persons or property as a matter of products liability, negligence or
otherwise, or from any use or operation of any methods, products, instructions, or ideas contained in the
material herein.

Library of Congress Cataloging-in-Publication Data
A catalog record for this book is available from the Library of Congress

British Library Cataloging-in-Publication Data
A catalogue record for this book is available from the British Library

ISBN: 978-0-12-810402-6

For information on all Academic Press publications
visit our website at https://www.elsevier.com

Working together
to grow libraries in
developing countries

www.elsevier.com • www.bookaid.org

Publisher: Nikki Levy
Acquisition Editor: J. Scott Bentley
Editorial Project Manager: Susan Ikeda
Production Project Manager: Nicky Carter
Designer: Matthew Limbert

Typeset by VTeX

Dedication

For
Alejandra and Sebastian
with love

Contents

Foreword   xi
Preface   xiii

1 **Overview**   1

   1.1 Introduction   1
   1.2 Summary   3

2 **Accounting for Official Capital Flows**   5

   2.1 Global imbalances   5
   2.2 Financial crises   8
   2.3 Financial integration   9
   2.4 Private versus official creditors   10
        2.4.1 Capital flows   13
        2.4.2 Stocks of foreign capital   19

3 **Current Account Imbalances: The Role of Official Capital Flows**   27

   3.1 Introduction   27
   3.2 Implications of reserve currency status   31
        3.2.1 Literature review   31
        3.2.2 Implications of the dual role of the reserve currency   32
        3.2.3 Reserve status and balance of payments accounting   33
        3.2.4 Reserve currency status in a portfolio balance model   33
   3.3 Empirical analysis of the role of official capital for the current account
        balance   37
        3.3.1 Who finances the US current account deficit? A statistical
               analysis   38
        3.3.2 What is the role of official capital in the current account balance?
               A regression analysis   39
        3.3.3 Which factors are major determinants of the US current account
               balance?   57
        3.3.4 How do official and private capital flows interact?   58
   3.4 Conclusions and policy implications   59
   Appendix 3.A Reserve currency status and balance of payments   61
   Appendix 3.B List of variables and data sources   63
   Appendix 3.C Sample of countries   66
   Appendix 3.D Regression results: Robustness using fixed samples   66

4   Determinants of the Public Budget Balance: The Role of Official Capital Flows   71

4.1 Introduction   72
4.2 Foreign exchange reserves in historical perspective   74
     4.2.1 A short history of reserve currencies   75
     4.2.2 A short history of asset classes used as reserves   79
4.3 Implications of reserve currency status   80
     4.3.1 Implications for interest rates   80
     4.3.2 Implications for the public budget   82
4.4 The role of official capital for the public budget balance – a regression
     analysis   85
     4.4.1 Description of data set and empirical approaches   85
     4.4.2 Time-series analysis: US and UK   90
     4.4.3 Analysis in a panel data set of industrialized countries   90
     4.4.4 Alternative identification: Are reserve currency countries
            outliers?   100
     4.4.5 Robustness checks   107
4.5 Conclusions   107
Appendix 4.A List of variables and data sources   109
Appendix 4.B Sample of countries   112
Appendix 4.C Data sources: Shares of reserve currencies in total foreign
              exchange reserves   112
Appendix 4.D Regression results: Robustness using fixed sample sizes   112

5   Reserve Accumulation and Financial Crises: From Individual Protection to Systemic Risk   119

5.1 Introduction   119
5.2 Reserves and crises: The links   121
     5.2.1 Reserves and domestic crises   122
     5.2.2 Reserves and crises in the reserve currency country   123
     5.2.3 Reserves and global crises   126
5.3 The optimal amount of reserves   127
     5.3.1 The benchmark model   128
     5.3.2 Modeling the behavior of the reserve currency country   131
     5.3.3 Optimal reserve level in the presence of local and global crises   132
     5.3.4 Optimal reserve level in the presence of a global social planner   134
     5.3.5 How can the socially optimal level of reserves be implemented?   135
     5.3.6 Robustness analysis   136
5.4 Quantitative implications of the model – a calibration analysis   140
5.5 Conclusions   151
Appendix 5.A Uses of reserve income: Investment vs. consumption   151
Appendix 5.B Probit analysis of financial crises   154

6   Global Aspects of Central Bank Policies   **161**

   6.1 Reform of the international monetary system in light of our findings   **161**

   6.2 Global liquidity and central bank cooperation   **164**

      6.2.1 Global liquidity spillovers   **164**

      6.2.2 The political economy of central bank cooperation   **165**

   6.3 The Target system in the Euro area   **168**

   6.4 Outlook   **171**

Bibliography   **173**

Index   **185**

For additional content please see the Companion Website:
http://booksite.elsevier.com/9780128104026

Foreword

The topic of global imbalances that have been built up over the past years has proved to be one of the biggest theoretical and empirical challenges in modern open macroeconomics. In the book, Dr. Steiner identifies problems in the international financial architecture that have contributed to this development and derives suggestions for the solutions of these problems. In my view, his observations are highly valuable for policy makers. The book is an impressive combination of theoretical analysis, empirical research, and a detailed knowledge of institutional arrangements in international finance.

I would like particularly to highlight one aspect of the book that I find noteworthy and rare in macroeconomics. The starting point of this research on reserve holdings is a welfare question and allocative approach to finding an answer: What is an optimal allocation of reserves? Are there externalities that prevent a welfare maximizing allocation of reserves? The book is therefore rooted in the German tradition of public economics that views the field of macroeconomic policy as a sub-discipline, next to the analysis of the welfare state and the issues of taxation or public goods.

The results derived from such an approach and the policy recommendations that follow from it are particularly strong. Dr. Steiner demonstrates the Pareto improvements that can be achieved with an improved reserve management by central banks. With a variety of different empirical and simulation techniques, he sheds further light on the issues. This book is highly original and forces the reader to re-evaluate the conventional wisdom on the topic.

Frank Westermann, Professor, Ph.D.

Preface

When central banks turned to policies of massive reserve accumulation in the aftermath of the Asian financial crisis, this gave rise to a literature that examines the causes of rising reserves and their economic implication for the domestic economy. This literature, however, widely neglected the fact that reserve accumulation is a two-sided phenomenon: While some countries accumulate reserves, others have to supply safe reserve assets. Given that the number of reserve-providing countries is usually small, the foreign demand for their assets might have major repercussions on their domestic economies.

This book intends to fill this gap: It shows empirically that reserve accumulation lowers both the current account balance and the public budget balance of the reserve-currency provider significantly. This increasing indebtedness may ultimately lead to a crisis in the reserve-providing country and destabilize the entire system. As a result, reserve accumulation imposes a negative externality.

These ideas, which resulted in this book, evolved while I was an assistant professor at the Chair of International Economic Policy at the School of Business Administration and Economics, University of Osnabrück. I am particularly grateful to Frank Westermann for his encouraging guidance, constant support and helpful advice during each stage of my work. I enjoyed the freedom of developing my own research ideas, which he accompanied with his thoughtful care of being on the right track. Special gratitude goes also to Valeriya Dinger for being my second assessor as well as to the other members of the assessment panel.

The writing of this book was a continuous process. It has benefited from the ideas, helpful comments and valuable suggestions of colleagues at home and abroad, at universities and conferences where I presented my work. I am particularly grateful to colleagues who read and commented earlier drafts of this book. Given that parts of the book have been published in academic journals, it has benefited from the input of a number of anonymous referees and editors. Finally, seven anonymous referees have reviewed this book and provided helpful comments to make it complete and well-rounded.

Special thanks go to the team at Elsevier, especially the editor Scott Bentley, who accompanied the publication process in a smooth and helpful way.

Finally, I would like to thank my family for their continuous support. They have always shown appreciation and trust for my work here in Germany and in Chile. The love, patience and encouragement of my wife and son accompanied me during each day of writing this book. It was only this inflow of happiness that made this book possible.

Andreas Steiner

Overview

1

Contents

1.1 Introduction   1
1.2 Summary   3

1.1   Introduction

When in the mid-1980s a new wave of financial globalization started, countries' willingness to remove capital controls and to become part of the world capital market was associated with the anticipated benefits from financial liberalization. Theory predicts that an efficient allocation of capital, better risk-sharing opportunities and technological spillovers linked to foreign investment raise domestic welfare. Its contributions to the development of the domestic financial sector, to macroeconomic policy discipline and efficiency have been referred to as indirect, collateral benefits. Besides theory, international organizations like the IMF were advocates of financial liberalization (see Joyce and Noy, 2008).

The series of financial crises during the 1990s and the Asian financial crisis of 1997/98 in particular, however, mark a turning point in countries' attitude toward financial liberalization. By highlighting the flip side of increasing financial integration, these crises made countries rethink the benefits and costs of their integration in the international financial system.

International capital flows to emerging and developing countries have been proven to be temporary and volatile. They can be large relative to the size of the domestic economy. First, capital-receiving countries have faced periods of surges of capital inflows, which might cause appreciating exchange rates, asset price bubbles and overheating of the domestic economy. In this wake, the expression "the capital inflow problem" was coined (Calvo et al., 1994). Second, these capital flows may reverse suddenly. Episodes of sudden stops of capital flows, capital flow reversals and the loss of reserves have been pervasive. They were often associated with financial crises.

These experiences indicated the need for a reappraisal of the effects of financial globalization (see Kose et al., 2009a). Based on a large number of papers and the use of different approaches (cross-sectional, panel and event studies) the empirical literature on the effects of financial liberalization provides mixed results with respect to direct or indirect positive net effects of financial opening on welfare (see, among others, Obstfeld, 2009; Prasad et al., 2007; Rancière et al., 2008).

Despite these mixed blessings of financial openness, measures of de jure and de facto financial openness show that in the aggregate the policy of financial liberalization has not been reversed. Countries rather tried to reap the benefits of financial integration while being better prepared to cope with capital outflows and crises. A large stock of international reserves was considered as a form of self-insurance that provides a buffer

Global Imbalances, Financial Crises, and Central Bank Policies
Copyright © 2016 Elsevier Inc. All rights reserved.

in the face of volatile capital flows. Reserves have been found to reduce the incidence and severity of financial crises.

This policy manifests itself in the remarkable increase in central banks' international reserves during the last two decades. This increase is observable both in the level of reserves and in indicators of reserve adequacy, which use to scale the level of reserves by GDP, a measure of broad money (M2) or imports.

A variety of papers on the causes, costs and benefits of foreign exchange holdings emerged during the 2000s. Besides mercantilist explanations, precautionary motives have been identified as an important driver of countries' demand for reserves. One common feature of this literature is its focus on individual countries: Papers explain the domestic motives for reserve accumulation, provide an analysis of domestic costs and benefits and highlight the effects of reserves on domestic variables like the probability of crises, capital flows and inflation. This country-centered partial equilibrium analysis neglects spillovers across countries.

The present book starts with this observation and tries to turn the tables by focusing on the global effects of central banks' reserve policies independently of their motivation. This perspective concentrates on two related aspects: First, reserve policies in one country affect the reserve-providing country. This is due to the fact that the present international monetary system uses national currencies as reserves. Reserve accumulation constitutes an official capital flow between two countries. Second, global reserve accumulation might increase the indebtedness of the reserve-providing countries and destabilize the international monetary system. In this view, reserve accumulation has a negative externality, which affects all countries depending on their real and financial linkages.

In the following chapters I am going to elaborate on the international dimension of central banks' reserve policies and official capital flows. I first show that reserve accumulation increases the indebtedness of the dominant reserve currency country (Chapters 3 and 4): Reserve accumulation lowers both the current account balance and the public budget balance of the reserve-currency provider. This relationship is theoretically motivated and empirically tested. These findings motivate the reconsideration of the optimal amount of reserves: Chapter 5 integrates the idea that reserve accumulation creates systemic risk in a standard model of the optimal demand for reserves.

In sum, I track how central bank policies contribute to global imbalances and sovereign debt, which, in turn, are a backdrop of financial crises. I thereby contribute to different strands of the literature in international macroeconomics and international finance: The analysis of current account balances adds to the literature on the determinants of trade and capital flows. The chapter on public budget balances bridges the gap between the fields of international economics and public economics. Finally, we contribute to the literature on the consequences of international capital flows and add a new perspective by focusing on the source of capital flows: To better understand the behavior of capital flows, it is important to distinguish between private and official sources. Motivation, intention and decision-making processes of these different types of investors might differ fundamentally.

1.2 Summary

Chapter 2 is descriptive and provides an illustration of the importance of official capital flows. While the literature on cross-border capital flows focuses on private flows, we show that official flows cannot be treated as marginal. They rather constitute an important determinant of net capital flows across countries.

Chapter 3 entitled "Current Account Imbalances: The Role of Official Capital Flows" explains the US current account deficit and global imbalances as the natural outcome of a monetary system based on the dollar as key currency. The empirical results are corroborated by an application of the portfolio balance model.

Our panel data analysis over the period 1970–2009 confirms the hypothesis that the global demand for reserve assets by central banks lowers the current account balance of the reserve-issuing country: Any dollar of provided reserve assets decreases the US current account by more than one dollar. On average, the demand for dollar reserves has lowered the US current account by 1 to 2 percentage points relative to GDP. The flip side of this effect is a higher current account balance in reserve-accumulating countries. These novel findings show that the worldwide demand for international reserves has contributed to the buildup of global imbalances.

Chapter 4 examines the relationship between global reserve accumulation and public finances of reserve-providing countries. Since central banks invest their foreign exchange reserves predominantly in government bonds, their global accumulation affects the equilibrium in the market for government bonds of reserve currency countries.

By means of a panel data analysis we examine this relationship during different constellations of the international monetary system: the sterling period (1890–1935) and the dollar dominance (since World War II). We show for both periods that reserve currency status significantly lowers the fiscal balance. Any additional dollar of reserves lowers the center's balance by 0.7–1.4 dollars. These new findings show that reserve currency status increases sovereign debt of the center country.

A consequence of these empirical findings is that the center country of the international monetary system gets increasingly indebted over time. As such, these papers provide a first empirical test of the Triffin dilemma, which argues that the use of national currencies as reserve assets is destabilizing in the long run. Chapter 5 integrates these findings in a model of the optimal demand for reserves. It provides a new perspective on the relationship between countries' international reserve holdings and financial crises: While the "local" view holds that reserves may prevent domestic crises, it overlooks that the accumulation of reserves eases the financing constraint of the reserve currency country and may cause a financial crisis in the center, which is transmitted globally. According to this "global" view reserve accumulation might destabilize the international financial system. Since the crisis affects all countries alike, the accumulation of reserves imposes a negative externality on non-accumulating countries.

Based on the model, we illustrate the gap between local and global optimality: The consideration of systemic risk lowers the demand for reserves. Moreover, if a supranational authority determines the optimal level of reserves, it internalizes the negative externality and accumulates fewer reserves. A macroprudential tax on reserve hoardings might implement the socially optimal solution. Our calibration analysis shows that these considerations are economically significant: They lower the optimal amount of reserves in the benchmark case remarkably.

Chapter 6, the final part of this book, relates our findings to various aspects of global central banking: First, based on our theoretical and empirical results, we provide suggestions for a reform of the international monetary system. Second, we show how financial integration and global liquidity spillovers have increased the importance of central bank cooperation. This section provides some examples of how central banks have coordinated their actions in the past. Finally, by illustrating the interbank payment system of the European Union (Target) we show that Target balances arise from net cross-border capital flows. These balances are a form of official financing and may be considered as a substitute for reserves. They have contributed to balance-of-payments imbalances.

Accounting for Official Capital Flows

2

Contents

2.1 Global imbalances   5
2.2 Financial crises   8
2.3 Financial integration   9
2.4 Private versus official creditors   10
    2.4.1 Capital flows   13
    2.4.2 Stocks of foreign capital   19

This chapter provides an empirical illustration of global imbalances, capital flows and countries' international investment positions. Its purpose consists in illustrating the importance of official institutions relative to private investors in shaping international financial markets and countries' net foreign asset positions.

2.1   Global imbalances

In this book the term global imbalances refers to a situation of persistently positive or negative current account balances that lead to diverging net foreign asset positions.

Despite the long and ongoing debate between academics, policymakers and economic advisors about the causes of global imbalances and their sustainability, there is no consistent and precise definition of the term. While a broad definition sets global imbalances equal with large current account balances (see Chinn et al., 2014), in a narrow way they are characterized as "external positions of systemically important economies that reflect distortions or entail risks for the global economy" (Bracke et al., 2008, p. 7). The first definition focuses on flows, while the latter identifies imbalances by stocks of foreign capital. Our definition combines both views by its focus on persistent current account balances, which, in the absence of unidirectional exchange rate changes or valuation effects, cause diverging external positions. Hence, it is important to identify imbalances within a wide time window, characterized by a sequence of current account balances of equal sign.

We leave open the question whether the observed current account balances reflect distortions. An unbalanced current account may be the optimal response of agents to temporary shocks or expected future changes in income. As such, unbalanced accounts are the by-product of integrated financial markets, which allow for intertemporal consumption smoothing and an efficient allocation of capital. According to Feldstein and Horioka (1980) the strong correlation between saving and investment is puzzling for

Global Imbalances, Financial Crises, and Central Bank Policies
Copyright © 2016 Elsevier Inc. All rights reserved.

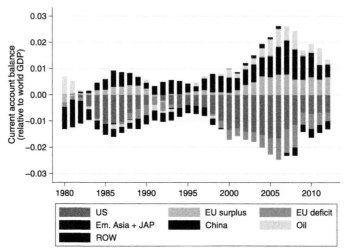

Figure 2.1 Global imbalances. *Notes:* The graph shows the balance of the current account relative to world GDP for selected country groups. The composition of country groups follows Blanchard and Milesi-Ferretti (2010) and is given by: *EU surplus*: Austria, Belgium, Denmark, Finland, Germany, Luxembourg, Netherlands, Sweden, Switzerland. *EU deficit*: Bulgaria, Czech Republic, Estonia, Greece, Hungary, Ireland, Italy, Latvia, Lithuania, Poland, Portugal, Romania, Slovak Republic, Spain, Turkey, Ukraine, United Kingdom. *Emerging Asia*: Hong Kong, Indonesia, Korea, Malaysia, Philippines, Singapore, Thailand. *Oil exporting countries*: Algeria, Angola, Azerbaijan, Bahrain, Republic of Congo, Ecuador, Equatorial Guinea, Gabon, Iran, Kazakhstan, Kuwait, Libya, Nigeria, Norway, Oman, Qatar, Russia, Saudi Arabia, Sudan, Syria, Trinidad and Tobago, United Arab Emirates, Venezuela, Yemen. *ROW*: Rest of the world.
Data sources: IMF (2013) and World Bank (2013).

open economies. Financial integration manifested by larger current account balances might weaken this relationship.

In the long run, however, temporary deficits have to be settled by surpluses. In the absence of valuation effects, permanently positive or negative current account balances lead to diverging net foreign asset positions. These developments might ultimately proof unsustainable.

We refrain from focusing on systemically important economies. It seems rather to be vital that the group of countries characterized by imbalances is economically significant in the aggregate.

Figure 2.1 provides a graphical representation of global imbalances: By depicting the evolution of the current account balance relative to world GDP for selected country groups, it visualizes how balances have grown over time. They have been somewhat reduced only by the recent global financial crisis. Balances have been persistently in surplus in emerging Asia and Japan and persistently in deficit in the US. The economically significant surpluses of China and oil-exporting countries are a phenomenon of the 2000s.

Figure 2.2 provides an alternative way to illustrate global imbalances: It shows the unconditional distribution of current account balances (in % of GDP) in selected years for all countries for which data are available in IMF (2013). Histogram and

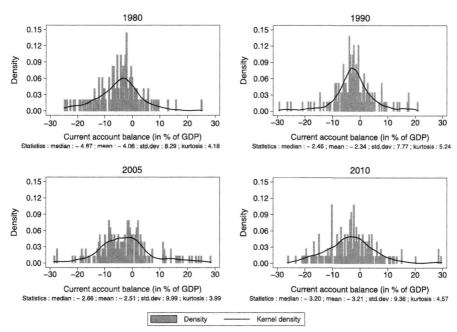

Figure 2.2 Distribution of current account balances. *Notes:* This histogram shows the distribution of current account balances (in % of GDP) for selected years. Each graph includes all countries for which data are available in IMF (2013). The bin width amounts to 0.5 percentage points. The line graph plots a kernel density estimate for current account balances. As kernel-weight function the function of Epanechnikov is used. The width of the density window is calculated as that width that would minimize the mean integrated squared error if data were from a normal distribution and a Gaussian kernel were used.
Data source: IMF (2013).

kernel density portray an increasing dispersion of current account balances between 1990 and 2005: While mean and median have not changed much, observations have become less concentrated around the mean.[1] The distribution has become flatter with more mass being concentrated in the tails. The decrease in the kurtosis confirms that values are spread wider around the mean. As the data for 2010 reveal, this trend – and hence global imbalances – has been reduced as an effect of the global financial crisis. Mean and median current account balance have been negative in all presented years. Since current accounts have to balance at the global level, this shows that the average deficit country is economically smaller than the average surplus country.

The empirical literature on the determinants of global imbalances (see, among others, Chinn et al., 2014 and Gruber and Kamin, 2007) focuses on fundamentals that drive private investors' decisions. Chapter 3 sheds new light on this issue by showing how, besides private agents, official capital flows have contributed to global imbal-

---

[1] Faruqee and Lee (2009) show in a data set starting in 1960 that the dispersion of current account balances has steadily increased since 1960 if one disregards 1980. They explain the temporary increase and subsequent fall in the dispersion in 1980 as an effect of the oil price shock.

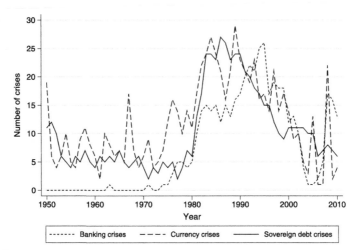

Figure 2.3 Financial crises. *Notes:* The graph shows the number of crises in a given year for a sample of 69 countries. Banking crises are defined either as the public unwinding of at least one financial institution after a bank run or the public unwinding of several financial institutions. A currency crisis corresponds to a depreciation of the nominal exchange rate with respect to the US dollar or other relevant currencies that exceeds 15%. Sovereign crises occur if the sovereign defaults on payment of debt obligations, repudiates them or if debt is restructured into less favorable conditions to the lender than in the original contract. In the case of domestic debt, freezing of bank deposits and forced conversion of deposits from foreign to local currency are also labeled sovereign debt crises.
Data source: Reinhart and Rogoff (2011).

ances. Central bank policies may not only take account of global imbalances and devise appropriate responses, they also have contributed to their buildup.

2.2 Financial crises

Alike global imbalances, there exists a two-way relationship between central bank policies and financial crises: On the one hand, central bank policies affect the incidence of financial crises. Examples are the choice of exchange rate regime, its international reserve policies and the regulation of the domestic financial system. On the other hand, financial crises require a response by the central bank, which has to manage the crisis and formulate an exit strategy.

We define a financial crisis as the occurrence of at least one of the following crises: a banking crisis, a currency crisis and/or a sovereign debt crisis. Figure 2.3 depicts the incidence of these crises since 1950. It is based on the data set and crisis definition of Reinhart and Rogoff (2011) and considers 69 economies (for the empirical definition of crises refer to the notes to Figure 2.3 and to Appendix 5.B).

The number of sovereign debt crises has increased sharply in the 1980s and reached its peak in 1986. A similar behavior can be observed for currency crises: Their number was extraordinarily high during the decade of the 1980s. While banking crises were

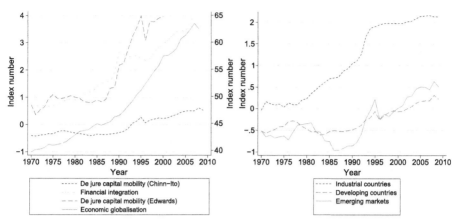

Figure 2.4 Measures of financial openness. *Notes:* The graph on the left-hand side shows the evolution of the following measures of financial openness: (1) Chinn–Ito index of de jure openness, (2) financial integration based on Lane and Milesi-Ferretti (2007) and defined as the ratio of foreign assets and liabilities over GDP, (3) de jure openness based on Edwards and (4) a measure of economic globalization, which considers flows of goods and capital, as defined by Dreher (2006). For the Chinn–Ito index (multiplied by ten) and financial openness the left-hand axis applies; for the index of Edwards and economic globalization values are displayed on the right-hand axis. The graph on the right illustrates the evolution of the unweighted mean of the Chinn–Ito index for different country groups. Sample countries and their classification are presented in Appendix 3.C. For these four measures larger index values denote financially more open economies. *Data sources:* Chinn and Ito (2006); Dreher (2006); IMF (2013); Lane and Milesi-Ferretti (2007) and update.

almost absent until the early 1970s, their incidence reached levels comparable to those of sovereign debt and currency crises in the 1990s.

2.3 Financial integration

Past decades have been characterized by financial globalization. International financial integration[2] has been increasing. This development is revealed by measures of both de facto and de jure financial openness. De facto financial openness is commonly measured by stocks or flows of international capital relative to GDP. De jure financial openness measures the extent to which a country imposes legal restrictions on its cross-border capital transactions. Figure 2.4 illustrates the evolution of selected measures of de jure and de facto financial openness over time. Two conclusions might be drawn: First, all presented measures point to an increasing degree of financial openness over time; although at different levels, this trend can be observed in industrial, emerging and developing countries alike.[3] Second, financial openness of emerging

---

[2] In this book the terms *financial integration* and *financial openness* are used as synonyms.

[3] Unless otherwise indicated, the classification of countries in industrial, emerging and developing countries follows the pattern presented in Appendix 3.C.

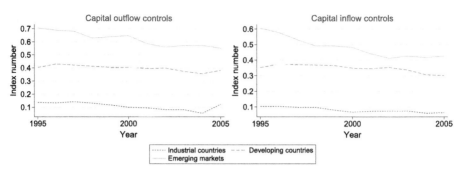

Figure 2.5 De jure financial openness. *Notes:* The graph shows the evolution of de jure controls on capital outflows (left) and inflows (right) for different country groups. Larger values indicate more pervasive controls.
Data source: Schindler (2009).

market countries does not significantly differ from that of developing countries. Industrial countries are more open to capital flows than the other two country groups.

Measures of de jure financial openness cover the extent of controls on capital inflows and capital outflows in subcategories. If controls are used in a macroprudential fashion, they should be adjusted depending on the stance of the business cycle and foreigners' willingness to invest in the domestic economy (see Fernández et al., 2015): A macroprudential capital account policy discourages net capital inflows during waves of capital inflows and economic expansions to countercyclically mitigate their effects (e.g. an appreciating real exchange rate, rising asset prices and wages). That is, during a boom countries might increase controls on inflows and remove controls on outflows. An aggregate measure of capital controls is unable to account adequately for this policy because these changes might cancel out. It is therefore crucial to study controls on inflows and outflows separately. One of the few indices accounting for this difference is an index developed by Schindler (2009). Figure 2.5, which is based on the Schindler index, shows that controls on both inflows and outflows have been reduced in industrialized, emerging and developing countries over the period 1995–2005.[4]

2.4   Private versus official creditors

The majority of the literature on capital flows implicitly refers to private flows. This section illustrates the magnitude of official relative to private capital. In the chapters that follow, we then concentrate on the effects of official capital flows. In particular, we show that reserve flows lower current account balances and fiscal balances of the center country of the international monetary system.

Empirical approaches to international financial integration examine international capital along several dimensions:

---

[4] The original version of the Schindler index only covers the period 1995–2005. It has been updated by other authors in the meantime, however, their data are not publicly available.

- *Flows versus stocks*: Capital flows might finance current account transactions. With increasing financial integration capital flows have become more autonomous (de-linked from trade) and are a symptom of portfolio diversification. Hence, flows are related to the competitiveness of the real sector of an economy, to changes in the global demand for its products and to its attractiveness as investment location. Stocks of foreign capital result from cumulated flows, interest income and valuation effects.

- *Net versus gross positions*: The empirical literature on countries' international investment position traditionally focuses on net foreign assets (NFA). The important distinction is whether a country is a creditor or a debtor. More recently, the recurrence of crises related to capital flight and sudden stops of capital flows has shown that gross positions of financial assets and liabilities provide additional information (Alberola et al., 2012; Broner et al., 2013). The potential magnitude of a capital reversal is related to gross positions, not net ones. Capital flows may be examined as net or gross flows as well. Small net flows in a given period may go along with large gross flows, namely large inflows and large outflows of capital. In this case, an increase in de facto financial integration is not necessarily linked to a substantial change in the country's net foreign asset position.

- *Composition of international capital*: A disaggregated analysis examines the type of asset in which the investment takes place: Statistics typically distinguish between foreign direct investment (FDI), portfolio investment and other investment. Portfolio investment covers transactions in equity and debt securities. Other investment subsumes categories like trade credits, loans and deposits. The type of investment reveals important information about intention and commitment of the investor, which, in turn, are related to the volatility and reversibility of the capital flow. FDI is considered to be resilient to crises because investors follow a long-run strategy. They might participate in the management of the firm, which facilitates the transfer of know-how. Portfolio equity flows, in turn, are related to hot money – investors' principal goal is the maximization of returns. Since returns of FDI and portfolio equity investment depend on the success of firms, both allow for risk-sharing between investors and producers. Debt flows, however, involve a contractual interest payment.

- *Maturity and currency structure*: International assets and liabilities may be divided in long-term and short-term debt. They may be denominated in domestic or foreign currency units. Both the maturity and currency structure of international capital may differ between assets and liabilities. These mismatches make an economy more vulnerable to financial crises. In particular, if foreign assets and liabilities are denominated in different currencies, exchange rate movements affect the net foreign asset position even in the absence of net capital flows. More importantly, on the microeconomic level of firms and households, these mismatches might induce insolvency.

A distinction that has been widely disregarded so far concerns the type of investor. In particular, there exist private investors and official ones. Motivations for their activities on the international financial market differ fundamentally.

Private investors base their investment decisions on expected returns and risk. Capital flows are shaped by a search for yield and risk diversification. Official investors, in turn, do not maximize expected returns in a narrow sense. Official capital flows are the by-product of other policies (e.g. exchange rate policy, self-insurance through stock of international reserves, economic cooperation through development assistance). They provide benefits that go beyond pure return considerations.

In our definition, capital flows are denominated *official* if the following two conditions are fulfilled:

1. The creditor, source of the flow, is neither a natural person nor an entity (i.e. a fund) dealing in the interest of an individual person.
2. Return and income generation are not the primary goal of the investment.

As such, capital flows resulting from central banks' reserve policies are labeled *official*. The central bank is an official entity and its reserve holdings are explained by motives other than return. Transactions undertaken by sovereign wealth funds, however, are not considered as official capital flows. While they are official entities acting in social interest, their primary investment goal consists in increasing the real value of the fund. This is precisely the reason why these resources are separated from the mandate of the central bank. In our definition, development aid granted by a natural person directly to the recipient – without collecting and channeling it through an official agency – is denoted a private flow. Development aid provided by official agencies or multilateral institutions, however, is considered as official flows.

Data allow us to identify two types of official capital:

1. *Development aid*: Official development aid (ODA) consists of loans made on concessional terms (net of repayments of principal) and grants, which meet the following criteria: (1) Donors are official agencies or multilateral institutions, (2) loans convey a grant element of at least 25 percent and (3) the objective of the loan or grant is to promote development and welfare in developing countries. Our empirical analysis is based on data collected by the Development Assistance Committee (DAC) of the OECD. These data contain transactions of official agencies of the members of the DAC, of multilateral institutions and of non-DAC countries. For statistical reasons, capital flows are grouped in two categories: (1) Net official development assistance and (2) official aid received. Net official development assistance covers flows to countries and territories in the DAC list of ODA recipients,[5] while net official aid refers to aid flows (net of repayments) provided to countries and territories in part II of the DAC list. Data is available for flows and stocks of development aid. The data provide a narrow measure of official aid flows because they do not include so-called "beyond ODA flows", which are, among other flows, private grants extended by NGOs and foundations. Moreover, they do not include non-concessional development loans granted by official entities. The amount

---

[5] The DAC maintains a list including all countries eligible to receive ODA. These consist of all low and middle income countries (according to the World Bank classification based on gross national income (GNI) per capita) and the Least Developed Countries (LDCs) as defined by the United Nations. G8 members, EU members and future EU members are excluded.

of outstanding development aid corresponds to the variable "concessional external debt stocks", which is listed in the World Bank's International Debt Statistics.

2. *International reserves*: The IMF (2009c, p. 111, paragraph 6.64) defines reserves as "external assets that are readily available to and controlled by monetary authorities for meeting balance of payments financing needs, for intervention in exchange markets to affect the currency exchange rate, and for other related purposes (such as maintaining confidence in the currency and the economy, and serving as a basis for foreign borrowing)." In practice, reserves consist of gold, foreign exchange reserves and IMF-related assets like members' reserve position in the IMF and their holdings of SDRs. There is data on stocks of reserves and – from the balance of payments – on sales and purchases of reserves (flows).

In the following subsections we use this definition to illustrate the magnitude of official relative to private capital. We first focus on capital flows and then turn to capital stocks.

2.4.1 Capital flows

The distinction between capital inflows and outflows is based on the residency of creditor and borrower (cf. Broner et al., 2013). Capital inflows are defined as net purchases (difference between purchases and sales) of domestic assets by non-residents. Capital outflows equal net purchases of foreign assets by domestic agents excluding the central bank. In particular, data allow us to distinguish between foreign direct investment flows, portfolio flows and other investment flows. Hence, capital inflows are the sum of inflows of foreign direct investment in the domestic economy, inflows of portfolio investment liabilities and other investment liabilities. Accordingly, capital outflows are the sum of outflows of foreign direct investment abroad, changes in portfolio investment assets and changes in other investment assets. In our measures of inflows and outflows we do not include capital account transactions because they contain development grants and remittances, which both do not reflect investments in a narrow sense. Official flows are defined as net purchases of reserve assets by the central bank plus development aid received.

Figure 2.6 shows the magnitude of capital flows for geographic regions over the period 1970–2012. A common feature across regions is the strong increase in gross capital flows between the mid-1990s and the global financial crisis of 2008–10. To better visualize them, we present two graphs for each region that use different scales: The first up to the year 2000 (Asia 1995) and the second beginning in that same year, but using a larger scale.

Industrial countries are characterized by a strong comovement of inflows and outflows of capital. This reflects increasing financial integration and a reduction in home bias: Net purchases of domestic assets by foreigners go hand in hand with purchases of foreign assets by domestic agents. Official flows do not play a substantial role.

Compared across regions, capital flows are the lowest to and from African countries. More importantly, in Africa official flows are the dominant type of flows. In most years, official flows are larger than inflows or outflows of capital.

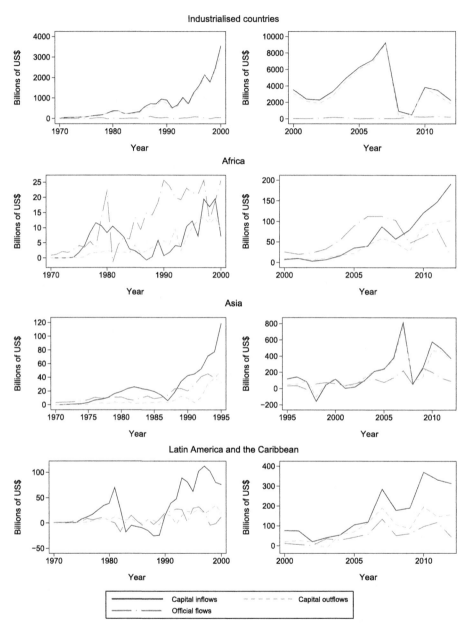

Figure 2.6 Capital flows (in billions of US$). *Notes:* Capital inflows are net purchases of domestic assets by foreigners. Capital outflows equal net purchases of foreign assets by domestic agents. Official flows are defined as net purchases of reserve assets by the central bank plus development aid received.
Data source: IMF (2013).

The graphs for Asia show similarities with industrial countries with respect to the waves of capital flows: There is a sharp increase in capital inflows in the early 1990s. The run-up to the East Asian financial crisis of 1997 is characterized by net capital inflows because inflows exceed outflows. The Asian financial crisis manifests itself by capital repatriation: Both inflows and outflows turn negative, that is, domestic and foreign agents sell assets from outside their jurisdiction on a net base.

In Latin America and the Caribbean capital inflows are consistently larger than outflows. The magnitude of private outflows and official flows are comparable. The Latin American debt crisis induced foreign investors to withdraw their capital: Capital inflows turn negative in 1983 and remain so for a relatively extended period. Net capital inflows do not return before 1990.

Increasing capital flows might result from growth in world GDP. To examine whether growth in capital flows exceeds economic growth, Figure 2.7 scales capital flows by trend GDP. Trend GDP is calculated by smoothing the series of nominal GDP by the Hodrick–Prescott filter with a smoothing parameter of 100. We take the unweighted mean across countries and group data according to their per capita income following the classification used in the World Bank's World Development Indicators. That is, data reveal the importance of capital flows for an average country of the respective income group. While the graph on the left-hand side visualizes three types of capital flows, the right-hand side graph shows the median (across countries) of the ratio of official to private flows and the mean value of this ratio over the entire period.

For the entire sample, the average magnitude of official flows (relative to GDP) has been similar to that of private capital inflows, which are again larger than private capital outflows. An exception has been the period since the year 2000 when private flows decoupled from official ones because of the enormous growth in private inflows. This increase is primarily due to flows to and from high income countries, as can be inferred from the second graph. Official flows play a marginal role in high income countries. For countries that do not belong to the high income group (see third panel of Figure 2.7) capital flows are substantially lower than in high income countries: The median high income country registered gross flows equal to 10.9% of trend GDP on average over the period 1970–2012, the same measure amounts to 6.45% in non-high income countries. However, in many years, official flows stand out as the largest component of capital flows in the group of non-high income countries. The importance of official flows is reflected in the average value of the median (across countries) of the ratio of official to private flows, which amounts to 0.58. That is, were private capital inflows and outflows of equal size, official flows would be as large as each type of private flows.

Figure 2.8 provides more detailed information about the group of non-high income countries by dividing them in upper middle, lower middle and low income countries. Remarkable is the finding that the larger the magnitude of official flows relative to private inflows and outflows, the lower the income of the respective group is. This may be explained by the fact that aid flows are primarily dedicated to low income countries.

After this analysis of gross flows, we now turn to a statistical description of net capital flows. In particular, Figure 2.9 compares the balance of the financial account

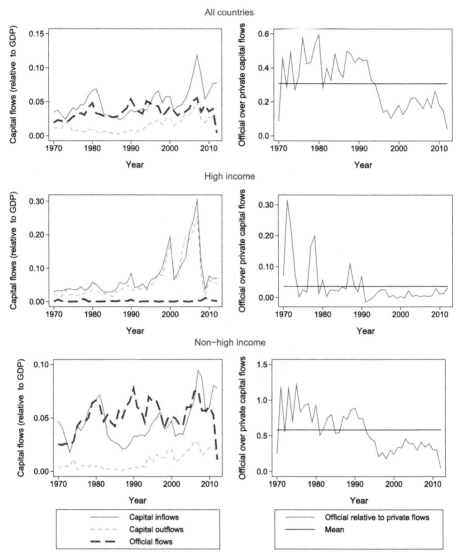

Figure 2.7 Average capital flows (relative to GDP): Coarse country classification. *Notes:* Capital inflows are net purchases of domestic assets by foreigners. Capital outflows equal net purchases of foreign assets by domestic agents. Official flows are defined as net purchases of reserve assets by the central bank plus development aid received. All capital flows are scaled by trend GDP. The right-hand panel shows the median (across countries) of the ratio of official over private flows, where private flows are defined as the sum of capital inflows and outflows. The straight line plots the average value of this ratio over time. Country groups are defined according to the World Bank classification presented in the World Development Indicators. *Data sources:* IMF (2013) and World Bank (2013).

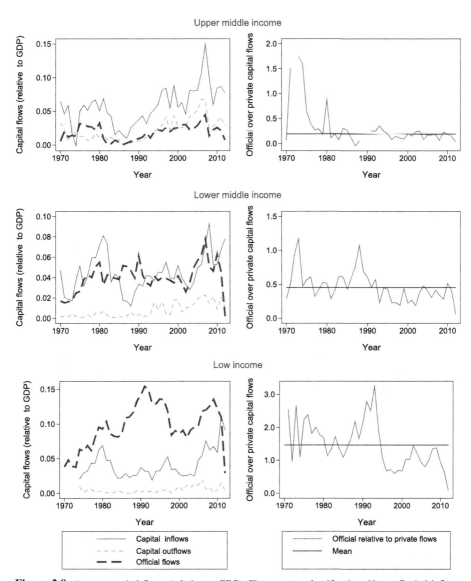

Figure 2.8 Average capital flows (relative to GDP): Fine country classification. *Notes:* Capital inflows are net purchases of domestic assets by foreigners. Capital outflows equal net purchases of foreign assets by domestic agents. Official flows are defined as net purchases of reserve assets by the central bank plus development aid received. All capital flows are scaled by trend GDP. The right-hand panel shows the median (across countries) of the ratio of official over private flows, where private flows are defined as the sum of capital inflows and outflows. The straight line plots the average value of this ratio over time. Country groups are defined according to the World Bank classification presented in the World Development Indicators. *Data sources:* IMF (2013) and World Bank (2013).

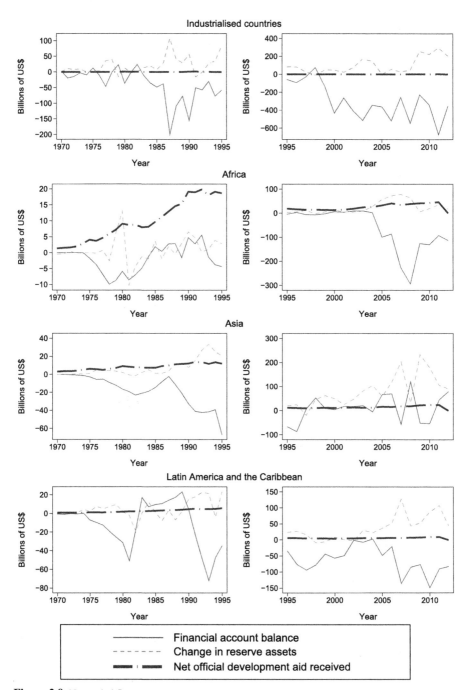

Figure 2.9 Net capital flows.
Data sources: IMF (2013) and World Bank (2013).

with flows in reserve assets and net flows in development aid. Flows are measured in billions of US$ and aggregated over the respective country group. A positive balance of the financial account equals net lending to the rest of the world. Alike in the previous graphs, we present for each country group two graphs: The first runs until 1995, while the second starts in that year. This allows us to use a larger scale for the second period, when net flows are significantly larger.

In industrialized countries, the average financial account balance oscillated around zero until the mid-1980s and has mostly been negative since then. Reserves and aid flows play a minor role. In Africa, development aid constituted the most important net flow until the early 2000s. In midst of the global financial crisis, African countries borrowed heavily from the rest of the world when the financial account balance amounted to −300 billion US$. The graphs for Asia highlight increasing net borrowing in the run-up to the East Asian financial crisis of 1997/98. Since then, the financial account has been relatively balanced and reserve flows have become the most important net capital flow. The financial account balance in Latin America and the Caribbean traces the region's experience with crises: The financial account balance fell strongly in the early 1980s and in 1994, the year of the Mexican Tequila crisis. Aid and reserve flows were relatively low. Reserves have become important only recently in the 2000s when they reached a magnitude similar to that of the financial account balance.

Table 2.1 presents summary statistics of net capital flows, total gross capital flows, reserve flows and aid flows for different time periods and across country groups. Net capital flows have mostly been negative and their volatility – measured by the median of the standard deviation – has increased over time. Gross capital flows relative to trend GDP have been multiplied over time in all country groups. This process went hand in hand with an increase in their volatility. Reserve flows also tend to rise over time. The strongest increase can be observed in low income countries. Net ODA flows reached their maximum (relative to trend GDP) in the 1980s and have been falling since then. They are concentrated toward low income countries where they constituted 9.2% of trend GDP over 1970–2012 for the average country.

2.4.2 Stocks of foreign capital

By examining net foreign asset (NFA) positions (see Figure 2.10), we now turn to international investment positions of countries and regions. These indicate whether a country is a creditor or a debtor country with respect to the rest of the world.

Since 1974 the average industrial country is a net debtor. Its NFA position has again deteriorated prior to the global financial crisis. African countries became heavily indebted until the mid-1990s. The year 1995 marks a turning point: Since then, Africa has reduced its indebtedness with respect to the rest of the world. The average Asian country was a debtor country until recently. After the NFA position has been decreasing in the 1990s and hit a bottom in 1996, its claims toward the rest of the world have increased during the 2000s and turned the average country in a creditor in 2004. Latin America and the Caribbean relied on net capital inflows during the 1980s, which reduced its NFA position. Since 1990 its NFA position has risen, but remains

Table 2.1 **Summary statistics of capital flows**

	All countries		High-income countries		Middle-income countries		Low-income countries	
	Median average	Median std. dev.	Median average	Median std. dev.	Median average	Median std. dev.	Median average	Median std. dev.
Net capital flows								
All sample	−2.49	6.50	−0.61	4.54	−3.00	6.45	−2.28	6.82
1970s	−3.64	2.58	−0.95	1.60	−4.66	3.25	−3.44	1.94
1980s	−2.30	4.02	−1.25	2.59	−1.25	2.59	−2.26	3.86
1990s	−1.78	3.89	−0.77	3.11	−1.85	3.99	−2.17	3.61
2000s	−1.68	5.48	0.50	4.27	−3.08	5.63	0.10	6.35
Total gross capital flows								
All sample	6.25	8.83	10.94	13.82	6.10	8.69	4.33	7.40
1970s	2.67	3.51	3.35	2.72	3.19	4.79	1.36	2.62
1980s	3.85	4.62	7.02	3.90	7.02	3.90	3.22	4.68
1990s	5.34	5.55	8.42	4.93	5.93	5.73	3.51	3.91
2000s	10.54	8.82	16.76	15.89	10.56	8.07	6.20	6.68

Table 2.1 *(continued)*

	All countries		High-income countries		Middle-income countries		Low-income countries	
	Median average	Median std. dev.	Median average	Median std. dev.	Median average	Median std. dev.	Median average	Median std. dev.
Reserve flows								
All sample	1.12	2.74	0.39	1.59	1.23	3.03	0.92	2.53
1970s	0.62	1.80	0.45	1.45	1.03	2.12	0.07	1.53
1980s	0.28	1.90	0.38	1.25	0.38	1.25	0.09	1.79
1990s	0.98	2.35	0.39	1.24	1.24	2.38	1.16	2.27
2000s	1.43	2.68	0.61	1.43	1.47	2.87	1.74	2.66
Net ODA flows								
All sample	3.92	2.99	0.10	0.24	2.48	1.99	9.19	5.55
1970s	3.21	1.19	0.03	0.02	2.29	0.72	4.99	2.48
1980s	5.16	1.52	0.04	0.09	0.04	0.09	10.81	2.60
1990s	3.74	1.65	0.08	0.12	1.49	0.79	11.19	3.72
2000s	2.03	1.15	0.25	0.05	1.25	0.51	9.35	1.86

Notes: Country groups are defined according to the World Bank analytical classification as presented in the World Development Indicators (thresholds of GNI per capita define income groups). Net capital flows are the sum of the balance of the capital and financial account. Negative values denote net capital flows. Total gross capital flows are the sum of capital inflows and capital outflows, which encompass FDI, portfolio investment and other investment flows as well as flows of reserve assets by both domestic and foreign agents. Reserve flows are net flows in reserve assets as derived from the balance of payments. Net ODA flows are the sum of net official development assistance and official aid received. All capital flows are scaled by trend GDP. We first calculate country averages and country standard deviations for the indicated time period. We then show the median value across countries for both measures. The sample dates from 1970 to 2012 and contains a maximum of 186 countries (sample size of specific values depends on data availability).

Data sources: IMF (2013) and World Bank (2013).

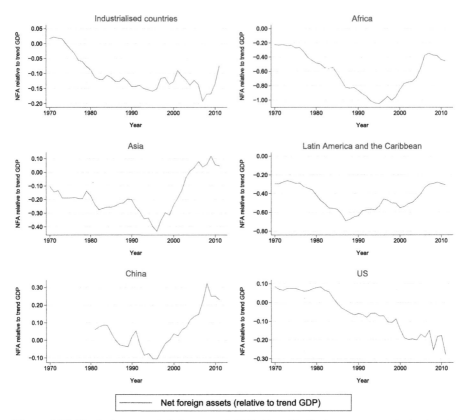

Figure 2.10 Net foreign assets (relative to trend GDP). *Note:* Net foreign assets are calculated as the difference between total assets and total liabilities. The Hodrick–Prescott filter is used to obtain trend GDP from nominal GDP.
Data sources: Lane and Milesi-Ferretti (2007) and update and World Bank (2013).

still relatively low compared to other regions: Net liabilities of the average country amounted to 29% of its trend GDP in 2010.

The lower panel of Figure 2.10 depicts the evolution of the NFA positions of China and the US. We have chosen these two countries because they are considered as major players in a simplified story of global imbalances where China's accumulation of international reserves finances the US current account deficit. This behavior is reflected in a decreasing NFA position in the US and increasing NFAs in China since the late 1990s.

We now turn to a consideration of gross stocks of foreign capital. The sum of foreign assets (FA) and foreign liabilities (FL) over GDP has been proposed as a measure of de facto financial openness by Lane and Milesi-Ferretti (2003, 2007).[6] The use of stocks instead of flows has the advantage that stocks reflect outstanding amounts of

[6] See Section 2.3 and Obstfeld and Taylor (2003).

international capital, while flows provide a snapshot, which is unable to provide information about long-run trends. This measure weights foreign assets and liabilities equally; that is, large creditor countries and highly indebted countries may both be financially open. Typical examples of financially open economies are financial centers with large foreign assets and liabilities. These illustrations show that the measure is independent of a country's NFA position.

This measure has been applied as dependent variable (e.g. Becerra et al., 2012) and covariate in many empirical studies, e.g. to explain economic growth and growth volatility (e.g. Kose et al., 2009a), crisis incidence and crisis transmission (e.g. Lane and Milesi-Ferretti, 2011), economic productivity (e.g. Eichengreen et al., 2011; Friedrich et al., 2013; Kose et al., 2009b), characteristics of international capital flows and economic policies (e.g. Furceri and Zdzienicka, 2012b; Spiegel, 2009).

This definition of financial openness does not distinguish whether claims are held by private agents or official agencies. That is, it makes no difference whether liabilities stem from private foreign investors' activities in the domestic economy or from foreign agencies' development aid.

We therefore propose an alternative measure called *private financial openness*, which measures the de facto openness of an economy with respect to private capital. Following our definition of official capital in Section 2.4, we exclude official claims and liabilities from this measure. In this sense, private financial openness measures private agents' willingness and ability to invest abroad and to incur foreign debt. Large inflows of development aid or a central bank's accumulation of reserves do not stem from private investors' decisions and are excluded from this measure. Both do not affect private investors' space for potential activities. In our interpretation, private financial openness refers to the extent to which expected-return-maximizing investors are active in international transactions.

Formally, private financial openness is defined as:

$$IFIPRGDP_{it} = \frac{(FA_{it} - IR_{it}) + (FL_{it} - DA_{it})}{GDP_{it}} \qquad (2.1)$$

where IR is the stock of international reserves and DA the amount of outstanding development loans.

We proceed by studying whether our measure of *private financial openness* differs significantly from the standard measure. Figure 2.11 shows the evolution of financial openness averaged over different country groups. The standard measure follows Lane and Milesi-Ferretti (2007) and computes the share of total assets and liabilities in GDP. We then first exclude international reserves and then additionally concessional external debt (development aid) from assets and liabilities. The last measure corresponds to our definition of private financial openness.

The graph highlights two points: De facto financial openness has increased in all country groups. Industrial countries are the most open country group, while emerging and developing countries exhibit a similar level of openness. Whereas emerging markets opened up during the 2000s, financial openness in the average developing country has been relatively stable since the 1990s. Second, whether there is a significant difference between total and private financial openness depends on the country

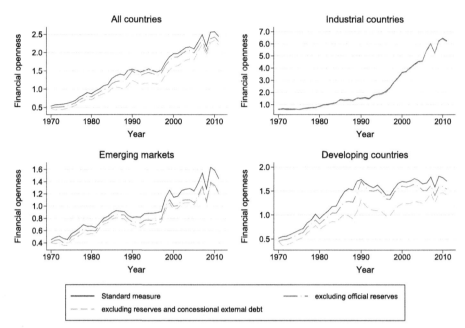

Figure 2.11 Total versus private financial openness – country groups.
Data sources: IMF (2013) and World Bank (2013).

group. Official claims and liabilities in industrial countries are small relative to total ones such that the difference is only marginal. The difference between both measures is remarkable in developing countries and in emerging markets, in the latter especially since the 2000s. While in emerging markets the difference is mainly due to reserve assets, in developing countries outstanding development loans are accountable for the discrepancy between total and private financial openness. In developing countries, the average total financial openness equals 1.78 in the year 2010, while private financial openness amounts to 1.46, a difference of 18%.

Country case studies, which are presented in Figure 2.12, show that the difference between total and private financial openness varies a lot across countries: While it is remarkable in some countries, it is negligible in others. Each plot shows the evolution of both measures for two countries of the same geographic region. Countries are selected such that in one the difference between both measures seems to be unimportant, whereas it matters in the other country, both in absolute terms and relative to the other country.

The upper left panel figures South Africa and Burundi. For South Africa the difference between both measures of financial openness is marginal. For Burundi, however, it makes a large difference, especially compared to South Africa: According to total financial openness Burundi was financially more open than South Africa from 1986 to 2008. South Africa only could catch up with Burundi after a strong increase in assets and liabilities in the late 1990s. However, if we compare both countries on the basis of private financial openness, South Africa has always been more open than Burundi.

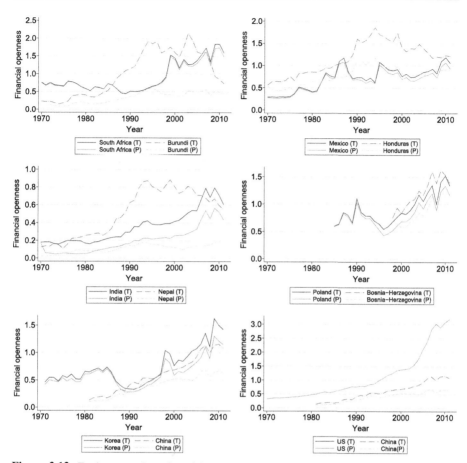

Figure 2.12 Total versus private financial openness – case studies. *Note:* (T) stands for the standard measure of total financial openness whereas (P) denotes private financial openness.
Data sources: Lane and Milesi-Ferretti (2007) and update and World Bank (2013).

Similar conclusions can be drawn for the country pairs in the remaining plots. In the upper right panel Mexican financial openness is not affected by the chosen measure. However, according to the standard measure, except for one year Honduras is financially more open than Mexico. If we consider private financial openness, Honduras and Mexico show comparable levels. Enlightening is also the comparison of China and Korea in the panel on the bottom left. For Korea the difference between both measures is relatively small. Since 1990 Chinese total financial openness is similar to that in Korea. However, if we consider private financial openness China is much more closed than Korea because private financial openness does not incorporate its large holdings of international reserves. Chinese financial openness is almost halved: In 2010 total financial openness equals 1.16 and private one 0.67.

The difference between total and private financial openness might be important in empirical applications. An example is the literature that examines whether financial openness spurs economic growth. Since theory suggests that financial openness improves the allocation of capital, reduces risks and lifts credit constraints, studies search for positive effects of financial openness on growth. On theoretical grounds, the relevant measure for openness would be the private one. It reflects firms' access to foreign financial resources and measures the extent to which potential financial constraints have been eased. While a large stock of reserves may indirectly raise growth through its positive effects on economic stability, reserves are not expected to enhance allocative efficiency. Future research may examine whether the relationship between financial openness and growth depends on the definition used.

Current Account Imbalances: The Role of Official Capital Flows[1]

Contents

3.1 Introduction   27
3.2 Implications of reserve currency status   31
   3.2.1 Literature review   31
   3.2.2 Implications of the dual role of the reserve currency   32
   3.2.3 Reserve status and balance of payments accounting   33
   3.2.4 Reserve currency status in a portfolio balance model   33
        Channel 1: Adjustment via exchange rate   36
        Channel 2: Adjustment via interest rates   37
3.3 Empirical analysis of the role of official capital for the current account balance   37
   3.3.1 Who finances the US current account deficit? A statistical analysis   38
   3.3.2 What is the role of official capital in the current account balance? A regression analysis   39
        Baseline results   42
        Instrumental variables approach   45
        Robustness   46
        Policy variables   48
        Private versus official current account financing   48
        Alternative measures of global reserve demand   51
        Alternative sample period   51
        Asymmetric effects   53
        Secondary reserve currency countries   55
   3.3.3 Which factors are major determinants of the US current account balance?   57
   3.3.4 How do official and private capital flows interact?   58
3.4 Conclusions and policy implications   59
Appendix 3.A   Reserve currency status and balance of payments   61
Appendix 3.B   List of variables and data sources   63
Appendix 3.C   Sample of countries   66
Appendix 3.D   Regression results: Robustness using fixed samples   66

3.1   Introduction

The global financial crisis of 2008–10 has revived the discussion about the causes and consequences of global imbalances and the net capital flows they involve. Global imbalances are considered to be among the causing factors of the global financial crisis (see Aizenman, 2010; Belke and Gros, 2010; Ferguson and Schularick, 2011; IMF,

---

[1] This is an extended and updated version of Steiner (2014a). Publication with permission from Elsevier. Differences in the quantitative results may arise from revised data.

Global Imbalances, Financial Crises, and Central Bank Policies
Copyright © 2016 Elsevier Inc. All rights reserved.

2009a; Obstfeld and Rogoff, 2010; Portes, 2009). They facilitated macroeconomic developments that led to the US housing boom and the accumulation of debt in the US.

A central question in international macroeconomics is how these imbalances can be explained.[2] While the literature traditionally centers on the question whether imbalances are caused by low US saving rates or an East Asian savings glut, this chapter provides empirical evidence for a new interpretation: Central banks' demand for reserves sustains global imbalances. First, reserve-accumulating countries run larger current account balances. Second, the US current account deficit can partly be explained by its reserve currency status.[3] This is a crucial finding since according to the savings glut and low US savings hypotheses the US external imbalance is a temporary phenomenon, whereas we show that it is rather a structural outcome of the international monetary system. From this vantage point, the reserve currency status of the US is one of the macroeconomic factors that contributed to the unfolding of the global financial crisis.

Two stylized facts, which are illustrated in Figure 3.1, motivate this chapter:

1. During the past 30 years the US has been characterized by a persistent current account deficit, which has negatively affected its net foreign assets position[4]: In 1970 the US was a creditor country with net foreign assets amounting to 4.1% of US output. Current account deficits turned this positive net foreign investment position into a debtor position. In 2010 the US owes the rest of the world 17% of its output.[5]

2. Over the same period, central banks in the rest of the world have accumulated an enormous amount of foreign exchange reserves, which are predominantly invested in US assets. Since 1970 they have accumulated dollar reserves equal to 60% of US GDP in 2010.

To some extent the constellation with a current account deficit in the reserve-providing country is the natural outcome of the architecture of the international monetary system. Countries at the periphery have to export capital to the reserve currency country in order to buy the insurance provided by foreign exchange reserves. Their accumulation of dollar reserves constitutes an inflow of capital to the US and sustains net capital flows to capital-rich countries – the Lucas paradox.

---

[2] For a review of the evolution of imbalances and the dominant players refer to Belke and Schnabl (2013).

[3] In our terminology a country enjoys reserve currency status if its assets are held by foreign central banks as part of their international reserves. As such it is a narrow concept of the international role of a currency, which focuses on its importance for official uses as opposed to private uses. The terms "key currency status" or "financial center" are defined by the role of currencies in private transactions. A financial center provides intermediation services to the rest of the world and is characterized by large stocks of foreign assets and liabilities relative to GDP. Key currency status refers to the international role of a currency manifested by its private use for the invoicing of trade or on the foreign exchange market.

[4] While it is true that the dollar served as major reserve currency long before the US current account turned into deficit, we argue that the current account surplus would have been larger without reserve status.

[5] Data are based on Lane and Milesi-Ferretti (2007) and update, and World Bank (2011).

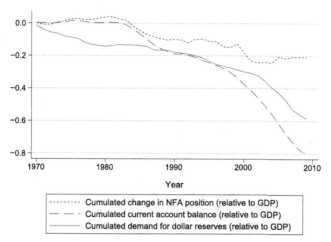

Figure 3.1 US current account deficit, NFA position and global dollar reserve accumulation.
Data sources: NFA position: Lane and Milesi-Ferretti (2007) and update; current account: World Bank (2012); global dollar reserve demand: own calculations based on the COFER database, IMF Annual Reports and World Bank (2012).

By examining whether the international role of the dollar has contributed to the US current account deficit and its deteriorating net foreign asset position, this chapter offers an empirical evaluation of the mechanics surrounding the Triffin dilemma. Triffin (1960, p. 9) notes that "the additions to international liquidity [...] are entirely dependent on the willingness of the key currency countries to allow their own net reserve position to deteriorate, by letting their short term liabilities to foreigners grow persistently and indefinitely at a faster pace than their own gold assets". Kindleberger (1969, p. 8) refers to Triffin stating that "reserves can be added only by new gold production, which is inadequate in some sense [...], and through deficits of the reserve-currency countries".

As a corollary of the insight that the provision of reserves might cause a deficit in the balance of payments, Triffin (1960) argues that any international monetary system that uses a national currency as its reserve asset will be unstable.[6] The objectives to fix the dollar value in terms of gold and to satisfy an increasing demand for dollar reserves are mutually exclusive. In its modern version, the Triffin dilemma asserts that the value of the reserve currency may be undermined if sufficient reserves are provided to the rest of the world.

This chapter is related to various strands of the literature. First, we base our analysis on the literature on the determinants of the current account (see Chinn and Prasad, 2003; Chinn et al., 2014; Gruber and Kamin, 2007). These papers examine how private agents' decisions with regard to savings and investment give rise to private capital flows, which, in turn, shape current account balances. We take this literature as our benchmark and extend it by explicitly taking account of official capital flows and

---

[6] Triffin (1960, p. 87) concludes that "the use of national currencies as international reserves constitutes indeed a "built-in destabilizer" in the world monetary system".

countries' reserve currency status. The literature usually finds that the main reserve currency country, the US, is an outlier (see Chinn et al., 2014; Gruber and Kamin, 2007). Her current account is persistently overpredicted. Using in-sample and out-of-sample predictions, Chinn and Ito (2007) conclude that the US current account is systematically overpredicted since the mid-1990s, a fact not observed for any other country. Balakrishnan et al. (2009) find a positive residual for the US signaling an unexplained preference for US assets. Whether this observation is linked to the US status as reserve currency provider has not been examined empirically so far.

Second, by illustrating the importance of central banks' reserve policies for current account balances, our study affiliates to a literature that highlights the importance of policies and interdependencies in explaining global imbalances. Schnabl and Freitag (2012) show that monetary policies in center and periphery countries have shaped imbalances. Prades and Rabitsch (2012) emphasize the role of differences in financial openness. Aizenman and Jinjarak (2009) document that US imports affect the current account balance in the rest of the world. An increase in lagged US imports raises the current account balance in surplus countries.

Conceptually this study is related to a recent literature that stresses the role of official capital flows in explaining global imbalances (see Alfaro et al., 2014; Gagnon, 2012, 2013; IMF, 2013). Gagnon (2013) shows empirically that current account imbalances are linked to official purchases of international reserves. His approach differs from ours in that he examines whether official capital flows are offset by private ones while we estimate the effect on the current account directly. Chinn et al. (2014) find that the impact of the lagged level of reserves on the current account is negative for industrialized and positive for developing countries. Bayoumi and Saborowski (2014) emphasize that the degree of capital account openness matters for the impact of reserve accumulation on the current account. While there is no effect in financially open economies, in countries with closed capital accounts every dollar of accumulated reserves raises the current account by 50 cents. The authors also identify a weaker US current account as the counterpart of global reserve accumulation. Finally, Farhi et al. (2011) note that imbalances might reflect rather imbalances in the demand and supply of reserve assets across nations than a disequilibrium in trade.

The main innovation of this study is to extend the literature on the determination of the current account by taking account of the role of official capital flows. Our findings are twofold: First, we confirm the positive relationship between reserve accumulation and current account balance for reserve-accumulating countries using an instrumental variables approach. Any dollar of accumulated reserves increases the current account balance by 40 to 50 cents. Second, we explicitly consider the effect of global reserve accumulation on the current account of reserve-providing countries. Our evidence shows that any dollar of globally accumulated reserves decreases the US current account by more than one dollar. Private capital flows rather reinforce than offset official flows. While the average demand for US reserve assets amounted to 0.9% of US GDP per annum over the period 1970–2009, its entire estimated effect equals 2.2% of US GDP. Current accounts of other reserve-providing countries besides the US are not significantly affected.

The remainder of this chapter is organized as follows. The next section discusses the theoretical implications of being the reserve currency provider. Section 3.3 provides an empirical analysis of the link between current account balances and reserve policies. It focuses on the question whether reserve currency status can be held accountable for a downward shift in the current account. Concluding remarks are offered in Section 3.4.

3.2 Implications of reserve currency status

This section discusses the theoretical argument that the reserve-providing country faces relaxed external financing constraints. The reserve currency provider is often considered to benefit from an exorbitant privilege (Gourinchas et al., 2010): Thanks to the foreign demand for reserve assets, its balance of payments constraint is relaxed and it can more easily run current account deficits. The flip side of this soft constraint may be a rising level of external debt.[7]

3.2.1 Literature review

A number of theoretical models explore the implications of key currency status. In contrast to our approach, these models usually do not distinguish between private and official investors[8] because the effects of the demand for reserve assets on the issuing country arise independently of the nature of the investor.

Caballero et al. (2008) derive low US interest rates and a US current account deficit as the equilibrium outcome of different levels of financial development. Mendoza et al. (2009) explain global imbalances as the result of different degrees of financial market development. By means of a calibration analysis they examine the transition dynamics from autarky to full global financial integration. The US current account (relative to GDP) drops on impact by 4 percentage points and gradually converges to its long-run equilibrium (a balanced current account) over a period of 50 years.

Maggiori (2013) shows that the emergence of a key currency country within the global monetary system can be modeled as the equilibrium outcome of countries with different levels of financial development: The country with the most developed financial market holds a relatively large share of risky assets while it provides safe assets to the rest of the world. In the long run, the key currency country runs a trade deficit, which is financed through net earnings on its net foreign assets thanks to a safety premium.

Ghosh (2011) presents a microfounded model of imperfect asset substitutability between countries in the spirit of the portfolio balance approach. In this setting, an

---

[7] Aliber (1964) and Tavlas (1997) provide balanced discussions of the implications of being the reserve currency country.

[8] In Section 3.2.4 we explicitly introduce central banks as investors in a portfolio balance model.

exogenous increase in the share of wealth invested in one country leads to a current account deficit in that country on impact.

Benigno and Fornaro (2012) argue that reserve accumulation might be a second-best policy in an economy characterized by growth externalities and crises. In this scenario, a liberalization of the capital account increases the optimal amount of reserves. Compared to a situation without central bank intervention, the current account balance increases. As a corollary, the current account balance of the reserve currency country decreases.

The presented theoretical models concur that the global demand for safe assets creates a current account deficit in the region with a highly developed financial market. Optimizing (representative) individuals are the drivers of these capital flows. With limited financial integration, however, individual agents might be unable to satisfy their demand for foreign assets. In this case, the central bank might provide intermediation services between domestic creditors and foreign borrowers that mimic the situation of full capital mobility: The central bank issues domestic assets and uses these funds to buy foreign exchange reserves. Hence, with limited capital mobility the demand for safe assets might be reflected in an increase in central banks' reserves (see Bacchetta and Benhima, 2015; Song et al., 2011).

3.2.2 Implications of the dual role of the reserve currency

A reserve currency country is characterized by the unique situation that its currency fulfills two roles: First, alike any other currency, it is the unit of denomination of financial assets. Second, it provides insurance to other countries in states of financial crisis and is therefore used as reserve asset by central banks.

As a consequence of this dual role, lending is provided by two types of agents for different reasons: First, alike any financially integrated economy, the reserve currency country receives loans from private foreign lenders as a result of their portfolio optimization. Second, in contrast to the rest of the world, foreign central banks provide loans to the reserve currency country equal to the amount of foreign exchange reserves they hold.[9] Thus, the reserve currency country faces an additional demand for its loans. In line with a simple demand–supply framework, the amount of debt and the price of loans are higher than without reserve currency characteristic. Equilibrium may be restored by lower interest rates or an appreciated exchange rate.

Theses exceptional features of reserve currency bonds have been documented empirically: Krishnamurthy and Vissing-Jorgensen (2012) conclude that foreign central banks invest their reserves in US Treasuries regardless of their return relative to other US fixed income assets. Caballero and Krishnamurthy (2009) stress that capital inflows to the US have been sustained by the rest of the world's demand for a safe store of value. This contributes to global imbalances and leads to a concentration of risky

---

[9] Foreign central banks may increase their reserve hoardings to maintain the pegged exchange rate (see Blanchard et al., 2005) or to build a buffer stock for potential future crises (see Aizenman and Lee, 2007).

assets in the US. As a consequence, US asset prices are higher and interest rates are lower.[10]

3.2.3   Reserve status and balance of payments accounting

The demand for reserves need not be associated with a current account deficit in the reserve currency country. It may be financed through counterbalancing private capital outflows from the reserve currency country. According to the balance of payments constraint, the sum of current account balance (CA) and capital account balance (KA)[11] equals the change in international reserves (R). If the capital account is further divided into the balance of private (KA^{PR}) and official capital flows (KA^{OF}), the balance of payments constraint can be written as:

$$CA + KA^{PR} + KA^{OF} = \Delta R \qquad (3.1)$$

For the center country, this balance of payments constraint can alternatively be expressed as (see Appendix 3.A for the details):

$$CA + KA^{PR} = -\Delta R^{ROW} \qquad (3.2)$$

where ΔR^{ROW} denotes the change in reserve assets in the rest of the world. This equation shows that any demand for additional reserves from the rest of the world may be satisfied by one of the following two counterbalancing operations in the center country: (1) a current account deficit or (2) private capital outflows. When the supply of reserves is financed by private capital outflows, the effect on financial fragility in countries other than the reserve currency provider, however, is inconclusive: While the country increases its buffer stock of reserves, its external vulnerability also grows since private capital inflows increase its external debt. Hence, it is true that the center has to run a current account deficit when the rest of the world wants to raise its net foreign asset position by the accumulation of *net* reserve assets.

3.2.4   Reserve currency status in a portfolio balance model

This section presents a simple portfolio balance model in the spirit of Blanchard et al. (2005) to illustrate how reserve currency status affects current and capital account of the center country. The model shows that any additional demand for reserves causes one of the following changes in the short run: Either the exchange rate of the reserve currency country appreciates and the current account balance decreases or interest rates diverge causing net private capital outflows from the center country.

---

[10] Estimates of the interest rate effect of foreign official demand of Treasury bonds are provided by Kitchen and Chinn (2011), Krishnamurthy and Vissing-Jorgensen (2012) and Warnock and Cacdac Warnock (2009).

[11] In our definition, all cross-border financial transactions are recorded in the capital account. The IMF uses a different classification where, according to their type, financial flows enter either the financial or capital account. In our definition, the capital account is the aggregate of the IMF's financial and capital account. Unless otherwise stated, this definition applies throughout the rest of this book.

According to the portfolio balance approach the equilibrium in international asset markets is restored by exchange rate adjustments. The model is based on imperfect substitutability between assets. In the long-run equilibrium the current account is balanced: Debtor countries run a trade surplus to finance interest payments on their net debt.[12]

Our contribution to the model is to explicitly introduce central banks as actors. While the standard model assumes that the equilibrium is determined by market forces, we allow central banks to affect supply and demand of both assets via foreign exchange market intervention. While private investors base their portfolio determination on risk–return considerations, central banks invest in reserve assets of safe havens independently of their return.

Our model considers two regions, the reserve currency country – for simplicity labeled US – and the rest of the world, which will be called foreign. There are two assets, US and foreign bonds. The wealth of US investors (W), measured in units of US goods, can be expressed as

$$W = X - F \tag{3.3}$$

where X denotes the stock of US assets and F is the US net debt position with regard to the rest of the world.

The same relationship holds for the rest of the world, whose variables are denoted by an asterisk and are expressed in terms of foreign goods. The net debt position of the US (F) equals the net foreign asset position of the rest of the world because both form a closed economy:

$$\frac{W^*}{E} = \frac{X^*}{E} + F \tag{3.4}$$

where the real exchange rate (E) is defined as the price of foreign goods in terms of US goods (a decrease in E corresponds to a depreciation of the dollar).

The gross real rate of return on assets depends on their rate of interest and valuation changes due to exchange rate movements. The expected gross real rate of return of US relative to foreign assets can be expressed as:

$$R^e = \frac{1+r}{1+r^*} \frac{E^e_{+1}}{E} \tag{3.5}$$

where r and r^* denote US and foreign real interest rates, respectively. E^e_{+1} is the expected real exchange rate one period ahead. Due to the assumption of imperfect asset substitutability, uncovered interest parity need not be satisfied. To this setting with US and foreign private investors we add central banks as additional investors in each country. The total amount of assets is supplied by private investors (X^{PR}) and the central bank (X^{CB}):

$$X = X^{PR} + X^{CB} \tag{3.6}$$

[12] For the foundations of the portfolio balance model refer to Branson (1977), Henderson and Rogoff (1982) and Kouri (1983) among others.

where the same relationship holds in the rest of the world (equation with asterisks). Investors choose between US and foreign assets. US private investors allocate a share α^{PR} of their wealth to US assets and a share $(1 - \alpha^{PR})$ to foreign assets. Foreign private investors dedicate a share α^{PR*} of their wealth to foreign assets and invest a share $(1 - \alpha^{PR*})$ in US assets. These shares increase in the expected relative gross return of the respective asset:

$$\alpha^{PR} = \alpha^{PR}(R^e), \quad \alpha^{PR*} = \alpha^{PR*}(R^e) \quad \text{with} \quad \alpha^{PR}_{R^e} > 0, \alpha^{PR*}_{R^e} < 0$$
$$\text{and} \quad 0 \leq \alpha^{PR}, \alpha^{PR*} \leq 1$$

The asset composition of central banks, in turn, is independent of the relative return. It depends entirely on the reserve status of the respective currency. Let $(1 - \alpha^{CB*})$ denote the fraction of total foreign central bank wealth X^{CB*} devoted to US assets. The US central bank, in turn, holds a share $(1 - \alpha^{CB})$ of its wealth in foreign assets. We assume that central banks sterilize their interventions: A purchase of foreign reserves is financed by a sale of domestic assets.

The market for US assets is in equilibrium if the supply of US assets (X) equals the demand for US assets by private investors and central banks in both regions:

$$X = \alpha(R^e)W + (1 - \alpha^*)\frac{W^*}{E} \tag{3.7}$$

where α is a weighted average of α^{PR} and α^{CB} and α^* is a weighted average of α^{PR*} and α^{CB*}. Using equations (3.3), (3.4) and (3.6), this condition can alternatively be expressed as[13]

$$X = \alpha^{PR}(R^e)(X^{PR} - F) + \alpha^{CB}X^{CB} + (1 - \alpha^{PR*})\left(\frac{X^{PR*}}{E} + F\right)$$
$$+ (1 - \alpha^{CB*})\frac{X^{CB*}}{E} \tag{3.8}$$

We now turn to the evolution of the net foreign asset position of the rest of the world, which is given by

$$dF = rF + (1+r)(1-\alpha)\left(1 - \frac{1+r^*}{1+r}\frac{E}{E_{+1}}\right)(X - F) + D(E) \tag{3.9}$$

where $D(E)$ is the US trade deficit.[14] $D(E)$ is assumed to increase in E. The three terms on the right-hand side account for the following effects: The foreign country accumulates assets thanks to (1) interest income in the presence of an existing positive net foreign asset position, (2) excess returns on its gross holdings of foreign assets and (3) a trade surplus. By definition, the change in the net foreign asset position equals the current account balance.

---

[13] We assume that profits or deficits of central banks are carried over to the public. This allows us to hold X^{CB} and X^{CB*} constant over time. This simplification does not affect our major findings.

[14] By implication $D(E)$ represents the trade surplus of the rest of the world.

Assume that there are three periods: In period 1 the reserve asset is provided by one country in the rest of the world. Due to exogenous reasons, in period 2 the reserve currency status moves to the US. Central banks adjust their reserve holdings accordingly. In period 3 there are no further changes in the composition of central banks' balance sheets. The exchange rate gradually moves to its long-run equilibrium.

In period 1 both central banks hold their desired amounts of reserves. The exchange rate is in its long-run equilibrium and the current account is balanced. Assume for simplicity that the net foreign asset position F equals 0. Furthermore, central banks credibly fix the real exchange rate such that $E = E^e_{+1}$. As a consequence, the relative return R^e is given and, by implication, asset shares α^{PR} and α^{PR*} are predetermined. Equation (3.8) can be solved for the equilibrium real exchange rate:

$$E = \frac{(1 - \alpha^{PR*})X^{PR*} + (1 - \alpha^{CB*})X^{CB*}}{(1 - \alpha^{PR})X^{PR} + (1 - \alpha^{CB})X^{CB} + (\alpha^{PR} + \alpha^{PR*} - 1)F} \quad (3.10)$$

In period 2, for given interest rates the US central bank reduces the share of foreign assets in total assets (α^{CB} increases) and the central banks of the rest of the world exchange foreign assets for US ones (α^{CB*} decreases). We proceed by considering two different adjustment scenarios to this change in preferences.

Channel 1: Adjustment via exchange rate

Assume that interest rates are given. Investors do not anticipate the reserve status shock and expect the exchange rate to be constant. Since private investors' asset shares are constant, the whole burden of adjustment is carried by the exchange rate. The effect on the exchange rate can be assessed by the first derivative of equation (3.10):

$$\frac{\partial E}{\partial \alpha^{CB*}} = -\frac{X^{CB*}}{(1 - \alpha)X + (\alpha + \alpha^{PR*} - 1)F} < 0 \quad (3.11)$$

The exchange of assets of the rest of the world for US assets by foreign central banks is equivalent to a decrease of α^{CB*}. Hence, the transition of reserve status to the US appreciates the exchange rate. This lowers the US trade balance $D(E)$ and the current account on impact. The US central bank, in turn, exchanges foreign assets for US assets:

$$\frac{\partial E}{\partial \alpha^{CB}} = \frac{[(1 - \alpha^{PR*})X^{PR*} + (1 - \alpha^{CB*})X^{CB*}]X^{CB}}{[(1 - \alpha^{PR})X^{PR} + (1 - \alpha^{CB})X^{CB} + (\alpha^{PR} + \alpha^{PR*} - 1)F]^2} > 0 \quad (3.12)$$

A move to US assets, which corresponds to an increase in α^{CB}, leads to a dollar appreciation. That is, actions of both central banks reinforce each other. The country that has become the reserve currency provider runs a current account deficit.

In period 3, α^{CB} and α^{CB*} reach their new equilibrium and the net foreign asset position of the US, F, has decreased. As a consequence, the exchange rate depreciates. In the long-run equilibrium with a balanced current account, the exchange rate is below its initial value in period 1: To finance interest payments on its increased foreign indebtedness, the US runs a trade surplus.

Channel 2: Adjustment via interest rates

After a changeover of reserve currency status, asset market equilibrium may alternatively be restored by changes in interest rates. The lower demand for foreign assets by central banks has to be offset by an increasing private demand. This may be accomplished by a fall in r and a rise in r^* such that α^{PR} decreases and α^{PR*} increases while world savings are constant. US private investors increasingly invest in the rest of the world and foreign investors reduce their US asset position. Asset markets are in equilibrium at the given exchange rate. The trade balance is unaffected.

Due to the interest rate differential $(\Delta(r - r^*) < 0)$ US income from foreign assets rises and payments on foreign liabilities decrease. In the long run equilibrium, the exchange rate appreciates. The rest of the world runs a larger trade balance to finance its interest payments. The current account is balanced.

So far, we have considered the exchange rate and interest rate channels separately. In reality, both might be at work jointly. The empirical facts described above suggest that the increasing demand for dollar reserves has gone hand in hand with a decreasing net foreign asset position of the US (channel 1) and a decreasing interest rate on US assets (channel 2). Provided that the exchange rate reacts in response to the reserve preference shock and that the process of reserve accumulation is not completed, the current account balance of the reserve currency country is lowered.

These results are confirmed by alternative models. In a new open economy macroeconomic model with imperfect substitution between assets, Canzoneri et al. (2013) examine the effects of central banks selling part of their dollar reserves. The calibration shows that an increasing demand for reserves lowers the US current account, decreases the US interest rate and raises foreign interest rates. Similar results are derived by Sá and Viani (2013) in a calibrated portfolio balance model.

3.3 Empirical analysis of the role of official capital for the current account balance

The relationship between reserve accumulation, US reserve status and current account balances is examined in empirical terms in the following section. It empirically tests the Triffin dilemma, according to which reserve currency status systematically lowers the current account balance.

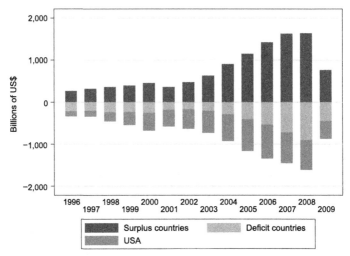

Figure 3.2 US current account deficit in relation to global current account balances.
Data source: World Bank (2012).

3.3.1 Who finances the US current account deficit? A statistical analysis

Figure 3.2 visualizes the importance of the US current account deficit relative to the rest of the world: For each year, the US current account deficit is compared with (1) the sum of the current account balances of all deficit countries and (2) to the sum of the current account of all surplus countries. It shows that a substantial part of the global deficit is concentrated in one country, namely the US. This concentration is even more pronounced if one compares countries' average balances in the long run: While the US current account deficit has been persistent,[15] other countries have switched from the surplus to the deficit group and vice versa during this period. To put it into perspective, the current account deficit of the US accounted for 47% (51%) of the global deficit over the period 1970–2012 (1995–2012).

In light of this observation, the question arises who finances the US current account deficit. Official and private external investors might provide credits. Whereas official capital inflows are the result of reserve currency status, private capital inflows are not directly linked to this status. Private inflows might be explained by economic and institutional variables like the presence of well developed financial markets. Figure 3.1, which may be found at the beginning of this chapter, compares the magnitude of US external financing with the global change in dollar reserves. It depicts the cumulated balance of the current account and the cumulated change in the net foreign asset position of the US since 1970. The difference between both series is a measure of the exorbitant privilege (see Gourinchas et al., 2010). Thanks to favorable exchange rate movements, the net external asset position of the US deteriorated less than the cumu-

---

[15] The US current account has been in deficit since 1982 with the exception of a small surplus in 1991.

lated sum of current account deficits. The third line highlights the cumulated demand for dollar reserves over the same period. The change in dollar reserves is calculated on the basis of data taken from the COFER database of the IMF and IMF Annual Reports, which provide information on the currency composition of foreign exchange reserves. The figure shows that a substantial part of the US current account deficit has been financed through the purchase of reserves by foreign central banks. Hence, official capital flows are an important driver of net capital flows.

3.3.2   What is the role of official capital in the current account balance? A regression analysis

This section examines how reserve policies affect the current account balance. We distinguish two effects: First, any change in reserves affects the current account of the country where reserve changes take place if these changes are not offset by private capital flows. Second, since the accumulation of reserves constitutes a capital export, it might affect the current account balance of the reserve-providing country. Following the seminal papers on the determinants of current accounts by Chinn and Prasad (2003), Chinn et al. (2014) and Gruber and Kamin (2007), we regress the current account balance relative to GDP on a set of possible determinants. This setting is augmented by two variables: First, the change in foreign exchange holdings is added for each individual country. Second, the regressions for reserve-providing countries are augmented by the global demand for reserve assets denominated in the country's currency.

The empirical study is carried out on the basis of a pooled data set of cross-country and time-series observations. It contains annual data from 1970 to 2009. Variable definitions and data sources can be found in Appendix 3.B. After dropping small countries (population smaller than 3 millions in the year 2005), the sample contains 125 countries, which are listed in Appendix 3.C.

Since the current account balance equals the difference between national saving and national investment, all variables that affect saving or investment are potential determinants of the current account balance. In particular, the set of controls encompasses the following variables:

Government budget balance relative to GDP: If Ricardian equivalence holds, any public deficit will increase private saving so that overall saving and the current account balance are unaffected. However, if Ricardian equivalence is not perfect, national saving may increase in government saving. As a corollary, the twin deficit hypothesis states that government budget deficits go along with deficits in the current account.

Net foreign asset (NFA) position relative to GDP: The NFA position of a country reflects the sum of its current account balances in the past and valuation changes in assets and liabilities. It affects the current account balance through two channels: First, the higher the NFA position, the higher the returns, which positively enter the current account balance. Second, in the long run a positive NFA position reduces a country's incentives for precautionary savings and relaxes the current account constraint. Countries with a comfortable NFA position might prefer lower current account balances.

Financial deepening: The development of financial markets, its instruments and institutions positively affect both saving and investment. Investment returns increase while credit costs are lower. However, developed financial markets may also reduce private agents' borrowing constraints and lower private saving. Deep financial markets may attract foreign saving. Countries whose financial markets are characterized by a comparative advantage relative to other countries might therefore face capital inflows, which place downward pressures on the current account balance. Financial deepening is measured by M2 relative to GDP.

Oil-exporting countries: The current account balance of exporters of natural resources might on average be more favorable. We include exports of fuels as a percentage of merchandise exports to control for this fact.

Stage of development: Theory suggests that the catch-up process of countries at low stages of development may be characterized by capital imports and current account deficits. More advanced countries may run current account surpluses in order to pay off the external liabilities they accumulated while catching up or in order to benefit from high returns in capital-poor countries. The stage of development is measured by real per capita income relative to the rest of the world. Due to possible nonlinearities its squared term is also included.

Demographics: Both young and old societies are expected to save less. This affects the current account balance insofar as the demographic structure of a society differs across countries. We include young and old dependency ratios and measure them relative to the average ratio across all countries.

GDP growth: Consumption-smoothing agents may save in periods of high GDP growth and dissave if economic activity is hit by a negative shock. Therefore, the current account balance is expected to be positively affected by GDP growth.

Trade openness: Real openness of an economy could affect the current account balance via two channels: First, more open economies are more exposed to external shocks. This might increase precautionary savings. Second, real openness measures a country's integration with the rest of the world. It reflects the macroeconomic policy stance toward trade. The effect of a trade-friendly policy environment on the current account balance, however, is theoretically undetermined. Trade openness is measured as the sum of exports and imports over GDP.

Finally, we add our variables of interest, the change in foreign exchange holdings for each individual country and for reserve currency countries in addition the global demand for their reserve currency assets (both relative to GDP). Given that central banks usually do not disclose the currency composition of their reserves, the change in global foreign exchange holdings denoted in a given currency is estimated. By way of example, the amount of reserves denominated in dollars is calculated as the worldwide level of reserves excluding the US multiplied by the share of the dollar in foreign exchange reserves in that year. The change in this variable between two consecutive years is the official demand (or supply if the change is negative) of dollar reserves.[16]

---

[16] Data of the currency composition of foreign exchange reserves is based on IMF Annual Reports (1970–1994) and on the COFER database of the IMF (1995–2009). Since central banks disclose their reserve composition on a voluntary basis, the COFER measure is only based on a fraction of total world reserves

Any additional demand for foreign exchange allows the US to import goods or purchase foreign assets in exchange for the reserve asset. We interact this global demand for dollar reserves with the US dummy. In addition, we combine the global demand for other major reserve currencies – British Pound, French Franc, German Mark, Japanese Yen, Netherlands Guilder and Swiss Franc – in the variable "Official capital inflows (without US)". This variable equals the official demand for reserve assets in the respective currency (relative to GDP) and is zero for all countries without reserve status.

This specification allows for time-varying effects of reserve currency status: The higher the demand for reserve assets in a given year, the stronger the effect of reserve currency status on the current account balance. For hypothetical years where the global demand for reserves is constant, the specification correctly assumes that there is no direct effect on the current account balance.[17] Finally, the specification also allows for loss of reserve status: If central banks sell their reserve assets of country i, the global demand for its reserve assets is negative.

Besides the change in world total central bank foreign exchange reserves denominated in the respective reserve currency, we use two alternative measures of official capital inflows: the change in US Treasuries held by foreign central banks and the quantity change in central banks' foreign exchange reserves denominated in the respective reserve currency, which is provided by the Annual Report of the IMF. Quantity changes have the advantage that they map active central bank reserve policies characterized by sales and purchases of reserves. Observed changes in reserves, however, are the outcome of both quantity and price changes.

Figure 3.3 shows our three measures of official capital inflows to the US: The figure highlights the comovement of the three series. Although we will use all three measures in the regression analysis to test the robustness of our results, we do not expect that our findings depend on a certain measure.

According to the quantity change in reserves, which, as shown in Figure 3.3, has been a rather conservative measure of the global reserve demand in recent years, official capital inflows to the US have financed on average 0.9% of US GDP per annum over 1970–2009. Its importance has been rising: While the average contribution was 0.6% of GDP over 1970–1989, it amounted to 1.3% during 1990–2009.

Using this set of explanatory variables, we estimate the following fixed-effects specification

$$\left(\frac{CAB}{GDP}\right)_{it} = \alpha X_{it} + \beta \left(\frac{\Delta IR}{GDP}\right)_{it} + \gamma \left(\frac{\Delta IR^d}{GDP}\right)_{it} + c_i + \epsilon_{it} \qquad (3.13)$$

where CAB/GDP is the ratio of the current account balance to GDP, X is a vector of control variables, ΔIR is the change in foreign exchange reserves in country i between $t-1$ and t, ΔIR^d measures the demand for reserve assets of country i by foreign

---

(56% in 2012). For any given year we assume that the sample is representative in the sense that the global reserve composition equals the reserve composition of those countries disclosing it.

[17] There still exists the indirect effect of low interest rates, the exorbitant privilege.

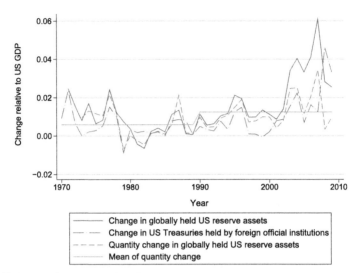

Figure 3.3 Global official demand for US reserve assets.
Data sources: Change in globally held US reserve assets is calculated as the change in global foreign exchange holdings denominated in US dollars and held by central banks (IFS, COFER database); change in US Treasuries held by foreign official institutions from Flow of Funds, Federal Reserve, Table L.106, line 11; quantity change in globally held US reserve assets from IMF Annual Report; mean of quantity change calculated over the periods 1970–1989 and 1990–2009.

central banks,[18] c is a fixed country effect and ϵ is the error term.[19] i denotes a specific country and t represents the time period. The slope parameters, represented by the vectors α, β and γ, are assumed to be constant across countries and time. We use the fixed effects estimator with a cluster-robust variance estimator.[20] Standard errors are corrected for within-country correlations.

Baseline results

The results of the baseline regressions are presented in Table 3.1. We first examine the results of OLS regressions for the full sample using different sets of explanatory variables and different country samples. Columns (1) to (4) make use of the entire sample. For the sake of comparison, column (1) presents the baseline regression as presented in Chinn et al. (2014). We then subsequently add our variables of interest: the change in foreign exchange reserves in each individual country (column (2)), the global demand for dollar reserves (column (3)) and the global demand for other reserve currencies (column (4)).

---

[18] ΔIR^d is zero for all countries besides those enjoying reserve currency status.

[19] We do not include fixed time effects because they are not meaningful in this context. Current account balances have to add up to zero globally.

[20] The Hausman test rejects a random effects specification.

Table 3.1 Determinants of the current account – OLS

	Full sample				Industrialized countries				Emerging markets	Developing countries
	(1)	(2)	(3)	(4)	(5)	(6)	(7)	(8)	(9)	(10)
Government budget balance (relative to GDP)	-0.0001*** (-3.85)	-0.0001*** (-3.75)	-0.0001*** (-3.67)	-0.0001*** (-3.67)	-0.0000 (-1.28)	-0.0000 (-1.28)	-0.0000 (-0.95)	-0.0000 (-0.96)	-0.0001*** (-3.53)	0.0786** (2.64)
NFA to GDP ratio	0.0197*** (3.18)	0.0189*** (3.23)	0.0188*** (3.26)	0.0188*** (3.25)	0.0830*** (4.15)	0.0831*** (4.13)	0.0719*** (4.36)	0.0719*** (4.36)	0.0167 (1.32)	0.0204*** (3.27)
Financial deepening	0.0004** (2.15)	0.0004* (1.95)	0.0004* (1.96)	0.0004* (1.96)	0.0000 (0.18)	0.0000 (0.17)	0.0000 (0.10)	0.0000 (0.10)	0.0010** (2.51)	-0.0004 (-0.99)
Fuel exports	0.0003 (0.99)	0.0002 (0.91)	0.0002 (0.87)	0.0002 (0.86)	0.0015 (0.88)	0.0015 (0.88)	0.0014 (0.85)	0.0014 (0.85)	-0.0003 (-0.76)	0.0006* (1.82)
Relative income	-0.0318 (-0.45)	-0.0194 (-0.28)	-0.0194 (-0.28)	-0.0195 (-0.28)	0.1252*** (4.06)	0.1253*** (4.05)	0.1199*** (4.16)	0.1194*** (4.19)	-0.0176 (-0.18)	-0.1304 (-0.93)
Relative income (squared)	0.0064 (0.58)	0.0044 (0.40)	0.0047 (0.43)	0.0046 (0.43)	-0.0178*** (-4.15)	-0.0178*** (-4.15)	-0.0168*** (-4.17)	-0.0167*** (-4.21)	0.0032 (0.12)	0.0271 (1.04)
Relative dependency ratio (old)	-0.0021 (-1.04)	-0.0024 (-1.23)	-0.0026 (-1.28)	-0.0026 (-1.28)	-0.0029* (-2.13)	-0.0028* (-2.09)	-0.0028* (-2.05)	-0.0028* (-2.04)	-0.0119 (-1.18)	0.0005 (0.12)
Relative dependency ratio (young)	-0.0005 (-0.85)	-0.0002 (-0.41)	-0.0001 (-0.26)	-0.0001 (-0.25)	0.0016 (1.62)	0.0016 (1.61)	0.0022*** (3.30)	0.0022*** (3.30)	0.0013 (1.51)	-0.0018*** (-2.54)
GDP growth	0.0277** (2.02)	0.0077 (0.56)	0.0075 (0.55)	0.0075 (0.55)	-0.0025 (-0.14)	-0.0019 (-0.10)	-0.0040 (-0.21)	-0.0037 (-0.20)	0.0137 (0.84)	0.0236 (1.30)
Trade openness	0.0324* (1.73)	0.0180 (1.00)	0.0185 (1.03)	0.0185 (1.03)	0.0291 (0.68)	0.0291 (0.68)	0.0227 (0.61)	0.0232 (0.63)	0.0476 (1.49)	-0.0183 (-1.00)
Change in foreign exchange (relative to GDP)		0.3549*** (5.26)	0.3553*** (5.26)	0.3554*** (5.26)					0.2689*** (3.52)	0.3803*** (4.27)
Official capital inflows to US * US dummy			-0.9469*** (-4.97)	-0.9464*** (-4.96)			-1.3424*** (-5.52)	-1.3421*** (-5.52)		
Official capital inflows (without US) * RCC dummy				-0.1565 (-0.83)				-0.1236 (-1.73)		
Observations	1645	1636	1636	1636	271	271	271	271	426	977
R-squared	0.08	0.13	0.14	0.14	0.42	0.42	0.46	0.46	0.28	0.16
Number of countries	99	98	98	98	11	11	11	11	18	71

Notes: The dependent variable is the current account balance to GDP ratio. RCC is a dummy variable that takes on the value one for the following reserve currency countries: France, Germany, Japan, the Netherlands, Switzerland and the UK. Estimation by OLS including country fixed effects. Robust t-statistics are reported in parentheses. Standard errors are estimated robust to intragroup correlations. The symbols *, **, and *** denote statistical significance at the 10%, 5% and 1% levels, respectively.

A positive government budget balance is associated with a lower current account balance. This effect is not in line with our expectations, but in line with other studies.[21] Ricardian equivalence does not hold. Households more than offset government's effect on the current account. The negative coefficient may signal that in periods of economic boom government budget surpluses go along with higher import demand by domestic citizens. A country's net foreign asset position (relative to GDP) and the current account balance are positively correlated. This implies that the gap between creditor and debtor countries is rather increasing than vanishing. The current account balance is positively affected by the development of national financial markets: More liquid and sophisticated financial markets are considered to be beneficial for economic growth, which, in turn, improves the current account balance. The remaining control variables show the expected sign, but are not statistically significant. By and large, these findings are in line with the results reported in Chinn and Prasad (2003) and Gruber and Kamin (2007). The main difference is the sign of the coefficient of the government budget balance.

Our priors with respect to the link between reserve changes and current account balances are confirmed: A change in foreign reserves in an individual country is positively correlated with its current account. The coefficient on the change in foreign exchange in column (2) of Table 3.1 implies that each dollar of additional reserves translates into an increase in the current account balance by 35 cents. The marginal increase in R-squared from 0.08 to 0.13 shows that domestic changes in foreign exchange reserves are an important determinant of the current account balance. The effect of a change in global reserves on the US current account is statistically and economically significant. If the rest of the world accumulates one dollar of reserves, the US current account decreases by 95 cents in the full sample. Although negative, the demand for other reserve currencies than the dollar does not significantly affect the current account balance of the issuing countries.

As has been documented by Chinn and Prasad (2003) there might be significant differences in the determination of current accounts between industrialized and developing countries. More specifically, industrialized countries might be able to run lower current account balances: As a result of the quality of their institutions and the relative stability of their currencies they are regarded as safe investment places.

Columns (5) to (8) repeat our analysis for a restricted sample of 11 industrialized countries. The following differences are remarkable: The government budget balance and financial deepening lose their significance. Relative income becomes significant indicating that richer economies run larger current account balances although this effect is decreasing in the level of income (nonlinearity indicated by the squared term). Older societies are characterized by lower current account balances. Changes in foreign exchange reserves do not affect the current account balance of industrialized countries. Reasons might be the relatively small changes in reserves in the majority of these countries – with the exception of Japan – and the high degree of financial integration of this country group, which facilitates that private capital flows offset the

---

[21] Kim and Roubini (2008) report for the US that the current account improves when the fiscal balance worsens ("twin divergence").

effect of official ones on the current account balance. The negative effect of the global demand for dollar reserves on the US current account balance is confirmed. It is even larger in this small sample indicating that each dollar of provided reserves lowers the US current account by 1.34 dollars.

The positive correlation between the accumulation of foreign exchange and the current account balance is confirmed in a subsample of 18 emerging markets (column (9)) and in a sample of developing countries (column (10)). Since these samples do not include reserve currency countries, the global demand for reserves cannot be included as a regressor in these specifications. Remarkably, for developing countries the twin deficit hypothesis is confirmed – a positive relation between government budget balance and current account balance. Moreover, resource-rich developing countries have larger current account balances.

Instrumental variables approach

Our preceding analysis is subject to endogeneity concerns: Official capital flows and the current account balance might be determined simultaneously. Changes in reserves might rather be driven by the current account balance than vice versa. The central bank has to accumulate reserves when the current account is in surplus at the fixed exchange rate and when this surplus is not offset by private capital outflows. Alike, the global demand for reserve-currency bonds might result from a current account deficit of the reserve-providing country. At given exchange rates, the rest of the world has to accumulate dollar assets when the US runs a current account deficit. These dollar assets might be purchased by private agents or official entities.

In the presence of endogeneity, our OLS estimates are biased and inconsistent. We therefore apply an instrumental variables approach (2SLS). In a first step, we estimate the demand for reserves in an individual country by an auxiliary regression. The idea is to get a measure of the demand for reserves that is independent of the current account balance. In particular, we regress the change of reserves relative to GDP on our exogenous variables and, in addition, on the following first-differenced variables: real GDP, trade openness, a measure of volatility and an index of capital controls. To account for level effects, the absolute amount of foreign exchange (relative to GDP) is added. The partial R-squared of excluded instruments equals 0.28. The Kleibergen–Paap test rejects the hypothesis of underidentification and the F statistic of 47 shows that instruments are sufficiently strong (see Staiger and Stock, 1997). A test of endogeneity of the change in foreign exchange reserves rejects the hypothesis of exogeneity at the 10% level. We therefore conclude that the 2SLS approach is preferable. The predicted value of the change in foreign exchange is then used in the second step to instrument for the demand for reserves.

The global demand for reserve-currency bonds might also be characterized by reverse causality. We therefore replace it by an estimate. We estimate the demand for reserves for each country and take the sum over all countries to get the global demand for reserves in a given year. In particular, we regress the ratio of foreign exchange reserves to GDP on real GDP, trade openness, a measure of volatility, total and short-term external debt (relative to GDP), a dummy for fixed exchange rate regimes and economic globalization using a fixed effects estimator with a cluster-robust variance estimator. We then multiply this global reserve demand by the share of each reserve currency in total foreign exchange holdings and compute the change of this variable between two consecutive years. This is, we calculate the demand for reserves by country i based on fundamentals of country i, which are assumed to be exogenous from policies in reserve-providing countries.

Table 3.2 replicates the regressions of Table 3.1 with the difference that the three variables for the reserve demand are instrumented. The underidentification test of Kleibergen–Paap has a p-value below 1% across all specifications. The bottom of the table reports the Wald F statistic of the weak identification test according to Kleibergen–Paap and the p-value of the Hansen J test for overidentifying restrictions.

With respect to our variables of main interest, previous results are confirmed: In the whole sample the accumulation of reserves raises the current account balance significantly. The effect is slightly larger compared to the analysis without instrumentalization with each dollar of reserve accumulation being transmitted into an increase in the current account balance by 44 cents. While the current account balance is independent of reserve changes in industrial countries, emerging markets and developing countries show a positive correlation between both variables. The negative impact of the global demand for reserves on the US current account is confirmed. Its magnitude is larger after instrumentalization.

Using 2SLS implies the following main changes with respect to the set of control variables: In the whole sample, the current account balance increases with the government budget balance in all regressions controlling for the demand for reserves. This confirms the twin deficit hypothesis. Moreover, relatively old societies are characterized by significantly lower current account balances, which is in line with our priors. The share of fuel exports in total exports significantly raises the current account balance in industrial and developing countries. For the sample of emerging markets, demographic structure and trade openness become significant.

In the presented tables, the number of observations and countries, which are used in each column, varies not only between country groups, but also within a given country group. The reason for this is that when we add additional control variables, observations are not available for the entire sample that has been used before. Some data are missing such that we lose observations or countries drop out of the sample. By using all observations that are available for a specific specification, we consider the maximum amount of information. This approach, however, implies that we cannot draw unambiguous conclusions from a comparison of two regression outputs: Changes in coefficients might either be due to the added control variables or to the modified sample. For completeness we therefore provide results for the same specifications based on fixed samples within a given country group in Table 3.D.1 in the Appendix. That is, the number of observations is constant for regressions on the full sample and on industrial countries.

Robustness

This section examines whether our results are robust to the inclusion of additional control variables. To be more precise, we augment our specification by policy variables

Table 3.2 Determinants of the current account – 2SLS

	Full sample					Industrialized countries			Emerging markets	Developing countries
	(1)	(2)	(3)	(4)	(5)	(6)	(7)	(8)	(9)	(10)
Government budget balance (relative to GDP)	-0.0001**	0.0744*	0.0743*	0.0744*	-0.0000	-0.0444	-1.5321	-1.6456	-6.6517	0.0754**
	(-2.47)	(1.75)	(1.75)	(1.75)	(-1.11)	(-0.01)	(-0.22)	(-0.24)	(-0.68)	(2.47)
NFA to GDP ratio	0.0197***	0.0163***	0.0162**	0.0162**	0.0830***	0.0666***	0.0593***	0.0595***	0.0157	0.0200***
	(2.94)	(2.45)	(2.45)	(2.44)	(5.31)	(4.39)	(3.79)	(3.84)	(1.15)	(2.63)
Financial deepening	0.0004***	0.0003***	0.0003***	0.0003***	0.0000	-0.0001	-0.0001	-0.0001	0.0010***	-0.0003
	(3.90)	(2.80)	(2.82)	(2.84)	(0.33)	(-0.41)	(-0.63)	(-0.56)	(3.76)	(-1.48)
Fuel exports	0.0003	0.0001	0.0001	0.0001	0.0015*	0.0024***	0.0024***	0.0024***	-0.0002	0.0004**
	(1.56)	(0.90)	(0.85)	(0.85)	(1.86)	(3.03)	(3.00)	(2.96)	(-0.93)	(2.02)
Relative income	-0.0318	-0.0194	-0.0194	-0.0192	0.1252***	0.1015**	0.0970**	0.0972**	-0.0187	-0.1498*
	(-0.91)	(-0.50)	(-0.50)	(-0.49)	(3.20)	(2.25)	(2.09)	(2.10)	(-0.25)	(-1.81)
Relative income (squared)	0.0064	0.0056	0.0057	0.0057	-0.0178***	-0.0126*	-0.0119*	-0.0119*	0.0100	0.0346**
	(1.15)	(0.93)	(0.95)	(0.94)	(-2.86)	(-1.84)	(-1.68)	(-1.69)	(0.25)	(2.13)
Relative dependency ratio (old)	-0.0021**	-0.0026***	-0.0027***	-0.0029***	-0.0029***	-0.0022***	-0.0021**	-0.0022**	-0.0128**	0.0009
	(-2.32)	(-2.72)	(-2.80)	(-2.91)	(-4.49)	(-2.57)	(-2.54)	(-2.38)	(-2.26)	(0.35)
Relative dependency ratio (young)	-0.0005	-0.0003	-0.0002	-0.0002	0.0016***	0.0009	0.0015**	0.0015**	0.0009	-0.0015***
	(-1.54)	(-0.94)	(-0.70)	(-0.71)	(3.09)	(1.39)	(2.19)	(2.19)	(1.14)	(-3.50)
GDP growth	0.0277***	0.0063	0.0063	0.0064	-0.0025	-0.0038	-0.0028	-0.0028	0.0025	0.0313*
	(2.68)	(0.52)	(0.51)	(0.52)	(-0.19)	(-0.17)	(-0.13)	(-0.13)	(0.12)	(1.94)
Trade openness	0.0324***	0.0168	0.0172	0.0170	0.0291	0.0347	0.0288	0.0284	0.0421**	-0.0229
	(3.37)	(1.57)	(1.61)	(1.59)	(1.10)	(0.87)	(0.74)	(0.72)	(2.42)	(-1.52)
Change in foreign exchange (relative to GDP)		0.4379***	0.4383***	0.4362***		-0.0092	-0.0423	-0.0421	0.5035***	0.3724***
		(4.99)	(4.99)	(4.98)		(-0.04)	(-0.17)	(-0.17)	(2.83)	(3.52)
Official capital inflows to US * US dummy			-1.3711***	-1.3757***			-1.9217***	-1.9206***		
			(-3.66)	(-3.67)			(-4.29)	(-4.29)		
Official capital inflows (without US) * RCC dummy				2.2944				0.6852		
				(0.84)				(0.30)		
Observations	1643	1447	1447	1447	271	237	237	237	381	857
R-squared	0.08	0.11	0.11	0.11	0.42	0.37	0.40	0.40	0.26	0.13
Number of countries	97	89	89	89	11	11	11	11	18	62
Weak identification (F statistic)		47.16	47.12	47.41		10.46	10.57	10.46	13.98	32.15
Hansen J statistic (p-value)		0.06	0.06	0.06		0.18	0.28	0.28	0.00	0.79

Notes: The dependent variable is the current account balance to GDP ratio. RCC is a dummy variable that takes on the value one for the following reserve currency countries: France, Germany, Japan, the Netherlands, Switzerland and the UK. Estimation by 2SLS including country fixed effects. The following variables are instrumented by the first-stage predictions: change in foreign exchange, official capital inflows to US and official capital inflows (without US). Robust t-statistics are reported in parentheses. Standard errors are estimated robust to intragroup correlations. The symbols *, ** and *** denote statistical significance at the 10%, 5% and 1% levels, respectively.

and variables accounting for financial center status. We then test the robustness for different subperiods and for alternative measures of the global demand for reserves.

Policy variables

Since any current account balance has to be financed by capital inflows or capital outflows, determinants of the capital account affect the current account balance too. Therefore, we include two variables that reflect the ability of an economy to invest abroad and to attract foreign investment: Capital controls and civil liberties.[22]

Capital controls: Economies characterized by strict controls on capital inflows are less able to finance current account deficits whereas economies with controls on capital outflows are less able to run current account surpluses. Since our measure of de jure capital account openness (Chinn–Ito index) does not distinguish between inflow and outflow controls,[23] the sign of the coefficient on the index of capital controls is unclear a priori.

Civil liberties: Country risk is an important factor in investment decisions. Reliable institutions and a sound legal and political system can improve a country's attractiveness as investment place. The index of civil liberties measures personal freedom, human rights, rule of law and economic rights. Countries with better institutions are expected to be correlated with larger net capital inflows, which reduce the current account balance. Higher index values are assigned to countries where civil liberties are less present.

Private versus official current account financing

Creditors financing a current account deficit might be foreign private agents or foreign official entities like central banks. Since this chapter strives at determining whether current account imbalances are primarily sustained by private or official capital flows, it is important to adequately disentangle both types. Alike foreign central banks, private investors might benefit from deep and liquid financial markets of the reserve-providing country. In particular, the US has been described as the banker of the world that transforms short-term external liabilities into long-term external loans. Besides this maturity transformation, the US increasingly provides risk transformation services issuing short-term fixed income assets and investing the proceeds in riskier foreign long-term projects (see Gourinchas and Rey, 2007). Theoretically, these flows may be balanced: A reserve currency country can provide financial intermediation to the rest of the world while its current account is balanced. If, however, its feature as financial center is linked to domestic investment opportunities, financial center status might affect the current account balance.

Financial center: We control for the effect of financial centers by the inclusion of a dummy variable. It is defined on the basis of a country's gross positions of external assets and liabilities relative to GDP. If both positions are jointly larger than their

---

[22] See De Santis and Luehrmann (2009) for the determinants of the capital account.

[23] For our large set of countries and the considered time period there are no measures of capital controls available that distinguish between controls on inflows and outflows.

respective mean plus their standard deviation in the cross-section, the country is considered to be a financial center. The requirement that both positions have to exceed a threshold avoids capturing oil exporters who are huge creditors but not financial centers or poor developing countries with huge liabilities and no assets.[24] Interestingly, the US is not a financial center according to this definition. To capture a broader notion of financial center, we additionally include countries listed as top ten in the Global Financial Centers Index, which is published by the City of London Corporation and evaluates the competitiveness of financial center cities. In particular, Hong Kong, Japan, Switzerland, the United Kingdom and the US are coded as financial centers over the entire period.[25]

Market capitalization: As an alternative to account for the financial depth of international financial centers we include the size of the stock market relative to GDP as a proxy variable (as in Focarelli and Pozzolo, 2001). Large stock markets offer investment opportunities for foreign capital. As a result, countries with large stock markets might attract foreign capital. They might act as a "savings sink", where foreign excess savings are invested. An example is provided by oil-exporting countries that recycle their petrodollar income. The previous regressions have shown that oil exports positively affect the current account balance. By implication, their financial-cum-capital account balance is lower than without oil-export status. This implies that oil-exporting countries invest part of the proceeds abroad.

The augmented regressions are presented in Table 3.3.[26] They all use the instrumental variables approach (2SLS) of Table 3.2. In the full sample, neither capital account openness nor civil liberties significantly affect the current account balance (column (1)). Financial centers are correlated with higher current account balances (column (2)), which implies that capital inflows due to center status are more than offset by capital outflows. Market capitalization, in turn, lowers the current account balance significantly (see column (3)). The inclusion of market capitalization affects the estimated impact of some other controls: The effect of the government budget balance again turns negative, while fuel exports, relative income and trade openness become significant. Capital mobility and civil liberties both lower the current account. These changes might be due to the fact that market capitalization is only available for a limited number of countries such that its consideration reduces the number of included countries from 86 to 63.

In the sample of industrial countries, capital mobility raises the current account balance. Market capitalization is insignificant. In the group of emerging markets, capital

---

[24] By way of example, in 2005 the following countries are identified as financial centers: Belgium, Hong Kong, Ireland, the Netherlands, Singapore, Switzerland and the United Kingdom.

[25] While being in the top ten, Singapore's financial development is more recent. We therefore rely on the definition based on gross foreign assets and liabilities, according to which it has been a financial center since 1998.

[26] For completeness Table 3.D.2 in the Appendix reproduces these specifications based on fixed samples within each country group.

Table 3.3 Robustness: Additional controls

	Full sample			Industrialized countries		Emerging markets		Developing countries	
	(1)	(2)	(3)	(4)	(5)	(6)	(7)	(8)	(9)
Government budget balance (relative to GDP)	0.0620** (2.03)	0.0618** (2.01)	-0.2391*** (-4.74)	0.2943 (0.04)	-7.4573 (-1.10)	-5.4373 (-0.51)	-34.2375*** (-2.70)	0.0737*** (2.64)	-0.2371*** (-2.79)
NFA to GDP ratio	0.0159** (2.31)	0.0160** (2.33)	0.0322** (3.10)	0.0474*** (2.81)	0.0546*** (2.91)	0.0196 (1.16)	0.0202 (1.19)	0.0185** (2.43)	0.0347*** (2.79)
Financial deepening	0.0003*** (2.93)	0.0004*** (3.13)	0.0004*** (2.62)	-0.0001 (-0.39)	-0.0003** (-2.01)	0.0012*** (4.57)	0.0009*** (2.64)	-0.0005* (-1.74)	-0.0003 (-0.85)
Fuel exports	0.0001 (0.79)	0.0001 (0.85)	0.0014*** (4.83)	0.0022*** (2.70)	0.0036*** (4.48)	-0.0002 (-0.79)	0.0013** (2.05)	0.0004* (1.90)	0.0020*** (6.11)
Relative income	0.0183 (0.43)	0.0138 (0.33)	-0.2217*** (-5.31)	0.0808 (1.49)	0.2480*** (3.20)	-0.1450* (-1.71)	0.0179 (0.18)	-0.0799 (-0.79)	-0.3961*** (-5.58)
Relative income (squared)	0.0008 (0.12)	0.0015 (0.23)	0.0372*** (5.50)	-0.0116 (-1.42)	-0.0345*** (-3.05)	0.0878* (1.90)	-0.0453 (-1.00)	0.0192 (0.99)	0.0733*** (4.18)
Relative dependency ratio (old)	-0.0032*** (-3.15)	-0.0033*** (-3.23)	-0.044*** (-3.33)	-0.0012 (-1.35)	-0.0001 (-0.07)	-0.0078 (-1.38)	-0.0012 (-0.18)	-0.0011 (-0.39)	-0.0057 (-1.22)
Relative dependency ratio (young)	-0.0001 (-0.30)	-0.0001 (-0.39)	-0.0005 (-0.98)	0.0008 (1.16)	-0.0008 (-0.90)	0.0007 (0.78)	-0.0034** (-2.27)	-0.0014*** (-3.09)	-0.0017** (-2.32)
GDP growth	0.0000 (0.00)	0.0007 (0.06)	-0.0206 (-1.47)	0.0071 (0.34)	0.0054 (0.19)	0.0019 (0.09)	0.0149 (0.87)	0.0198 (1.17)	0.0076 (0.32)
Trade openness	0.0127 (0.99)	0.0141 (1.10)	0.0635*** (4.51)	0.0226 (0.57)	0.0744** (1.79)	0.0298* (1.74)	0.0725*** (3.79)	-0.0449** (-2.41)	-0.0154 (-0.73)
Capital controls	-0.0017 (-0.99)	-0.0019 (-1.08)	-0.0059** (-2.53)	0.0126*** (3.96)	0.0175*** (3.80)	-0.0094*** (-4.27)	-0.0063*** (-2.71)	0.0016 (0.63)	-0.0070* (-1.95)
Civil liberties	-0.0013 (-0.63)	-0.0016 (-0.80)	-0.0047* (-1.82)	0.0008 (0.18)	0.0259*** (3.46)	-0.0089*** (-3.72)	-0.0069** (-2.09)	0.0004 (0.13)	-0.0039 (-0.99)
Financial center (dummy)		0.0957* (1.90)							
Market capitalization			-0.0002*** (-3.32)		0.0001 (0.99)		-0.0003*** (-3.01)		-0.0003*** (-2.77)
Change in foreign exchange (relative to GDP)	0.4682*** (5.15)	0.4619*** (5.10)	0.4076*** (4.12)	-0.1646 (-0.66)	-0.0608 (-0.22)	0.5706*** (3.33)	0.3492*** (2.40)	0.4211*** (3.70)	0.3738*** (3.37)
Official capital inflows to US * US dummy	-1.4819*** (-3.76)	-1.4761*** (-3.74)	-0.8363* (-1.73)	-1.5093*** (-3.74)	-1.7085*** (-3.82)				
Official capital inflows (without US) * RCC dummy	2.5904 (0.90)	2.6757 (0.92)	2.6890 (0.82)	0.3085 (0.14)	-0.3104 (-0.16)				
Observations	1390	1390	855	237	183	359	278	822	418
R-squared	0.10	0.11	0.24	0.43	0.52	0.32	0.46	0.11	0.33
Number of countries	86	86	63	11	11	17	17	60	37
Weak identification (F statistic)	45.12	45.08	28.43	10.80	7.91	13.43	14.07	30.00	21.41
Hansen J statistic (p-value)	0.01	0.01	0.07	0.24	0.00	0.00	0.00	0.47	0.02

Notes: The dependent variable is the current account balance to GDP ratio. RCC is a dummy variable that takes on the value one for the following reserve currency countries: France, Germany, Japan, the Netherlands, Switzerland and the UK. Estimation by 2SLS including country fixed effects. The following variables are instrumented by the first-stage predictions: change in foreign exchange, official capital inflows to US and official capital inflows (without US). Robust t-statistics are reported in parentheses. Standard errors are estimated robust to intragroup correlations. The symbols * , ** , and *** denote statistical significance at the 10%, 5% and 1% levels, respectively.

mobility, civil liberties and market capitalization negatively affect the current account balance.[27]

More importantly, our results with respect to the demand for reserves are robust to the inclusion of additional controls. The accumulation of reserves increases the current account balance in all samples except industrial countries. The estimated coefficient varies between 0.35 and 0.57. The global demand for dollar reserves lowers the US current account balance significantly. In the full sample, the magnitude of this effect falls after controlling for market capitalization, but is with 0.84 still large.

Alternative measures of global reserve demand

The change in reported foreign exchange reserves is an imprecise measure for the demand of reserves. Besides sales and purchases of reserve assets it accounts for valuation changes resulting from changes in market prices of these assets and of exchange rate changes. Unfortunately, individual country data on the magnitude of exchange market intervention are not available for a broad sample. On the aggregate level, however, besides reporting the currency composition of reserves, the IMF provides data on the absolute change in official holdings of foreign exchange by currency. These data are broken down in quantity and price changes. Since quantity changes measure the demand for reserves resulting from active reserve policies, we use them as an alternative measure for the demand for reserve-currency bonds.

Columns (1) to (4) of Table 3.4 show the results making use of this alternative measure of global reserve demand. In both, the whole sample and the sample of industrial countries, the global demand for dollar reserves lowers the US current account balance. The absolute magnitude of the estimated coefficient is larger than one in all four specifications. The demand for secondary reserve currencies does not significantly affect the current account balances of the respective countries. The findings with respect to our set of standard control variables are basically unchanged.

The Flow of Funds of the FED provide a third measure of the global demand for US reserve assets. It reports the amount of US Treasuries that are held by foreign official entities. We use the change in US Treasuries held by foreign official institutions to proxy for the global demand for dollar assets. The negative impact of foreign Treasury accumulation on the US current account is confirmed.[28]

Alternative sample period

It might be interesting to examine how the determinants of the current account have evolved over time. To this end, we divide the sample into two subperiods, the first ranging from 1970 to 1989 and the second covering the period 1990 to 2009 (see Table 3.4, columns (5) to (8)). The results indicate that the determinants of the current account have changed over time. While financial deepening and trade openness are the only significant determinants in the first period, since 1990 the current account balance

---

[27] The dummy variable for financial center status can only be included in the whole sample; it is dropped due to collinearity or absence of financial centers in the country subsamples.

[28] We do not provide the results here; they may be obtained from the author upon request.

Table 3.4 Robustness: Measurement and subperiods

	Full sample		Industrialized countries		1970–1989		1990–2009	
	(1)	(2)	(3)	(4)	(5)	(6)	(7)	(8)
Government budget balance (relative to GDP)	0.0743* (1.75)	0.0619** (2.03)	−0.5694 (−0.08)	1.3942 (0.21)	0.0477 (1.59)	0.0452 (1.48)	−0.1322** (−2.27)	−0.1912*** (−3.04)
NFA to GDP ratio	0.0162** (2.44)	0.0159** (2.31)	0.0602*** (3.94)	0.0475*** (2.83)	0.0241 (1.35)	0.0234 (1.31)	0.0161** (2.22)	0.0182** (2.41)
Financial deepening	0.0003*** (2.79)	0.0003*** (2.87)	−0.0001 (−0.61)	−0.0000 (−0.37)	0.0012*** (2.90)	0.0012*** (3.00)	0.0002 (1.47)	0.0002 (1.14)
Fuel exports	0.0001 (0.85)	0.0001 (0.79)	0.0024*** (2.94)	0.0022*** (2.69)	−0.0001 (−0.50)	−0.0001 (−0.41)	0.0007*** (2.64)	0.0008*** (2.76)
Relative income	−0.0200 (−0.51)	0.0174 (0.41)	0.0935** (2.03)	0.0724 (1.32)	0.0296 (0.32)	0.0420 (0.45)	−0.1285* (−1.85)	−0.0863 (−1.06)
Relative income (squared)	0.0061 (1.00)	0.0012 (0.18)	−0.0111 (−1.58)	−0.0101 (−1.23)	−0.0226 (−1.49)	−0.0241 (−1.57)	0.0193* (1.68)	0.0141 (1.06)
Relative dependency ratio (old)	−0.0027*** (−2.76)	−0.0030** (−2.95)	−0.0020** (−2.47)	−0.0012 (−1.41)	0.0113* (1.65)	0.0105 (1.51)	−0.0023 (−1.54)	−0.0022 (−1.40)
Relative dependency ratio (young)	−0.0002 (−0.76)	−0.0001 (−0.35)	0.0013* (1.92)	0.0006 (0.83)	−0.0017 (−1.08)	−0.0016 (−1.01)	−0.0007 (−1.34)	−0.0008 (−1.50)
GDP growth	0.0062 (0.50)	−0.0002 (−0.02)	−0.0033 (−0.15)	0.0072 (0.35)	0.0278 (1.56)	0.0286 (1.59)	−0.0021 (−0.17)	−0.0076 (−0.58)
Trade openness	0.0171 (1.60)	0.0128 (1.00)	0.0299 (0.76)	0.0257 (0.65)	−0.0942** (−2.40)	−0.0927** (−2.28)	0.0108 (0.87)	0.0093 (0.60)
Capital controls		−0.0017 (−1.00)		0.0130*** (4.08)		−0.0034 (−0.64)		−0.0062*** (−2.75)
Civil liberties		−0.0013 (−0.64)		0.0017 (0.36)		−0.0001 (−0.03)		−0.0034 (−1.23)
Change in foreign exchange (relative to GDP)	0.4390*** (5.00)	0.4714*** (5.17)	−0.0407 (−0.16)	−0.1619 (−0.65)	1.1500*** (3.12)	1.1441*** (3.08)	0.3542*** (4.12)	0.3625*** (3.98)
Official capital inflows to US * US dummy	−1.2524*** (−3.88)	−1.3455*** (−3.89)	−1.3890*** (−3.73)	−1.0557*** (−3.29)	3.9481 (1.23)	3.9295 (1.26)	−1.2956** (−2.23)	−1.2012** (−2.03)
Official capital inflows (without US) * US dummy	−0.2716 (−0.19)	−0.3884 (−0.26)	−0.1037 (−0.08)	−0.1484 (−0.11)	11.8876 (1.33)	11.6073 (1.25)	1.1713 (0.47)	1.5251 (0.58)
Observations	1447	1390	237	237	279	279	1165	1108
R-squared	0.11	0.10	0.39	0.43	0.24	0.24	0.11	0.10
Number of countries	89	86	11	11	39	39	89	86
Weak identification (F statistic)	47.09	44.88	10.51	10.82	5.00	4.63	41.64	38.80
Hansen J statistic (p-value)	0.07	0.01	0.21	0.16	0.08	0.10	0.06	0.02

Notes: The dependent variable is the current account balance to GDP ratio. Estimation by 2SLS including country fixed effects. Columns (1) to (4) measure official capital inflows by the quantity change in global official reserves. In columns (5) to (8) the following variables are instrumented by their first-stage predictions: change in foreign exchange, official capital inflows to US and official capital inflows (without US). Robust t-statistics are reported in parentheses. Standard errors are estimated robust to intragroup correlations. The symbols *, **, and *** denote statistical significance at the 10%, 5% and 1% levels, respectively.

has been driven by the government budget balance, the NFA position, fuel exports and capital mobility. Domestic reserve accumulation increases the current account balance in both periods, although the effect is much larger during the first period. This decline over time might be explained by the increasing financial integration, which facilitates the financing of reserves by foreign capital inflows instead of current account surpluses. The US current account balance is lowered by the global demand for dollar reserves in the period since 1990 only. This suggests that in the early period the US used the demand for reserves to invest abroad rather than to finance imports. Results, however, have to be interpreted cautiously because the coefficient on the global demand for reserves is estimated on the basis of 20 data points only.

Asymmetric effects

The effects of reserve changes on the current account balance might be characterized by nonlinearities. In particular, the accumulation of reserves might have a different impact on the current account balance than the sale of reserves. We therefore proceed by examining both policies separately. The results are presented in Table 3.5.[29] All regressions use the instrumental variables approach (2SLS). The global demand for reserves is proxied by the quantity change provided by the IMF (see Table 3.4).

We first examine a subsample that contains all country–year observations when reserves increased. It is important to note that 70% of country–year observations are characterized by an increase in reserves. Column (1) uses the set of control variables of the benchmark regression, while column (2) adds political and financial variables. As before, a large share of old people has a negative effect on the current account balance. Capital openness and a low level of civil liberties decrease the current account balance. Financial centers are associated with a larger balance. The findings with respect to the impact of reserve changes confirm our previously reported results: Domestic reserve accumulation increases the current account balance with an impact coefficient between 0.4 and 0.5. The global demand for dollar reserves lowers the US current account, while this effect is not statistically significant in other reserve currency countries.

Columns (3) and (4) show the results for the subsample of observations characterized by a decrease in reserves. The results differ: First, while the dependency ratios, capital controls and civil liberties are insignificant, the net foreign asset position positively affects the current account balance. Second, a sale of reserves does not affect the domestic current account. These asymmetries might be explained by a fundamental difference between reserve accumulation and reserve decreases. Reserve accumulation may be described as an active central bank policy while the sale of reserves is often a consequence of lacking capital inflows or crises. In this respect, the sale of reserves might be used to sustain a historically given level of the current account balance when private financing comes short for reasons like financial instabilities and capital flight.

The global demand for reserves might have similar asymmetric effects on reserve currency countries. The effect on the current account might depend on the sign of the

[29] For completeness Table 3.D.3 in the Appendix reproduces these specifications based on a fixed sample size across specifications.

Table 3.5 Robustness: Asymmetric effects

	Asymmetries of domestic reserve changes				Asymmetries of global reserve changes			
	ΔIR > 0		ΔIR < 0		ΔIR^d > 0		ΔIR^d < 0	
	(1)	(2)	(3)	(4)	(5)	(6)	(7)	(8)
Government budget balance (relative to GDP)	−0.0498* (−1.68)	−0.0469 (−1.48)	0.0961 (1.52)	0.0529 (0.76)	0.0748* (1.76)	0.0621** (2.02)	0.0756* (1.72)	0.0625** (1.99)
NFA to GDP ratio	0.0106 (1.31)	0.0100 (1.27)	0.0215** (2.17)	0.0201* (1.94)	0.0163** (2.44)	0.0161** (2.33)	0.0156** (2.37)	0.0154** (2.25)
Financial deepening	0.0002 (1.60)	0.0002 (1.48)	0.0003 (0.99)	0.0003 (1.24)	0.0003*** (2.77)	0.0004*** (3.07)	0.0003*** (2.95)	0.0004*** (3.26)
Fuel exports	0.0001 (0.52)	0.0002 (0.86)	0.0000 (0.05)	−0.0000 (−0.01)	0.0001 (0.84)	0.0001 (0.86)	0.0001 (0.84)	0.0001 (0.88)
Relative income	−0.0076 (−0.15)	0.0214 (0.39)	0.0155 (0.26)	0.0176 (0.28)	−0.0210 (−0.54)	0.0120 (0.28)	−0.0162 (−0.41)	0.0194 (0.45)
Relative income (squared)	0.0046 (0.59)	0.0016 (0.18)	0.0008 (0.09)	0.0000 (0.00)	0.0065 (1.06)	0.0024 (0.36)	0.0070 (1.11)	0.0028 (0.41)
Relative dependency ratio (old)	−0.0023** (−2.32)	−0.0023** (−2.16)	−0.0030 (−0.71)	−0.0032 (−0.76)	−0.0028** (−2.48)	−0.0033*** (−2.73)	−0.0048*** (−3.29)	−0.0055*** (−3.68)
Relative dependency ratio (young)	0.0002 (0.43)	0.0002 (0.48)	−0.0006 (−0.98)	−0.0005 (−0.86)	−0.0002 (−0.74)	−0.0001 (−0.45)	−0.0002 (−0.73)	−0.0002 (−0.49)
GDP growth	0.0146 (0.96)	0.0112 (0.71)	−0.0350 (−1.25)	−0.0304 (−1.12)	0.0068 (0.55)	0.0011 (0.09)	0.0064 (0.52)	0.0006 (0.05)
Trade openness	0.0232* (1.88)	0.0201 (1.33)	0.0207 (0.85)	0.0222 (0.86)	0.0177* (1.65)	0.0149 (1.16)	0.0162 (1.50)	0.0130 (1.01)
Capital controls		−0.0035* (−1.67)		0.0015 (0.42)		−0.0020 (−1.14)		−0.0022 (−1.25)
Civil liberties		−0.0049** (−2.04)		0.0012 (0.26)		−0.0016 (−0.80)		−0.0018 (−0.86)
Financial center (dummy)		0.0310** (2.01)		0.1453*** (3.08)		0.0959* (1.90)		0.0969* (1.92)
Change in foreign exchange (relative to GDP)	0.4302*** (4.19)	0.4668*** (4.38)	0.0145 (0.02)	−0.0951 (−0.12)	0.4292*** (4.92)	0.4533*** (5.02)	0.4179*** (4.83)	0.4395*** (4.92)
Official capital inflows to US * US dummy	−1.3414*** (−3.57)	−1.4143*** (−3.36)	−1.4878* (−1.75)	−1.4245* (−1.70)				
Official capital inflows (without US) * RCC dummy	−0.6816 (−0.43)	−0.7372 (−0.45)	0.6190 (0.26)	0.8003 (0.34)				
Official capital inflows (all countries)					−0.9765*** (−3.22)	−1.0357*** (−3.22)	−7.4020*** (−2.72)	−7.7647*** (−2.74)
Observations	1034	991	398	386	1432	1375	1394	1337
R-squared	0.06	0.07	0.08	0.11	0.11	0.11	0.12	0.11
Number of countries	87	84	70	68	89	86	89	86
Weak identification (F statistic)	31.93	30.91	1.99	2.11	47.21	44.93	47.10	44.64
Hansen J statistic (p-value)	0.09	0.03	0.54	0.60	0.06	0.01	0.06	0.01

Notes: The dependent variable is the current account balance to GDP ratio. Estimation by 2SLS including country fixed effects. Robust t-statistics are reported in parentheses. Standard errors are estimated robust to intragroup correlations. The symbols *, **, and *** denote statistical significance at the 10%, 5% and 1% levels, respectively.

global change in reserves. We therefore proceed by splitting the sample of reserve currency countries into one with a positive demand for the respective reserve currency and another with a negative demand. These two subsamples are merged with the sample of non-reserve currency countries. Columns (5) and (6) of Table 3.5 report the effects of a global demand for reserves, while columns (7) and (8) focus on periods with decreasing global reserve levels. Due to a small number of observations, we merge the demand for US assets and that for other reserve currencies in one variable called "Official capital inflows (all countries)". It is significant with a negative sign over all four specifications. However, it is remarkable that the magnitude of the effect of global reserve sales is much larger than that of reserve accumulation. Reserve sales increase reserve countries' current accounts significantly. This highlights the insurance role of reserves and the asymmetric structure of the international monetary system. During crises, when reserves are sold, reserve currency countries provide goods and services to countries in crisis.

Secondary reserve currency countries

So far we controlled for secondary reserve currencies by one single variable that equals the global demand for reserve assets of the respective country except the US and is zero for all non-reserve countries. We find that the global reserve demand does not affect the current account of secondary reserve currency countries. Since the insignificance might result from opposing effects within the set of countries, we proceed by a disaggregated analysis that adds an individual variable for each secondary reserve currency country: For country i the variable "official capital inflows to country i" equals the global demand for reserve assets of country i; it is zero for all other countries. The results are presented in Table 3.6. Column (1) uses OLS, column (2) the instrumental variables approach where domestic and global reserve demands are instrumented. Dependent variable in the first-stage regression are observed reserve holdings. As an alternative dependent variable in the first stage, we use the quantity change in official reserve holdings provided in the Annual Report of the IMF to predict the global demand for reserves. Based on this first-stage regression, columns (3) and (4) present the results using OLS and 2SLS estimation techniques, respectively.

We find significant negative effects for France, Switzerland and the UK. This finding, however, is not robust across different estimation techniques, albeit the coefficient is negative in all our specifications. Results, however, have to be interpreted cautiously because the country-specific coefficients on the global demand for reserves are estimated on the basis of 30 data points only. Germany is an outlier: Its current account increases when the rest of the world accumulates reserves denominated in German Mark or Euro. This implies that the official demand for German reserve assets is more than compensated by private capital outflows to the rest of the world. An explanation might be that German investors are especially risk averse and invest in other countries when reserves signal sound economic conditions abroad.

We then replicate our initial analysis of secondary reserve currencies where we put all these currencies in one variable with the difference that we exclude both the US and Germany because the first is the dominant reserve currency country and the latter

Table 3.6 Robustness: Secondary reserve currencies – detailed analysis

Method	(1) OLS	(2) 2SLS P	(3) OLS PQ	(4) 2SLS PQ	(5) OLS	(6) 2SLS P	(7) OLS PQ	(8) 2SLS PQ
Government budget balance (relative to GDP)	−0.0001*** (−3.71)	0.0817* (1.91)	−0.0001*** (−3.73)	0.0817* (1.92)	−0.0001*** (−3.70)	0.0818* (1.92)	−0.0001*** (−3.74)	0.0817* (1.92)
NFA to GDP ratio	0.0188*** (3.26)	0.0168*** (2.54)	0.0188*** (3.25)	0.0168*** (2.55)	0.0189*** (3.27)	0.0169*** (2.55)	0.0188*** (3.26)	0.0168*** (2.55)
Financial deepening	0.0004* (1.94)	0.0003*** (2.92)	0.0004* (1.90)	0.0003*** (2.88)	0.0003* (1.92)	0.0003*** (2.86)	0.0003* (1.90)	0.0003*** (2.89)
Fuel exports	0.0002 (0.87)	0.0002 (0.91)	0.0002 (0.88)	0.0002 (0.92)	0.0002 (0.86)	0.0002 (0.92)	0.0002 (0.88)	0.0002 (0.92)
Relative income	−0.0178 (−0.26)	−0.0213 (−0.55)	−0.0184 (−0.27)	−0.0228 (−0.59)	−0.0180 (−0.26)	−0.0215 (−0.55)	−0.0180 (−0.26)	−0.0228 (−0.59)
Relative income (squared)	0.0044 (0.40)	0.0058 (0.94)	0.0044 (0.40)	0.0061 (0.99)	0.0043 (0.39)	0.0058 (0.95)	0.0044 (0.40)	0.0061 (0.99)
Relative dependency (old)	−0.0025 (−1.32)	−0.0026*** (−2.77)	−0.0024 (−1.24)	−0.0024** (−2.55)	−0.0024 (−1.24)	−0.0023*** (−2.63)	−0.0023 (−1.24)	−0.0024** (−2.57)
Relative dependency (young)	−0.0002 (−0.28)	−0.0003 (−0.90)	−0.0002 (−0.34)	−0.0003 (−0.97)	−0.0002 (−0.28)	−0.0003 (−0.97)	−0.0002 (−0.36)	−0.0003 (−0.97)
GDP growth	0.0074 (0.55)	0.0142 (1.26)	0.0076 (0.57)	0.0146 (1.29)	0.0075 (0.56)	0.0142 (1.27)	0.0075 (0.57)	0.0144 (1.28)
Trade openness	0.0187 (1.04)	0.0229* (2.16)	0.0188 (1.04)	0.0231** (2.18)	0.0191 (1.06)	0.0232** (2.18)	0.0189 (1.05)	0.0232** (2.19)
Change in foreign exchange (relative to GDP)	0.3553*** (5.26)	0.2968*** (5.27)	0.3550*** (5.25)	0.2964*** (5.26)	0.3554*** (5.27)	0.2967*** (5.27)	0.3550*** (5.26)	0.2965*** (5.27)
Official capital inflows to								
– US	−0.9411*** (−5.17)	−1.6275*** (−3.69)	−1.2144*** (−4.48)	−1.1982*** (−3.93)	−0.9345*** (−5.14)	−1.6057*** (−3.66)	−1.2124*** (−4.49)	−1.1991*** (−3.93)
– UK	−0.0889*** (−2.86)	−1.6133** (−2.48)	−1.1131 (−1.50)	−0.9894 (−1.51)				
– CHE	−0.2882*** (−7.22)	−0.1282 (−0.04)	−0.2500*** (−3.66)	−0.1105 (−0.05)				
– GER	0.6324*** (6.47)	−1.8364 (−1.14)	0.5350*** (6.04)	0.7717 (1.22)	0.6371*** (6.57)	−1.8253 (−1.13)	0.5339*** (6.04)	0.7709 (1.22)
– FRA	−1.3162*** (−3.33)	−0.5901 (−0.12)	−3.9112*** (−8.95)	−3.9066*** (−3.11)				
– JAP	2.0026** (2.48)	5.9063 (1.53)	−0.4844 (−0.62)	−0.3914 (−0.25)				
– all RCC except US and GER					−0.3633** (−2.40)	0.3059 (0.40)	−0.4651** (−2.41)	−0.9241 (−1.43)
Observations	1697	1506	1697	1506	1697	1506	1697	1506
Number of countries	101	92	101	92	101	92	101	92
R-squared	0.14	0.12	0.13	0.12	0.13	0.12	0.13	0.12

Notes: The dependent variable is the current account balance to GDP ratio. Robust t-statistics are reported in parentheses. Standard errors are estimated robust to intragroup correlations. The symbols *, **, and *** denote statistical significance at the 10%, 5% and 1% levels, respectively. RCC stands for reserve currency countries. Specifications based on 2SLS instrument the domestic demand for foreign exchange reserves. P at the head of a column signifies *predicted* and indicates that the global reserve demand is calculated in a first-stage regression to control for endogeneity, PQ indicates that this first-stage regression for the global reserve demand is based on the quantity change in official reserve holdings provided by the IMF Annual Report instead of the change resulting from globally observed reserve holdings.

seems to be an outlier. The results, which are shown in columns (5) to (8), are inconclusive: While the effect for this group of secondary reserve currencies is significantly negative in regressions using OLS, it becomes insignificant when an instrumental variables approach is used. In sum, we do not find significant robust effects for secondary reserve currency countries. The US current account balance, however, is significantly lowered by the global demand for dollar reserve assets across all specifications of Table 3.6.

What might explain this difference between major and secondary reserve currency countries? First, dominance and persistence might matter. Incumbents like the US with consolidated reserve status might behave differently than countries that gained reserve currency status more recently. The latter might try to prevent low current account balances as long as they build up a reputation as safe haven. France, Germany and Japan were aspiring countries that gained reserve status during our period of consideration, whereas the US was an established reserve currency country well before the 1970s. For the UK the situation is different because Pound sterling lost most of its share in international reserves. As our analysis in Table 3.5 shows, during periods of negative reserve demand there is no significant effect on the current account balance. Second, for the secondary reserve currencies we face the problem of how to treat the introduction of the Euro. Since the share of the Euro in total reserves basically makes up for the combined shares of German Mark, French Franc and Dutch Guilder before 1999, we take the relative importance of these three currencies in 1998, hold them constant and take these shares to divide Euro reserves between these three countries. That is, we assume that for instance Italy and Spain are not reserve-providing countries despite the introduction of the Euro. Due to this simplification the measurement of the global demand for reserve assets from France, Germany and the Netherlands might be flawed.

3.3.3 Which factors are major determinants of the US current account balance?

Until now we have focused on the statistical significance of possible determinants of the current account balance. To judge their economic importance, we follow Chinn et al. (2014) and calculate the contributions of the different factors based on our regression estimates (i.e. $\hat{\alpha}_i x_{it}$, $\hat{\gamma}_i (\Delta IR^d / GDP)_{it}$). We use the estimated coefficients of regression (3) of Table 3.3. To cope with the large number of explanatory variables we group them. We group the contributions of young and old dependencies into "Demographics" and relative income and its squared value into "Relative income". Factors whose average individual contribution is smaller than 0.5% of GDP are put into the group "Other".

The following determinants distinguish themselves: The relatively high income per capita of the US compared to other countries has a positive effect on the current account balance. Its deep financial market raises the current account balance. The demographic structure with relatively more old and less young people than the world average lowers its current account balance. The contributions of these three groups

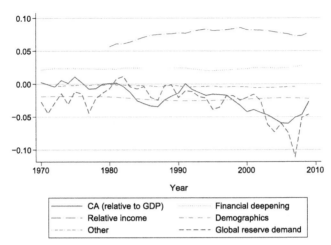

Figure 3.4 Estimated contributions to US current account balance.
Data sources: See Appendix 3.B.

are quite stable over time. The global reserve demand lowers the US current account balance and, according to our estimates, mimics the volatility of the balance quite well. Given that the sum of all contributions corresponds to the predicted current account balance, our model still overpredicts the US current account balance. However, it explains its volatility pretty well.

3.3.4   How do official and private capital flows interact?

Our results with respect to the US indicate that the effect of official capital flows on the current account balance is rather magnified than alleviated by private capital flows: The absolute value of the coefficient of the global demand for reserves on the US current account is consistently larger than one.

In a world with perfect capital markets where assets are perfect substitutes, a world interest rate exists. In equilibrium, any official capital flow would induce private flows in the opposite direction keeping the interest rate constant. As a consequence, the magnitude of official capital flows could not affect the capital account balance. Official capital flows and the capital account balance would be uncorrelated. By implication, official capital flows would not affect the current account balance either.

The relationship between the US capital account and foreign official capital flows is examined by means of a correlation and regression analysis. The results are presented in Table 3.7. Two measures for official capital inflows are used: (1) the change in global foreign exchange reserves denominated in dollars and (2) the net change in US Treasury bonds held by foreign official institutions. The correlation between either measure and the capital account balance is positive and relatively high. This implies that official capital inflows increase net capital inflows – the sum of official and private ones – to the US. Private flows do not offset official flows. This conclu-

Table 3.7 **Effect of official capital flows on the capital account of the US**

Capital account	Correlation	Regression
Official capital inflows	0.832	0.938*** (9.23)
Net change in Treasury bonds held by foreign official institutions	0.600	1.050*** (4.61)

Notes: t-statistics are reported in parentheses. The symbols *, ** and *** denote statistical significance at the 10%, 5% and 1% levels, respectively. Estimations are based on 40 observations (1970–2009).

sion is supported by a simple regression analysis: Bivariate regressions of the capital account balance on proxies for official capital inflows yield significant and positive coefficients. Both coefficients are not significantly different from one suggesting that private capital flows do not offset official flows. As a consequence, official capital inflows constitute an additional source of financing.[30] This is evidence for the low degree of substitution between US assets and assets of the rest of the world.[31]

3.4 Conclusions and policy implications

This chapter has revisited an old dilemma: Any international monetary system based on a reserve asset that is simultaneously used as national currency, may be characterized by increasing indebtedness of the center country. Whereas this dilemma has been identified long before, this study is the first to evaluate the effects of reserve currency status empirically. The evidence is striking: The accumulation of reserves in developing countries is correlated with a larger current account balance, while this effect is absent in industrial countries. This finding supports the mercantilist explanation for reserve accumulation. The global accumulation of reserves lowers the current account balance of the US, which is the major provider of reserve assets. Any additionally accumulated dollar of reserve assets lowers the US current account by 1 to 2 dollars. Private and official capital flows basically do not affect each other. If the US lost its reserve currency status, its current account balance relative to GDP would improve by 1 to 2 percentage points.[32] These numbers are economically significant. Expressed in absolute terms they are outstanding. The existence of the Triffin dilemma is confirmed empirically.

---

[30] Gagnon (2012) shows that the same conclusions hold for developing countries characterized by current account surpluses: Private capital flows do not offset changes in official capital flows. 40–50% of any change in official capital flows show up in the current account balance.

[31] This is in line with the observation that the demand for official reserves is insensitive to their return (see Krishnamurthy and Vissing-Jorgensen, 2012).

[32] To be precise, we do not argue that the reserve currency status of the US is responsible for its large current account deficit during the last three decades. We just conclude that the current account balance would be larger if the US did not provide the reserve currency.

The stylized constellation between the US and emerging markets, with the latter financing the current account deficit of the former by their accumulation of reserves, has its precedent in history (see Meissner, 2010): During the 1920s, France accumulated British sterling, the reserve currency at that time, and contributed to a secular decrease of the British current account.

Our empirical approach has focused on the reserve currency status of the US. Using a historical data set, further research might extend this case study and examine the relationship between reserve currency status and current account balance for the period of sterling dominance before World War II. Special insights might be provided by the changeover from the sterling to the dollar.

While the lower current account balance is an equilibrium outcome, persistent deficits and a deteriorating net external asset position may undermine the confidence in the reserve currency in the long run.[33] The theoretical and empirical literature concurs that persistent current account deficits are associated with a higher incidence of currency crises (see Frankel and Saravelos, 2012). As a result, the reserve currency status endogenously increases the vulnerability to financial crises in the long run. In conjunction with a decreasing US share in global economic activity and rising alternative reserve currencies this process might challenge the dollar's role in the long run. It has to be noted, however, that current account deficits in reserve currency countries might be less of concern than in other countries: Investors might react non-linearly to deficits depending on the status of the nation.[34]

In an early work Kenen (1960) examines the conditions under which the dollar might lose its role as reserve currency. In particular, he assesses the impact of changes in the US ratio of gold to foreign-owned dollar debt for the working of the gold–dollar standard of that time. The theoretical model shows that a lasting deficit of the US balance of payments may erode confidence in the dollar, cause countries to switch to gold and bring about global instability. Once reserve liabilities exceed the gold stock of the reserve currency country, the international monetary system enters a "crisis zone": Central bank runs, characterized by central banks substituting gold for dollar assets, become self-fulfilling (Officer and Willett, 1969). Under the present system without guaranteed gold conversion, one might argue that reserves are backed by US foreign assets or US GDP. The crisis zone is then characterized by foreign assets falling short of foreign liabilities. According to this definition, the dollar standard has been in a crisis zone since 1985. Alternatively, Farhi et al. (2011) argue that the confidence of the dollar standard is linked to the fiscal capacity of the US.[35,36] In an empirical study,

---

[33] In this respect it has to be noted that the net foreign asset position of the US can improve despite cumulative current account deficits because of valuation changes. This, however, requires a depreciation of the dollar, which again runs counter to the virtue of a reserve currency.

[34] This point is related to the concept of debt intolerance, introduced by Reinhart et al. (2003). The authors argue that the level of debt that is tolerated and sustainable varies a lot across countries. It depends on a country's experience with default and inflation in the past, its institutions and financial system.

[35] See also Obstfeld (2014).

[36] According to an alternative view (see Despres et al., 1966) the deficit is no reason for concern because it is the outcome of the US providing financial intermediation to the rest of the world. The provision of maturity and risk transformation, however, does not imply an unbalanced capital account. Capital inflows

which analyzes the determinants of safe haven currencies, Habib and Stracca (2012) find that safe haven status is positively associated with a country's net foreign asset position.

The finding that reserve currency status lowers the current account balance of the dominant center country, however, is not linked to the specific situation of the US being the reserve currency provider. The problem is a more fundamental one: It lies in the fact that a national currency is used as the global reserve currency (see Taylor, 2013). Therefore, shifting to another currency – with the Euro or Renminbi being viable choices – would not solve the underlying problem. While another country might provide a stable reserve currency in the short run, in the long run the Triffin dilemma strikes back: Any reserve currency, that provides the demanded assets in sufficient amounts to the rest of the world, is likely to face a deterioration in its current account and net foreign asset position.

Appendix 3.A   Reserve currency status and balance of payments

This note shows how the global demand for reserves affects the balance of payments of the reserve currency country. Special reference is made to the balance sheet of the reserve currency providing central bank.

According to the balance of payments constraint, the sum of current account balance (CA) and capital and financial account balance (KA) equals the change in international reserves (R). The capital account may be further divided into private and official capital flows where official capital flows are defined as changes in assets and liabilities held by foreign official institutions, mostly foreign central banks and governments. Hence, the balance of payments constraint can be written as:

$$CA + KA^{PR} + KA^{OF} = \Delta R \tag{3.14}$$

where the capital account balance is divided into the balance of private capital flows (KA^{PR}) and the balance of official capital flows (KA^{OF}).

All central bank transactions with foreign entities are recorded in the balance of payments. Accordingly, ΔR corresponds to the change in a central bank's foreign assets and liabilities.[37]

$$\Delta R = \Delta A^f - \Delta L^f \tag{3.15}$$

where A^f are foreign monetary assets and L^f denote foreign monetary liabilities.

are expected to be mirrored by capital outflows such that the capital account may be balanced. We show empirically that the status as a financial center does not lower the current account. Central banks' demand for reserves, in turn, does affect the current account.

[37] To be precise, we model ΔR as changes in foreign exchange reserves, which constitute the major component of international reserves in the current monetary system. We do not consider changes in gold.

For an ordinary central bank ΔR equals the change in its monetary assets, namely the change in its international reserve holdings because $L^f = 0$.[38] A deficit in the current-cum-capital account in this country has to be balanced by a sale of central bank reserves, which contracts its balance sheet. The central bank of the reserve currency country, however, features the particularity that part of its currency in circulation is held by foreigners. Domestic currency circulating in foreign countries is part of the central bank's foreign liabilities. Consequently, a deficit in the current-cum-capital account in a reserve currency country can additionally be financed by an equal increase in the central bank's liabilities without affecting its foreign assets: The central bank increases money supply and extends its balance sheet.

Whereas deficit financing in an ordinary country comes to a natural end when reserves are exhausted, the reserve currency country can finance a current-cum-capital account deficit through an increase in its foreign liabilities as long as these are accepted by the rest of the world.

Assume without loss of generality that the reserve currency country holds its stock of foreign monetary assets – which equals the stock of reserves for a non-reserve currency country – constant ($\Delta A^f = 0$). Then the following identity holds:

$$\Delta R = -\Delta L^f \qquad (3.16)$$

The change in its reserves equals the change in its foreign liabilities.[39]

An increase in foreign central banks' dollar reserves can take either of two forms: The central bank amounts dollar cash or in dollar denoted assets. In the balance of payments notation of the reserve currency country, the first transaction enters as a change in the central bank's liabilities with respect to foreigners (ΔL^f) and the second appears in the capital account as an official capital inflow. Accordingly, the accumulation of reserves by the rest of the world ΔR^{ROW} can be expressed as

$$\Delta R^{ROW} = KA^{OF} + \Delta L^f \qquad (3.17)$$

After plugging (3.16) and (3.17) in (3.14) we get

$$CA + KA^{PR} = -\Delta R^{ROW} \qquad (3.18)$$

This formulation shows that any demand for reserves from the rest of the world may be satisfied by one of the following two counterbalancing operations: (1) a current account deficit or (2) private capital outflows. It is true that the US has to run a current account deficit when the rest of the world wants to accumulate *net* dollar assets since private capital outflows increase the liabilities of the rest of the world toward the US. If the accumulation of reserves is financed by foreign private capital inflows [$-KA^{PR} = \Delta R$], net foreign asset positions are unaffected.

---

[38] The liabilities of a central bank are composed of currency in circulation and reserve holdings of commercial banks. For an ordinary country, both components are purely domestic.

[39] Note that the level of reserves cannot fall below zero for an ordinary central bank. The reserve currency providing central bank, however, may figure a negative gross reserve position in its balance sheet.

Appendix 3.B   List of variables and data sources

Variable	Source	Definition
Current account balance (relative to GDP)	WDI	Current account balance divided by nominal GDP
GDP	WDI	GDP measured at purchaser's prices is the sum of gross value added by all resident producers in the economy where product taxes are added and subsidies are deduced provided they are not reflected in the value of the products.
Capital account	IFS	Capital account balance according to the textbook definition as counterpart of the current account balance net of changes in official reserves. Calculated as the sum of the capital account balance and the financial account balance as defined by the IMF where the former comprises transfers and the provision of nonproduced, nonfinancial assets and the latter is the net sum of direct investment, portfolio investment, financial derivatives, and other investment.
Government budget balance (relative to GDP)	WEO, GFS, WDI	Data equals the variable general government net lending/borrowing provided in the WEO database, which is calculated as revenue minus total expenditure. Missing values are filled – where possible – by the variable *government cash surplus/deficit* of the GFS database (years from 1990 onward) and *overall deficit/surplus of consolidated central government* from the historical GFS database (for years prior to 1989). Data are converted to dollars by end of period exchange rates and divided by current GDP.
NFA to GDP ratio	Lane and Milesi-Ferretti (2007) and update	Total external assets minus total external liabilities divided by GDP
Financial deepening	WDI	Money and quasi-money (M2) as a percentage of GDP
Relative dependency ratio (young)	WDI	Ratio of young (0–15 years) to working (15–65 years) population measured as deviation from world average

(*continued on next page*)

Variable	Source	Definition
Relative dependency ratio (old)	WDI	Ratio of old (65+ years) to working (15–65 years) population measured as deviation from world average
Relative income	WDI	Relative income is measured as real GDP per capita as a ratio to its average value across all countries. GDP is measured as gross domestic product in constant international dollars with the year 2005 as base. An international dollar has the same purchasing power over GDP as the US dollar has in the United States.
Trade openness	WDI	Sum of exports and imports divided by GDP
Capital controls	Chinn and Ito (2006)	Measure of the de jure openness of the capital account (kaopen). Calculation is based on the binary dummy variable of the IMF's Annual Report on Exchange Arrangements and Exchange Restrictions (AREAER).
Civil liberties	Freedom House	The index of civil liberties is based on an evaluation of four subcategories, namely personal freedom, associational rights, rule of law and individual rights and autonomy. Higher index values indicate less free countries. Numerical ratings lie between 1 and 7.
Fuel exports	WDI	Fuel exports as a percentage of total merchandise exports
Financial center, dummy	Own calculations based on Lane and Milesi-Ferretti (2007) and update and GFCI	The dummy takes on the value one in a country year where the country is identified as a financial center. A financial center is defined as having both a ratio of foreign assets to GDP and of foreign liabilities to GDP that exceed the mean plus one standard deviation of the respective variables in a given year over the whole sample. Based on information provided by the Global Financial Centres index the following countries are labeled financial centers over the whole period independently of whether they meet the empirical criteria for financial centers (see above): Hong Kong, Japan, Switzerland, the United Kingdom and the United States.

Variable	Source	Definition
Market capitalization	Standard & Poor's and WDI	Market capitalization is the market value (share price times the number of shares outstanding) of domestic companies listed on the country's stock exchanges. Investment companies, mutual funds or other collective investment vehicles are not included.
Economic globalization	Dreher (2006)	Index based on actual flows of goods and capital and restrictions concerning these flows (subindex A)
Volatility	WDI	Measured as the standard deviation over the previous five years of the growth rate of exports as a capacity to import
Foreign exchange reserves	IFS	
Official capital inflows	IFS	Net capital inflows to reserve currency countries provided by official foreign institutions. Calculated as the worldwide level of foreign exchange reserves multiplied by that year's reserve currency share in total reserves, which is provided by the IMF in its Annual Report and the COFER database. The change in this variable between two consecutive years is the proxy for official capital inflows. Alternatively, the level of foreign exchange holdings is replaced by the quantity change in official holdings of reserve currency (IMF Annual Report, Appendix Table I.3). Flows are measured relative to GDP of the recipient country.
Net change in Treasury bonds held by foreign official institutions	Federal Reserve	Difference of Treasury securities held by non-US official institutions (Flow of Funds, Table L.107, line 11) between two consecutive years

Sources: GFCI: Global Financial Centres Index provided by Z/Yen; GFS: Government Finance Statistics (online and historical database); IFS: International Financial Statistics; WEO: World Economic Outlook Database; WDI: World Development Indicators.

Appendix 3.C   Sample of countries

Afghanistan	Czech Republic	Korea, Rep.^{b}	Russian Federation^b
Albania	Denmark^a	Kyrgyz Republic	Rwanda
Algeria	Dominican Republic	Lao PDR	Saudi Arabia
Angola	Ecuador	Lebanon	Senegal
Argentina^b	Egypt, Arab Rep.^{b}	Liberia	Serbia
Armenia	El Salvador	Libya	Sierra Leone
Australia^a	Eritrea	Lithuania	Singapore
Austria^a	Ethiopia	Madagascar	Slovak Republic
Azerbaijan	Finland^a	Malawi	South Africa^a
Bangladesh	France^a	Malaysia^b	Spain^a
Belarus	Georgia	Mali	Sri Lanka
Belgium^a	Germany^a	Mexico^b	Sudan
Benin	Ghana	Moldova	Sweden^a
Bolivia	Greece^a	Morocco	Switzerland^a
Bosnia and Herzegovina	Guatemala	Mozambique	Syrian Arab Republic
Brazil^b	Guinea	Nepal	Tajikistan
Bulgaria	Haiti	Netherlands^a	Tanzania
Burkina Faso	Honduras	New Zealand^a	Thailand^b
Burundi	Hong Kong	Nicaragua	Togo
Cambodia	Hungary^b	Niger	Tunisia
Cameroon	India^b	Nigeria	Turkmenistan
Canada^a	Indonesia^b	Norway^a	Uganda
Central African Republic	Iran	Pakistan	Ukraine
Chad	Iraq	Panama	United Arab Emirates
Chile^b	Ireland^a	Papua New Guinea	United Kingdom^a
China^b	Israel^b	Paraguay	United States^a
Colombia	Italy^a	Peru^b	Uruguay
Congo, Dem. Rep.	Japan^a	Philippines^b	Uzbekistan
Congo, Rep.	Jordan	Poland^b	Venezuela, RB
Costa Rica	Kazakhstan	Portugal^a	Vietnam
Cote d'Ivoire	Kenya	Romania	Yemen, Rep.
Croatia			

Notes: Countries that belong to the group of industrialized countries are marked by the index a. Classification is in line with the IMF classification in its International Financial Statistics. Emerging market countries are marked by the index b.

Appendix 3.D   Regression results: Robustness using fixed samples

The following tables reproduce results presented in the main text with the difference that all specifications for a given country group are estimated based on the same number of countries and observations. Changes in coefficients within a country group are hence due to the added control variables and not to a modified sample.

Table 3.D.1 Determinants of the current account – 2SLS (fixed number of observations per country group)

	Full sample				Industrialized countries			
	(1)	(2)	(3)	(4)	(5)	(6)	(7)	(8)
Government budget balance (relative to GDP)	0.0973**	0.0744*	0.0743*	0.0744*	-0.0477	-0.0444	-1.2428	-1.3085
	(2.22)	(1.75)	(1.75)	(1.75)	(-0.01)	(-0.01)	(-0.18)	(-0.19)
NFA to GDP ratio	0.0180***	0.0163**	0.0162**	0.0162**	0.0666***	0.0666***	0.0594***	0.0595***
	(2.66)	(2.45)	(2.45)	(2.44)	(4.59)	(4.39)	(3.79)	(3.84)
Financial deepening	0.0004***	0.0003***	0.0003***	0.0003***	-0.0001	-0.0001	-0.0001	-0.0001
	(3.32)	(2.80)	(2.81)	(2.83)	(-0.43)	(-0.41)	(-0.65)	(-0.60)
Fuel exports	0.0002	0.0001	0.0001	0.0001	0.0024***	0.0024***	0.0024***	0.0024***
	(1.09)	(0.90)	(0.85)	(0.85)	(3.08)	(3.03)	(2.99)	(2.95)
Relative income	-0.0296	-0.0194	-0.0195	-0.0195	0.1013**	0.1015**	0.0958**	0.0958**
	(-0.74)	(-0.50)	(-0.50)	(-0.50)	(2.30)	(2.25)	(2.07)	(2.07)
Relative income (squared)	0.0069	0.0056	0.0058	0.0058	-0.0126*	-0.0126*	-0.0117	-0.0117*
	(1.10)	(0.93)	(0.96)	(0.95)	(-1.88)	(-1.84)	(-1.64)	(-1.65)
Relative dependency ratio (old)	-0.0022**	-0.0026***	-0.0027***	-0.0028***	-0.0022**	-0.0022**	-0.0021**	-0.0021**
	(-2.32)	(-2.72)	(-2.80)	(-2.86)	(-3.05)	(-2.57)	(-2.50)	(-2.33)
Relative dependency ratio (young)	-0.0004	-0.0003	-0.0002	-0.0002	0.0009	0.0009	0.0014**	0.0014**
	(-1.39)	(-0.94)	(-0.72)	(-0.72)	(1.39)	(1.39)	(2.14)	(2.14)
GDP growth	0.0314***	0.0063	0.0062	0.0063	-0.0042	-0.0038	-0.0029	-0.0029
	(2.82)	(0.52)	(0.51)	(0.51)	(-0.26)	(-0.17)	(-0.13)	(-0.13)
Trade openness	0.0332***	0.0168	0.0171	0.0171	0.0348	0.0347	0.0290	0.0288
	(3.09)	(1.57)	(1.60)	(1.60)	(0.87)	(0.87)	(0.74)	(0.73)
Change in foreign exchange (relative to GDP)		0.4379***	0.4385***	0.4370***		-0.0092	-0.0438	-0.0437
		(4.99)	(4.99)	(4.99)		(-0.04)	(-0.17)	(-0.17)
Official capital inflows to US * US dummy			-1.6660***	-1.6692***			-2.2865***	-2.2857***
			(-3.68)	(-3.68)			(-4.32)	(-4.32)
Official capital inflows (without US) * RCC dummy				2.0707				0.4942
				(0.65)				(0.18)
Observations	1447	1447	1447	1447	237	237	237	237
R-squared	0.08	0.11	0.11	0.11	0.37	0.37	0.39	0.39
Number of countries	89	89	89	89	11	11	11	11
Weak identification (F statistic)		47.16	47.13	72.55		10.46	10.59	24.65
Hansen J statistic (p-value)		0.06	0.06	0.06		0.18	0.28	0.28

Notes: The dependent variable is the current account balance to GDP ratio. RCC is a dummy variable that takes on the value one for the following reserve currency countries: France, Germany, Japan, the Netherlands, Switzerland and the UK. Estimation by 2SLS including country fixed effects. The following variables are instrumented by the first-stage predictions: change in foreign exchange, official capital inflows to US and official capital inflows (without US). Robust t-statistics are reported in parentheses. Standard errors are estimated robust to intragroup correlations. The symbols *, ** and *** denote statistical significance at the 10%, 5% and 1% levels, respectively.

Table 3.D.2 Robustness: Additional controls (fixed number of observations per country group)

	Full sample			Industrialized countries		Emerging markets		Developing countries	
	(1)	(2)	(3)	(4)	(5)	(6)	(7)	(8)	(9)
Government budget balance (relative to GDP)	−0.2434*** (−4.35)	−0.2434*** (−4.35)	−0.2385*** (−4.72)	−3.4643 (−0.48)	−7.2434 (−1.07)	−42.8138*** (−3.24)	−34.2375*** (−2.70)	−0.2435*** (−3.16)	−0.2371*** (−2.79)
NFA to GDP ratio	0.0321*** (3.12)	0.0321*** (3.12)	0.0323*** (3.10)	0.0520** (2.48)	0.0548*** (2.93)	0.0295* (1.71)	0.0202 (1.19)	0.0355*** (2.88)	0.0347*** (2.79)
Financial deepening	0.0003* (1.80)	0.0003* (1.80)	0.0004*** (2.61)	−0.0002 (−1.48)	−0.0003** (−2.02)	0.0009*** (2.74)	0.0009*** (2.64)	−0.0006 (−1.53)	−0.0003 (−0.85)
Fuel exports	0.0014*** (4.94)	0.0014*** (4.94)	0.0014*** (4.83)	0.0034*** (4.22)	0.0036*** (4.48)	0.0012** (1.86)	0.0013** (2.05)	0.0021*** (6.09)	0.0020*** (6.11)
Relative income	−0.2255*** (−5.49)	−0.2255*** (−5.49)	−0.2221*** (−5.32)	0.2311*** (2.82)	0.2464*** (3.18)	−0.0737 (−0.77)	0.0179 (0.18)	−0.3803*** (−5.51)	−0.3961*** (−5.58)
Relative income (squared)	0.0375*** (5.69)	0.0375*** (5.69)	0.0373*** (5.53)	−0.0315*** (−2.63)	−0.0341*** (−3.02)	−0.0028 (−0.06)	−0.0453 (−1.00)	0.0701*** (4.98)	0.0733*** (4.18)
Relative dependency ratio (old)	−0.0035*** (−2.98)	−0.0035*** (−2.98)	−0.0043*** (−3.29)	−0.0002 (−0.16)	−0.0000 (−0.02)	0.0001 (0.01)	−0.0012 (−0.18)	−0.0059 (−1.26)	−0.0057 (−1.22)
Relative dependency ratio (young)	−0.0006 (−1.33)	−0.0006 (−1.33)	−0.0005 (−1.00)	−0.0006 (−0.74)	−0.0008 (−0.96)	−0.0035** (−2.21)	−0.0034** (−2.27)	−0.0015** (−2.00)	−0.0017** (−2.32)
GDP growth	−0.0242* (−1.79)	−0.0242* (−1.79)	−0.0206 (−1.47)	0.0065 (0.23)	0.0060 (0.22)	0.0182 (1.11)	0.0149 (0.87)	0.0012 (0.05)	0.0076 (0.32)
Trade openness	0.0580*** (4.11)	0.0580*** (4.11)	0.0635*** (4.52)	0.0817*** (2.01)	0.0750** (1.79)	0.0664*** (3.40)	0.0725*** (3.79)	−0.0194 (−0.88)	−0.0154 (−0.73)
Capital controls	−0.0072*** (−3.13)	−0.0072*** (−3.13)	−0.0059** (−2.53)	0.0167*** (3.71)	0.0175*** (3.80)	−0.0084*** (−3.79)	−0.0063*** (−2.71)	−0.0089** (−2.48)	−0.0070* (−1.95)
Civil liberties	−0.0044* (−1.70)	−0.0044* (−1.70)	−0.0047* (−1.82)	0.0235*** (3.83)	0.0260*** (3.49)	−0.0071** (−2.11)	−0.0069*** (−2.09)	−0.0037 (−0.94)	−0.0039 (−0.99)
Market capitalization			−0.0002*** (−3.32)		0.0001 (0.99)		−0.0003*** (−3.01)		−0.0003*** (−2.77)
Change in foreign exchange (relative to GDP)	0.3596*** (3.84)	0.3596*** (3.84)	0.4078*** (4.12)	−0.0472 (−0.16)	−0.0651 (−0.24)	0.2133 (1.48)	0.3492*** (2.40)	0.3535*** (3.38)	0.3738*** (3.37)
Official capital inflows to US * US dummy	−1.3523** (−2.17)	−1.3523** (−2.17)	−0.9882* (−1.74)	−1.9092*** (−3.92)	−2.0615*** (−4.00)				
Official capital inflows (without US) * RCC dummy	1.2609 (0.41)	1.2609 (0.41)	2.7190 (0.69)	−0.1332 (−0.05)	−0.4852 (−0.20)				
Observations	855	855	855	183	183	278	278	418	418
R-squared	0.22	0.22	0.24	0.51	0.52	0.43	0.46	0.31	0.33
Number of countries	63	63	63	11	11	17	17	37	37
Weak identification (F statistic)	29.16	29.16	28.42	7.89	7.90	14.19	14.07	20.70	21.41
Hansen J statistic (p-value)	0.01	0.01	0.07	0.00	0.00	0.00	0.00	0.06	0.02

Notes: The dependent variable is the current account balance to GDP ratio. RCC is a dummy variable that takes on the value one for the following reserve currency countries: France, Germany, Japan, the Netherlands, Switzerland and the UK. Estimation by 2SLS including country fixed effects. The following variables are instrumented by the first-stage predictions: change in foreign exchange, official capital inflows to US and official capital inflows (without US). Robust t-statistics are reported in parentheses. Standard errors are estimated robust to intragroup correlations. The symbols *, ** and *** denote statistical significance at the 10%, 5% and 1% levels, respectively.

Table 3.D.3 Robustness: Asymmetric effects (fixed number of observations)

	Asymmetries of domestic reserve changes				Asymmetries of global reserve changes			
	$\Delta IR > 0$		$\Delta IR < 0$		$\Delta IR^d > 0$		$\Delta IR^d < 0$	
	(1)	(2)	(3)	(4)	(5)	(6)	(7)	(8)
Change in foreign exchange (relative to GDP)	0.4823***	0.4668***	−0.1684	−0.0951	0.4629***	0.4533***	0.4503***	0.4395***
	(4.54)	(4.38)	(−0.20)	(−0.12)	(5.12)	(5.02)	(5.03)	(4.92)
Government budget balance (relative to GDP)	−0.0279	−0.0469	0.0497	0.0529	0.0657**	0.0621**	0.0664**	0.0625**
	(−0.99)	(−1.48)	(0.73)	(0.76)	(2.20)	(2.02)	(2.17)	(1.99)
NFA to GDP ratio	0.0093	0.0100	0.0204**	0.0201*	0.0155**	0.0161**	0.0148**	0.0154**
	(1.15)	(1.27)	(1.99)	(1.94)	(2.25)	(2.33)	(2.17)	(2.25)
Financial deepening	0.0002	0.0002	0.0003	0.0003	0.0003**	0.0004***	0.0004***	0.0004***
	(1.63)	(1.48)	(0.86)	(1.24)	(2.84)	(3.07)	(3.02)	(3.26)
Fuel exports	0.0001	0.0002	−0.0000	−0.0000	0.0001	0.0001	0.0001	0.0001
	(0.57)	(0.86)	(−0.05)	(−0.01)	(0.66)	(0.86)	(0.67)	(0.88)
Relative income	0.0235	0.0214	0.0253	0.0176	0.0172	0.0120	0.0245	0.0194
	(0.42)	(0.39)	(0.41)	(0.28)	(0.41)	(0.28)	(0.57)	(0.45)
Relative income (squared)	0.0004	0.0016	−0.0007	0.0000	0.0012	0.0024	0.0014	0.0028
	(0.04)	(0.18)	(−0.07)	(0.00)	(0.18)	(0.36)	(0.21)	(0.41)
Relative dependency ratio (old)	−0.0025***	−0.0023**	−0.0025	−0.0032	−0.0032**	−0.0033**	−0.0054***	−0.0055***
	(−2.47)	(−2.16)	(−0.61)	(−0.76)	(−2.72)	(−2.73)	(−3.62)	(−3.68)
Relative dependency ratio (young)	0.0003	0.0002	−0.0005	−0.0005	−0.0001	−0.0001	−0.0001	−0.0002
	(0.68)	(0.48)	(−0.81)	(−0.86)	(−0.24)	(−0.45)	(−0.25)	(−0.49)
Growth GDP	0.0116	0.0112	−0.0300	−0.0304	−0.0003	0.0011	−0.0009	0.0006
	(0.73)	(0.71)	(−1.06)	(−1.12)	(−0.02)	(0.09)	(−0.07)	(0.05)
Trade openness	0.0194	0.0201	0.0219	0.0222	0.0126	0.0149	0.0106	0.0130
	(1.35)	(1.33)	(0.88)	(0.86)	(1.03)	(1.16)	(0.86)	(1.01)
Capital controls		−0.0035*		0.0015		−0.0020		−0.0022
		(−1.67)		(0.42)		(−1.14)		(−1.25)
Civil liberties		−0.0049**		0.0012		−0.0016		−0.0018
		(−2.04)		(0.26)		(−0.80)		(−0.86)
Financial center (dummy)		0.0310**		0.1453***		0.0959*		0.0969*
		(2.01)		(3.08)		(1.90)		(1.92)
Change in foreign exchange (relative to GDP)	0.4823***	0.4668***	−0.1684	−0.0951	0.4629***	0.4533***	0.4503***	0.4395***
	(4.54)	(4.38)	(−0.20)	(−0.12)	(5.12)	(5.02)	(5.03)	(4.92)
Official capital inflows to US * US dummy	−1.4039***	−1.4143***	−1.5165*	−1.4245*				
	(−3.56)	(−3.36)	(−1.77)	(−1.70)				
Official capital inflows (without US) * RCC dummy	−0.7152	−0.7372	0.6441	0.8003				
	(−0.45)	(−0.45)	(0.27)	(0.34)				
Official capital inflows (all countries)					−1.0402***	−1.0357***	−7.5993***	−7.7647***
					(−3.27)	(−3.22)	(−2.73)	(−2.74)
Observations	991	991	386	386	1375	1375	1337	1337
R-squared	0.06	0.07	0.08	0.11	0.10	0.11	0.11	0.11
Number of countries	84	84	68	68	86	86	86	86
Weak identification (F statistic)	30.36	30.91	2.11	2.11	44.91	44.93	44.65	44.64
Hansen J statistic (p-value)	0.04	0.03	0.56	0.60	0.01	0.01	0.01	0.01

Notes: The dependent variable is the current account balance to GDP ratio. Estimation by 2SLS including country fixed effects. Robust t-statistics are reported in parentheses. Standard errors are estimated robust to intragroup correlations. The symbols *, ** and *** denote statistical significance at the 10%, 5% and 1% levels, respectively.

Determinants of the Public Budget Balance: The Role of Official Capital Flows

Contents

4.1 Introduction 72
4.2 Foreign exchange reserves in historical perspective 74
4.2.1 A short history of reserve currencies 75
  Sterling dominance (1880–1913) 75
  Dual reserve currency system (1920–1939) 76
  Dollar dominance (since World War II) 78
4.2.2 A short history of asset classes used as reserves 79
4.3 Implications of reserve currency status 80
4.3.1 Implications for interest rates 80
4.3.2 Implications for the public budget 82
  Demand side view 82
  Supply side view 83
4.4 The role of official capital for the public budget balance – a regression analysis 85
4.4.1 Description of data set and empirical approaches 85
  Data set 85
  Empirical approaches 89
4.4.2 Time-series analysis: US and UK 90
4.4.3 Analysis in a panel data set of industrialized countries 90
  Results spanning 120 years of history 92
  UK during sterling dominance 94
  US during dollar dominance 96
4.4.4 Alternative identification: Are reserve currency countries outliers? 100
  UK under sterling dominance 100
  US during dollar dominance 103
4.4.5 Robustness checks 107
4.5 Conclusions 107
Appendix 4.A List of variables and data sources 109
Appendix 4.B Sample of countries 112
Appendix 4.C Data sources: Shares of reserve currencies in total foreign exchange reserves 112
Appendix 4.D Regression results: Robustness using fixed sample sizes 112

Global Imbalances, Financial Crises, and Central Bank Policies
Copyright © 2016 Elsevier Inc. All rights reserved.

4.1   Introduction

This chapter provides an empirical examination of the relationship between reserve currency status and government finances. Since central banks hold their foreign exchange reserves preferably in the form of government bonds issued by the center country of the international monetary system, the reserve-providing country faces an additional demand for its government bonds. By implication, reserve currency status facilitates the financing of fiscal deficits.

The empirical importance of the relationship between public finances and reserve currency status is characterized by three stylized facts:

1. Central banks' international reserves have increased considerably. The annual average growth rate between 1880 (1970) and 2010 has been 7.2% (12.2%). Since this rate exceeds the US inflation rate, which averaged 2.4% between 1880 and 2010, reserves have risen in real terms. Reserves have also increased relative to the economic size of the US, which might be considered as a form of collateral for dollar exchange reserves. US real GDP has grown at an average annual rate of 3.2% during the period of consideration.
2. Central banks' reserves have been increasingly held in the form of foreign assets at the expense of gold. The share of foreign exchange reserves in total reserves[1] has risen from 9.5% in 1899 to 95.5% in 2010 (see left-hand panel of Figure 4.1).
3. A considerable share of foreign exchange reserves has been invested in government bonds of reserve currency countries. By way of example, in 2010 35.2% of global foreign exchange reserves were invested in US Treasuries (see right-hand panel of Figure 4.1).

These facts imply that foreign central banks are major players on the market for safe government bonds. They hold a considerable share of government debt of the center countries. Their rising demand for government bonds generates a dilemma: Triffin (1960) points out that the objectives of providing an increasing amount of reserve assets and of fixing the real value of these assets are incompatible in a monetary system that uses national currencies as reserves. While Triffin focused on the implications for the balance of payments of the center country (see Chapter 3), the modern dilemma is a fiscal problem arising from central banks' preference for government securities (Obstfeld, 2011a, 2011b; Prasad, 2011). Obstfeld (2011b, p. 10) concludes with respect to the US:

> *"So global reserve growth requires the ongoing issuance of gross government debt. This requires, in turn, that the government run continuing deficits, or that it issue debt to acquire assets likely to be inherently riskier than the corresponding liabilities. Just as in the classic Triffin dilemma, global reserve growth is largely driven by deficits – not national balance of payments deficits, but government deficits."*

---

[1] Total reserves are defined as the sum of gold, convertible foreign exchange, unconditional drawing rights with the IMF (the country's reserve position in the Fund) and special drawing rights (SDRs). While historically reserves consisted of gold and foreign assets, drawing rights with the IMF arise from countries' capital shares in the IMF and SDRs were created in 1969 as a response to the "dollar shortage".

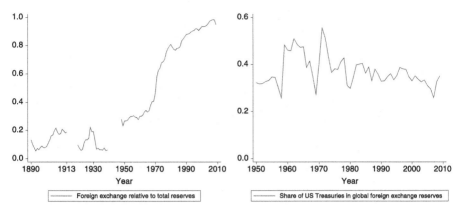

Figure 4.1 Relative importance of foreign exchange reserves and US Treasuries. *Data sources:* See Appendix 4.A.

Center countries have to run fiscal deficits if they want to satisfy the increasing demand for safe assets.[2] At the same time, the official demand for reserve assets lowers their interest rate, which, in turn, may lower fiscal discipline: Center countries' equilibrium response is to run lower fiscal balances.

If there exist perfect substitutes for government bonds of the center country, foreign central banks crowd-out the private demand for government bonds and the equilibrium on the government bonds market is unaffected. Under the more realistic assumption that there are no perfect substitutes,[3] the price of government bonds rises and lowers the effective interest rate. The public budget constraint of the center is relaxed. Its sovereign debt rises.

This chapter contributes to the preceding literature in several dimensions. First, we extend the literature on the determinants of the public budget balance by explicitly taking account of countries' reserve currency status. While the existing literature explains public budget balances by economic and political factors, it disregards that the supply of government bonds is not only supply-driven, but depends on private and official demand for such bonds alike. The equilibrium approach to fiscal policy pioneered by Barro (1979) focuses on economic factors that affect public finances. In this type of model, optimal tax rates are smooth over time. Deficits result from exceptional spending like the financing of wars and countercyclical policies. The importance of political and institutional factors for public finances is theoretically grounded by Alesina and Tabellini (1990). Empirical contributions of Roubini and Sachs (1989a, 1989b) show that coalition governments, left-wing parties and short terms of office are associated with larger deficits. While these findings are confirmed by Grilli et al. (1991), De Haan and Sturm (1997) and De Haan et al. (1999) do not find a robust relationship between

---

[2] In principle, the provision of government assets can be reconciled with a balanced public budget if the public sector purchases at the same time foreign assets.

[3] If home bonds and foreign reserve bonds were perfect substitutes, central banks could hold home bonds instead of foreign reserves (see Canzoneri et al., 2013).

political factors and government finances. To the best of our knowledge, the effect of reserve currency status on public finances has not been investigated before.

Our second contribution concerns the data set: Using various sources we have assembled a panel data set covering 120 years of public budget history, which allows us to examine the determinants of fiscal balances in the long run. Moreover, we can identify the changing influence of certain determinants over time. While existing panel studies examine more recent periods (i.e. Tujula and Wolswijk, 2007; Woo, 2003), long-run studies using historical data are usually time-series analyses focusing on a single country (i.e. Barro, 1986 and Bohn, 1998 for the US; Barro, 1987 for the UK). The analysis of the determinants of public budget balances in a historical panel is new.

Third, this chapter contributes to the literature that examines the consequences of reserve currency status. Reserve currency countries are often considered to enjoy an "exorbitant privilege" (see Gourinchas and Rey, 2007; Gourinchas et al., 2010), because they are able to issue debt in their own currency and at low interest rates. We focus on one aspect of this privilege, which has been undervalued so far: Reserve currency countries face a relaxed public budget constraint.

Finally, this chapter is linked to studies examining the relationship between the key currency role of the dollar and the financing of the US public deficit (i.e. Kitchen and Chinn, 2011; Krishnamurthy and Vissing-Jorgensen, 2012). While these studies focus on how reserve status affects the interest rate, we show that besides this price effect there is also a quantity effect: Reserve status increases the level of government debt. In this vein, Favilukis et al. (2012) report that the downward trend in the US net foreign asset position since 1994 can entirely be attributed to the purchase of US safe assets by foreigners.

This chapter makes reference to a recent literature investigating the scarcity of safe assets and its global implications (IMF, 2012; Dooley et al., 2004). Caballero and Farhi (2013) and Gourinchas and Jeanne (2012) provide theoretical approaches that emphasize the central role of governments and public debt in the production of safe assets. Blanchard et al. (2005) show in a portfolio balance model with imperfect asset substitutability that any additional demand for safe assets appreciates the exchange rate of the safe haven country.

The remainder of this chapter is organized as follows. The next section traces the evolution of the international monetary system since the establishment of central banks and explores the importance of government securities as central bank reserve assets. Implications of being the reserve currency provider are discussed in Section 4.3. Section 4.4 provides an empirical analysis of the effect of reserve currency status on the public budget balance. Concluding remarks are offered in Section 4.5.

4.2 Foreign exchange reserves in historical perspective

This section provides historical evidence of the increasing role of foreign exchange reserves in total reserves and illustrates the rise and fall of national currencies as reserve assets. It then summarizes the evidence on the asset classes in which central banks invest their foreign exchange reserves.

4.2.1   A short history of reserve currencies

The classical gold standard emerged during the 19th century as a by-product of the foundation of central banks, which were entitled to issue token coin and paper money. Monetary statutes bound central banks to cover circulating money to a predefined extent by gold.[4] Gold reserves fulfilled two tasks, a domestic and an external one: First, since central banks were committed to exchange paper money for gold, the gold cover ratio fostered confidence in the domestic fiat money. Second, gold could be used to cover deficits in the balance of payments and to defend the exchange rate. This arrangement gradually turned into a gold-exchange standard, where gold was supplemented by foreign assets denominated in gold-convertible currencies.

While the structure of the international monetary system with center and periphery is the outcome of an evolutionary process rather than supranational rules,[5] to attain reserve currency status countries have to fulfill certain key requirements: Economic size, openness to trade, developed and liquid financial markets and a stable value of the currency have been identified as important determinants.[6] Historically, the convertibility of the reserve currency into gold was a further prerequisite.

Sterling dominance (1880–1913)

In the period preceding World War I, apart from the Bank of England, most central banks held some foreign exchange reserves in addition to gold. A number of countries already hoarded sizable amounts of foreign exchange reserves and operated under a de facto gold-exchange standard (see Bloomfield, 1963).[7] Bordo and Eichengreen (2001) consider the transition from the gold to the gold-exchange standard as a post-1900 phenomenon. Foreign exchange enabled central banks to intervene directly in the foreign exchange market. According to the estimates of Lindert (1969) the share of foreign exchange assets in total reserves (sum of gold and foreign exchange) rose from 12.7% in 1880 to 23% in 1913. In 1913, India, Japan and Russia accounted for more than half of global foreign exchange holdings. The majority of these reserves were denominated in pound sterling. The United Kingdom naturally emerged as the center country because it fulfilled the key requirements for reserve currency countries: It was the world's largest economy measured in GDP (until 1872) and trade

---

[4] Refer to Federal Reserve System (1936, 1948) for summary tables of the legally enforced gold coverage across countries.

[5] Maggiori (2013) shows that the emergence of reserve currencies is the result of different levels of financial development across countries.

[6] See Chinn and Frankel (2007, 2008) and Habib and Stracca (2012) for empirical studies of the determinants of reserve currency status. Papaioannou et al. (2006) estimate optimal shares for the main reserve currencies.

[7] According to Bloomfield (1963) these countries are Austria–Hungary, Australia, Belgium, Canada, Finland, Japan, the Netherlands, New Zealand, Norway, Russia and South Africa.

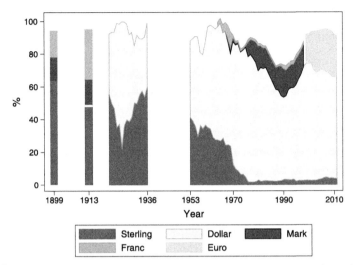

Figure 4.2 Shares of reserve currencies in total foreign exchange reserves. *Note:* This graph shows the temporal evolution of the share of the major reserve currencies in total foreign exchange reserves. Prior to World War I, data is only available for 1899 and 1913.
Data sources: See Appendix 4.C.

(until 1913). It was on a gold standard since 1819, while the US and continental European countries joined the gold standard not before the 1870s. Finally, London was the leading financial center. While the shares of German mark and French franc in total reserves both accounted for roughly 15% in 1899, the franc's share rose to 31% in 1913 at the expense of sterling.[8] Although US GDP surpassed that of the UK in 1872, the dollar was not yet used as global reserve currency. With Canada being the only country holding sizable dollar reserves,[9] the dollar share in global foreign exchange holdings was below 2% in 1913. Despite the rising importance of foreign exchange in total reserves, they were entirely covered by gold. In 1913, gold holdings of the three major reserve currency countries exceeded foreign exchange holdings in the rest of the world.

Dual reserve currency system (1920–1939)

While the monetary system after World War I was based on the same pillars as its predecessor, the evolution of the gold-exchange standard was characterized by two main changes: First, foreign exchange grew relative to total reserves. Second, the dollar emerged as important reserve currency. It shared the role of dominant reserve currency with pound sterling during the interwar years. The changing importance of key currencies in total foreign exchange reserves is illustrated in Figure 4.2.

---

[8] The growing share of the franc is mainly due to the accumulation of franc reserves in Russia. This Russian policy can be considered as counterpart to French lending to Russia.

[9] Although small in absolute terms, the entire foreign assets of the Philippine Treasury were denominated in dollar.

As a result of the scarcity of gold – historically gold production has been lower than increases in central banks' reserve holdings[10] – the Genoa conference in 1922 proposed to replace the gold standard officially by a gold-exchange standard. Central bank statutes were revised accordingly allowing central banks to report foreign assets denominated in gold-convertible currencies as reserves.[11] The share of foreign exchange in total reserves consequently rose from 9.5% in 1920 to 22.2% in 1928. After this peak, the share fell again to a low of 6.1% in 1939.[12] This return to gold resulted from an environment of increasing uncertainty: Both the convertibility in gold at fixed prices and the stability of exchange rates were put into question. These fears were corroborated by the devaluation of the pound sterling in 1931.

The demand for foreign exchange reserves was dominated by the behavior of the French central bank, which accounted for more than half of worldwide reserves in the late 1920s. Before the French franc became gold convertible in 1928, France resisted an appreciation of its currency by a massive accumulation of reserves. When the credibility of the pound sterling was questioned, the Banque de France sold sterling reserves in favor of gold and dollar between 1929 and 1931. The British devaluation in September 1931 reduced the share of sterling relative to dollar reserves on impact and also lowered the ratio of reserves to gold. Moreover, after the sterling crisis, the Banque de France liquidated the remaining sterling and dollar assets and concentrated its reserves in gold.[13]

Nurske (1944) notes that the increased demand for exchange reserves in the interwar period can be regarded as a substitute for privately owned mobile assets. In the period of the first financial globalization prior to 1914, private short-term capital flows balanced deficits and surpluses in the trade balance while gold transfers were relatively small. In the interwar period, however, private capital flows were much smaller because of capital controls and fears of volatile exchange rates. Central banks had to intervene more frequently to meet trade imbalances.[14]

The creation of the Federal Reserve System in 1913 is an important factor that facilitated the emergence of the dollar as key currency. Moreover, after 1914 the US turned from net debtor to net creditor, while the net foreign asset position of the UK deteriorated. According to the estimates of Eichengreen and Flandreau (2009), dollar reserves accounted for 18.2% of total foreign exchange reserves in 1920. In 1924, the dollar overtook sterling as most important reserve currency for the first time. In the 1930s, however, pound sterling regained its leading role.

---

[10] Eichengreen and Flandreau (2009) and Irwin (2012) argue that rather the distribution than the amount of gold was a problem.

[11] In Austria, Bulgaria, Danzig, Estonia, Greece and Hungary central banks were allowed to hold up to 100% of their reserves in foreign assets.

[12] Data are based on Lindert (1969). The numbers provided by Nurske (1944) are much larger, but show the same pattern over time.

[13] For an in-depth analysis of the French foreign reserve policy during the interwar period refer to Accominotti (2009).

[14] Mlynarski (1929) argues that after World War I foreign exchange reserves replaced circulating gold coins in their capacity as a first reserve.

Dollar dominance (since World War II)

After World War II, the dollar consolidated its role as key currency. Given that in 1948 72% of worldwide gold was concentrated in the US, the dollar was the only currency that could credibly announce its gold convertibility.

The rise of the dollar was backed by official US policy: The US historically encouraged foreign sovereigns to hold US assets. The exemption of foreign sovereigns from US income tax, set in section 892 of the US Internal Revenue Code, dates back to 1917. It was, however, disputed whether foreign central banks were legally to be considered as foreign sovereigns. In order to remove this uncertainty, US tax laws were amended in 1961 (section 895) stating that foreign central banks' income from obligations of the US should be exempt from taxation. This policy was motivated by the attempt to protect US gold reserves: Foreign central banks were encouraged to hold reserves in form of US Treasuries instead of gold. While this did not affect US net wealth, an outflow of gold might have shaken the confidence put on the dollar.

While foreign exchange reserves were usually borrowed before World War II, after the war reserve accumulation resulted of balance of payments surpluses and increased net foreign assets. The changeover from sterling to dollar was not abrupt, but rather extended over several decades. This gradual decline of sterling may be explained by inertia and official arrangements that committed members of the sterling area to hold a certain fraction of reserves in sterling (see Schenk, 2011).[15] In the 1950s sterling still accounted for more than 50% of total foreign exchange reserves. In the following years its share first decreased gradually but plunged in 1970 – from 23.7% to 12.5%. This sharp decrease was due to two forces: First, global dollar reserves increased as a result of a large US balance of payments deficit and, second, sterling reserves fell because the UK repaid $2 billion of central bank assistance to foreigners.

The gold–dollar standard collapsed in 1971 when the US revoked its commitment to exchange dollars for gold at the predefined price. This development was the result of various tensions: In the late 1960s private demand for gold rose in anticipation of a rising dollar price of gold and the FED and European central banks lost large amounts of gold. When the US entered a recession in 1970, the dollar was devalued, which also affected the fixed gold–dollar parity.

Despite the dollar devaluation, its share in foreign exchange reserves did not drop. On the contrary, it reached a peak in 1975, when 75% of global foreign exchange reserves were denominated in US dollars. This share then declined gradually and reached a lower floor of 50% in 1990. Since then, dollar assets accounted for a relatively stable share of two thirds of total exchange reserves.

The gradual decline of the pound sterling was so strong that in 1976 it was replaced by the mark as the second most important reserve currency. While the mark started its rise in the 1970s, the Japanese yen followed in the 1980s.

---

[15] Both the reserve currency country and foreign central banks have an interest in smoothing the reallocation of assets. Any abrupt shift in reserve asset preferences would go along with a devaluation of the reserve currency and erode the real value of foreign exchange reserves. The risk of massive capital flows resulting from the instability of the established reserve currency is stressed by Mlynarski (1929), Officer and Willett (1969) and Canzoneri et al. (2013).

This broad picture did not change with the creation of the Euro. While it was considered as a potential rival for the dollar's predominant role (Chinn and Frankel, 2007, 2008), the Euro share basically corresponds to the sum of shares of the currencies it replaced (German mark, French franc and Netherlands guilder).

With the growing importance of China in economic size and trade, the Renminbi has emerged as a new potential reserve currency. This tendency is intensified by the Chinese intents to internationalize the role of the Renminbi. In fact, however, while countries have shown interest in Renminbi reserve assets, only few hold them as part of their foreign exchange reserves so far. In addition, given the enormous amount of Chinese foreign exchange reserves, China itself has an interest in diversifying these reserves and in becoming less dependent on the dollar.

4.2.2   A short history of asset classes used as reserves

While individual central banks usually do not report the currency composition of their foreign exchange reserves, they provide even less information with respect to the type of assets they hold. Since reserves have to be readily available at known value in times of financial distress, the set of assets is restricted to safe short-term liquid assets.[16] Government bonds fulfill these conditions. Bloomfield (1963) notes for the period up to 1913 that external assets were held in the form of foreign bills, balances with foreign correspondents and foreign bonds. For the well studied case of Norway, Øksendal (2008) reports that exchange reserves were composed of British consols, French rentées and German government bonds for liquidity purposes.

Table 4.1 provides data on the share of government bonds in central banks' foreign assets in the interwar years for a number of selected countries for which data is available. It shows that government bonds were an important reserve asset although their share was rather unstable. The countries of the sterling area[17] invested their foreign exchange reserves predominantly in British Treasury bills (see Nurske, 1944, p. 60). This can be verified by the following observation: When reserves were sold in face of a balance of payments deficit abroad, the "outside" supply of Treasury bills grew. This effect could be observed in 1938: As a result of a balance of payments deficit in the sterling area, the share of Treasury bills in hands of London Clearing Banks increased at the expense of holdings abroad.

For the period preceding World War II, we can infer the role of government assets in total foreign exchange reserves only from those central banks that disclosed their reserve asset composition. More precise statements are possible with respect to the role of US Treasuries since World War II. The Flow of Funds data of the FED show

---

[16] The Group of Ten (1965, p. 21) defines reserves as "those assets of [a country's] monetary authorities that can be used, directly or through assured convertibility into other assets, to support its rate of exchange when its external payments are in deficit".

[17] The sterling area was formed by countries that decided to peg their exchange rate to the pound sterling after its devaluation in 1931. The group consisted of the British Commonwealth of Nations as well as independent countries, among them the Scandinavian countries, Japan and Portugal. The sterling bloc existed until World War II.

Table 4.1 **Share of government securities in total foreign assets held by central banks (in %)**

Central bank of:	1913	1920	1924
Australia	n.a.	72.5	73.7
Denmark	34.5	7.6	0.4
Finland	19.8	4.3	0.5
Japan	n.a.	9.9	n.a.
Italy	60.4	15.5	33.8
Norway	18.0	6.9	8.1
Portugal	n.a.	7.4	34.2
Sweden	21.1	8.7	27.5

Notes: n.a. = not available.
Data source: League of Nations (1925), pp. 150–159.

that official foreign institutions constitute a major source of demand for US Treasury bonds. The left-hand panel of Figure 4.3 visualizes the enormous increase in the real value of outstanding US Treasury debt since the early 1980s. This increased supply was absorbed by foreign official holders of Treasuries: Their share in total Treasury debt securities outstanding has risen from 6% in 1970 to 12% in 1990 (with a temporary maximum of 20% in 1978 after a period of global reserve accumulation in the aftermath of the breakdown of the Bretton Woods system). After a peak of 40% in 2009 (see right-hand panel of Figure 4.3), this share amounted to 35.9% in 2010. The declining share in recent years can be explained by the FED's massive purchase of US Treasuries resulting from its policy of quantitative easing. Notwithstanding, between 2000 and 2010, 49% of the increase in Treasuries was purchased by foreign official institutions. Foreign official investors hold the majority of total Treasuries in foreign hands (75% in 2010).

4.3 Implications of reserve currency status

This section discusses the theoretical argument that the reserve-providing country faces lower interest rates and a relaxed public budget constraint and summarizes the evidence.

4.3.1 Implications for interest rates

A reserve currency country is characterized by the unique situation that its assets are held by two types of foreign agents: private and official ones. Besides loans from private foreign investors, reserve currency countries receive loans from foreign central

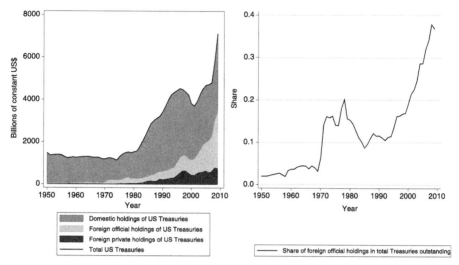

Figure 4.3 US Treasury debt. *Notes:* The left-hand panel shows the distribution of outstanding Treasury securities by holder. Data are deflated by the US GDP deflator (base year 2005 = 1), which is provided by IMF (2011a). The right-hand panel depicts the proportion of US Treasury securities that are held by foreign official entities (relative to total Treasuries).
Data source: Flow of Funds, Federal Reserve, Table L.106 (lines 11 and 12) and Table L.209 (line 1).

banks equal to the amount of foreign exchange reserves they hold.[18] These loans are primarily granted to the sovereign of the reserve currency country. Provided that private capital flows do not totally crowd-out official ones, the reserve currency country faces an additional demand for its assets, which translates into a higher amount of debt and higher asset prices.

These effects are intensified by the fact that the demand for safe reserve assets is relatively insensitive to their return because perfect substitutes are unavailable. For the early period of the dollar standard Aliber (1964) and Gemmill (1961) report that the share of foreign exchange in total reserves is independent of interest rates.[19] More recently, Krishnamurthy and Vissing-Jorgensen (2012) show that foreign central banks' investment decisions are insensitive to interest rates.

Moreover, the demand for Treasury bonds by foreign central banks substantially lowers their interest rate, which, in turn, softens the public budget constraint. This effect has been reported for different constellations of the international monetary system. Nurske (1944, p. 61) notes for the sterling dominance that a rising demand for UK Treasury bills as a result of trade lowered the discount rate of UK Treasury bills. For the more recent dollar dominance, a series of papers documents that foreign central

---

[18] For the benefits of foreign exchange holdings and their determinants refer, among others, to Aizenman and Lee (2007), Cheung and Qian (2009) and Jeanne and Rancière (2011).

[19] "The general conclusion from recent empirical investigations is that foreign official institutions do not shift funds from dollar assets into gold, or into reserve assets denominated in other currencies, in response to changes in interest rates" (Aliber, 1964, p. 448).

banks' asset demand lowers US interest rates. Krishnamurthy and Vissing-Jorgensen (2012) examine how US Treasury yields would react to a sale of all foreign official Treasury holdings. Their estimates point to an increase in US Treasury yields between 41 and 60 basis points depending on specification and maturity. Warnock and Cacdac Warnock (2009) find that annual official capital inflows of one percent of GDP are associated with a 40 basis point reduction in interest rates. These findings are qualitatively confirmed by Kitchen and Chinn (2011). Using consensus projections for the US they find that the share of foreign holdings in total Treasuries has to rise from 25% to 45% if interest rates are to be stabilized at around 5.5%. The estimates of Beltran et al. (2013) show that an increase in foreign official flows into US Treasury notes and bonds (relative to total Treasuries) by one percentage point decreases the return on 5-year Treasuries by 13 basis points.[20]

On theoretical grounds, Caballero and Krishnamurthy (2009) show that the global demand for a safe store of value rises US asset prices and lowers interest rates. Caballero et al. (2008) derive low US interest rates and an increase in the share of US assets in global portfolios as the equilibrium outcome of different levels of financial development.

4.3.2 Implications for the public budget

Demand side view

The purchase of Treasury bonds is a form of lending to the sovereign of a foreign country. According to standard theory on sovereign borrowing (see, among others, Eaton and Gersovitz, 1981; Grossman and Van Huyck, 1988; Bulow and Rogoff, 1989), external government financing is limited by a credit ceiling due to an incentive compatibility constraint: The benefits of sovereign default must not exceed its costs. Under the special circumstances of a reserve currency country this credit ceiling might be eased for several reasons. First, lenders might disregard the ceiling. Second, sequential lending from multiple sources involves the danger of overlending.

Lenders might disregard the credit ceiling because they do not consider the purchase of reserves as an investment. Countries rather think of reserve purchases as buying a self-insurance that hopefully enables them to prevent and manage financial crises. As a consequence, they do not expect repayment by the sovereign in the future. They rely on the acceptance of the reserve currency in the foreign exchange market. Moreover, since the reserve currency is perceived to be the safest haven, there are no alternatives available.

Because countries continuously adjust their hoardings of international reserves, lending is rather sequential than a one-time operation. Sequential lending from multiple sources may lead to debt dilution, i.e. the devaluation of existing debt. Since each unit of additional debt increases the probability of default, it imposes a negative externality on the outstanding amount of debt, which is not internalized in its price.

---

[20] According to these estimates the return on 5-year Treasuries would have been two percentage points higher in 2010 if China had not accumulated any dollar reserves between 1995 and 2010.

Consequently, the social cost of additional lending is larger than the private cost. The negative external effect implies that in the absence of a social planner lending to the reserve currency country is socially too high.

As a consequence of the neglect of the credit ceiling and of the presence of debt dilution, lending to the reserve currency country exceeds lending to a country with the same characteristics but without reserve currency status. Put differently, the public budget balance in the reserve currency country is expected to be lower.

Supply side view

The previous section has shown that the market for government bonds of reserve currencies is characterized by an additional demand, which might even discard the credit ceiling. This section takes a supply-side view and demonstrates that it is in the own interest of the reserve-providing country to run lower public budget balances compared to countries without reserve status. In response to low interest rates, households and the government endogenously increase consumption and lower savings.

Our starting point is the public budget identity, which is given by

$$D_t = (1 + i_t)D_{t-1} - S_t \tag{4.1}$$

where D_t denotes the level of public debt at the end of year t, i the nominal interest rate and S the primary government surplus. Scaled by nominal GDP, the dynamics of public debt can alternatively be expressed as

$$d_t = \left(\frac{1 + i_t}{1 + g_t}\right) d_{t-1} - s_t \tag{4.2}$$

where variables denoted by lower cases are scaled by GDP (e.g. $d = D/Y$) and g is the growth rate of nominal GDP. After adding standard assumptions and some algebraic manipulation (see Bohn, 1995, 2005), the intertemporal budget constraint of fiscal policy can be obtained as

$$d_t = \sum_{j=0}^{\infty} \frac{1}{(1+r_j)^j} E_t[s_{t+j}] \tag{4.3}$$

where the "return on debt" is defined as $r_t = (1 + i_t)/(1 + g_t)$. E_t denotes conditional expectations. The constraint requires that the present value of future primary surpluses equal the initial level of debt.

If a country attains reserve currency status, its interest rate decreases. We denote this lower interest rate by i^{RC}. Equation (4.3) shows that for lower future interest rates the intertemporal budget constraint is satisfied for a higher level of public debt d. In other words, for a given stream of future surpluses, a larger level of current debt is compatible with the intertemporal budget constraint. This also holds if reserve currency status is considered to be temporary: If the country enjoys reserve status from now until period N, in equation (4.3) i is replaced by i^{RC} for $0 \leq j \leq N$. By implication, in the limit the budget constraint is satisfied for a higher current level of sovereign debt. To put differently, for a given level of public debt lower future public budget balances are compatible with the constraint.

According to simple economics of intertemporal choice, an unexpected fall in interest rates induces substitution and income effects. According to the substitution effect, optimizing agents exchange future consumption for present one. The income effect depends on the sign of agents' net wealth: The effect is positive for borrowers and negative for creditors. This textbook analysis of intertemporal choice assumes that there exists one homogeneous asset with given interest rate. In our case it is more plausible to assume that there exist various assets with limited substitutability. A decease in interest rates of government bonds need not affect the return of other assets in which the sovereign itself may invest. This implies that the income effect of the sovereign is positive if it has outstanding liabilities and zero if it is a creditor without liabilities. The net effect of combined substitution and income effect is unambiguously positive. The optimal government response to a lower interest rate is an increase in present consumption.

There exists, however, a caveat with respect to our theoretical result: The theory on public spending explains deviations from a balanced budget by economic shocks or political considerations (e.g. Barro, 1979; Alesina and Tabellini, 1990). According to this reasoning, governments do not optimize intertemporally; expenditures are determined independently of interest rates.

However, even if interest rates do not enter the government's objective function directly, they affect the intertemporal budget constraint and link present balances to future ones. As shown by equation (4.3), lower interest rates imply that a given stream of surpluses is compatible with a larger current deficit. Put differently, balancing of a given deficit in the current period, which may be explained by an economic shock, requires lower future surpluses. This is, reserve currency status affects the relationship between current and future public balances in any case. In addition, Ricardian equivalence implies that private agents correct the intertemporally suboptimal allocation of government spending. Private agents increase present consumption in place of government when the cost of government debt decreases.

These considerations raise the question whether fiscal policies of reserve currency countries are sustainable. First, we have shown that higher present consumption is compatible with the intertemporal budget constraint. According to an alternative approach, debt is sustainable if the ratio of government debt over GDP is constant over time. Equation (4.1) can be expressed in changes as

$$\frac{dD_t}{dt} = i D_t - S_t \tag{4.4}$$

After taking the first derivative and setting dD equal to zero, we obtain

$$s_t = (i_t - g_t)d_t \tag{4.5}$$

This condition highlights that for a given level of debt a lower interest rate increases the space of sustainable primary surpluses. If the growth rate of GDP exceeds the interest rate (according to Bohn, 2011, this has been the case for the average US rate between 1792 and 2003), a stable debt to GDP ratio may even be accomplished by primary deficits. These deficits may be the larger, the lower the interest rate is. In sum, reserve currency countries can sustain higher levels of sovereign debt and run lower budget balances.

4.4 The role of official capital for the public budget balance – a regression analysis

4.4.1 Description of data set and empirical approaches

Data set

To study the effect of reserve currency status on the public budget balance we assembled a new annual data set covering 24 industrialized countries over the years 1890–2009. The focus on industrialized countries is due to data availability and to the attempt to form a relatively homogeneous country group, which warrants pooling. For each variable we use one main data source, which provides data from the start of the respective series until 2009 (International Financial Statistics start in 1948 at the earliest, for World Development Indicators the longest series date back to 1960). These series are complemented by alternative sources that provide historical data: The most important are Bordo et al. (2001), Lindert (1969) and Mitchell (2007). The definitions of the variables and their data sources are listed in Appendix 4.A. Appendix 4.B enumerates the countries of our sample.

At the core of our data set are yearly data of central banks' international reserves and their composition (gold vs. foreign exchange reserves). In contrast to the main data set, which contains country-specific data for our 24 sample countries, foreign exchange reserves are measured as the sum of reserves aggregated over all countries where data is available. Aggregation across countries is indicated because from the point of view of reserve currency countries the aggregate global net demand for their reserve assets is the variable of interest. The information which individual countries accumulate reserves is secondary. In particular, besides industrial countries our data on foreign exchange include the reserve stocks of emerging and developing countries, where the major part of reserve accumulation has taken place since the East Asian financial crisis of 1997/98. Beginning with their first-time publication in 1948, we use the IMF world series on foreign exchange. For the period 1890–1913 world reserves are calculated as aggregate reserves of 35 countries (see Lindert, 1969). Aggregate reserves in the interwar period are the sum over 21 countries as provided in the Statistical Yearbooks of the League of Nations (see Bordo and Eichengreen, 2001).

Currency shares in these foreign exchange reserves shed light on the dynamics of reserve currency status. These shares are based on various sources, which are listed in Appendix 4.C. Data on currency shares are not available at the global level; they rather reflect reserve choices of a selected number of central banks reporting them.[21] We therefore calculate the disaggregated demand for foreign exchange reserves denominated in individual reserve currencies. The procedure, which is the same for all reserve currencies, is illustrated by way of example for sterling reserves: Changes in total reserves and changes in their composition result from valuation changes (exogenous) and active reserve policy (endogenous). Since only purchases and sales of

---

[21] While some central banks report the annual change in the holdings of foreign exchange reserves listed by currency of denomination, others do not provide this breakdown.

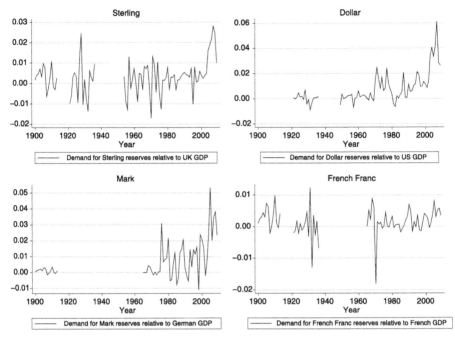

Figure 4.4 Change in global official holdings of major reserve currencies. *Note:* These graphs show the annual change in the level of globally held foreign exchange reserves denominated in four key currencies. The level of reserves denominated in the respective key currencies in a given year is computed as the global level of foreign exchange reserves multiplied by the share of the key currency in total foreign exchange reserves. To strip out the effect of exchange rate changes, reserves are converted in the respective currency before taking the difference.

reserves affect the bonds market of the center country, we try to isolate reserve changes due to active reserve policy. To this end, the total level of foreign exchange reserves is first converted into sterling and then multiplied by the sterling share in total foreign exchange reserves. The difference in sterling reserves between two years is our measure of sterling demand. While this method filters out the effect of exchange rate changes, we are unable to separate the effect of changes in the market value of reserve assets from active reserve policy.

This demand for assets of the major reserve currencies is illustrated in Figure 4.4.[22] It highlights several facts: First, the demand for reserve assets is highly volatile. Second, annual reserve changes amounting to 1% of GDP of the respective reserve country are rather the rule than the exception. This is an economically significant value. Third, changes in provided reserves measured relative to national GDP have been small in France, but large in the US and Germany. Fourth, the time series illustrate the fall of the sterling and the rise of the dollar as reserve currencies. While the official demand for sterling assets is often negative, dollar assets were sold on a

---

[22] The analysis of this chapter focuses on those reserve currencies that represented a remarkable share in total reserves over a substantially long time period within our historical data set. That is, we do not show the effects of, among others, the Japanese Yen, the Netherlands Guilder and the Swiss Franc.

Table 4.2 Demand for reserves relative to GDP of issuing country (in %, mean over periods)

	Sterling	Dollar	Mark	French franc
1899–1913	0.29	n.a.	0.11	0.32
1920–1936	0.08	0.03	n.a.	−0.04
1948–1969	0.14	0.11	0.16	0.45
1970–1994	0.19	0.85	0.53	0.04
1995–2009	0.94	2.48	1.93	0.28

Notes: n.a. = not available.

net basis only in few occasions. Since 1983 the demand for dollar reserves has been positive in any year.

Table 4.2 provides data on the demand for reserves relative to GDP of the issuing countries. The largest relative demand for reserve assets has been recorded in Germany and the US since 1995. Before 1970 the demand for reserve assets was economically less significant relative to GDP.

Since foreign exchange reserves are not entirely invested in government bonds, our measure of reserve demand provides an upper bound for the demand of government bonds. Given the lack of more precise data, we rely on this proxy variable for the period before World War II. Beginning in 1948, the Flow of Funds provide data on the amount of US Treasuries held by foreign official institutions, which we use in the robustness analysis.

The dependent variable of our regression analysis is the public budget balance expressed as a ratio of GDP. The choice of control variables follows the seminal papers of Roubini and Sachs (1989a, 1989b), De Haan and Sturm (1997) and Woo (2003). In particular, the following determinants of government surpluses/deficits are considered:

Inflation: Inflation erodes the real value of taxes if there is a collection lag, defined as a time difference between the moment the tax obligation arises and the moment of tax payment. Moreover, if tax law specifies a value expressed in national currency, inflation decreases its real value. In contrast, in the presence of progressive tax rate schedules government income benefits from higher inflation rates. The overall effect of inflation has to be determined empirically.

Growth of GDP: If government spending is used as an anticyclical instrument to smooth the business cycle, deficits emerge when GDP growth is temporarily low. In periods of relatively high GDP growth, governments may reduce their spending and amount surpluses in their budget balance. The built-in stabilizer of fixed tax rates works in the same direction: Whereas tax income is high during booms, it decreases during recessions.

Demographic structure: Economies with relatively old societies spend a larger share of income for social welfare like pensions and health. The dependency ratio of persons over 65 years (relative to its world average) is expected to negatively affect government finances.

Unemployment rate: If the rate of unemployment is high, government spending is high due to social assistance transfers. At the same time, low economic activity depresses tax revenue. Therefore, the unemployment rate is expected to negatively affect the public budget balance.

External shocks: Negative external shocks might be accommodated by an increase in government spending. The growth rate of the terms of trade multiplied by trade openness is used as a proxy for external shocks.

Relative income: Real per capita GDP relative to the world average is introduced to control for the stage of development. Relatively poor countries are more likely to have inefficient tax and spending systems. As a result, public budget deficits might arise.

Military expenditure: The involvement of a country's armed forces in wars and peacekeeping operations generates costs, which are often transitory and unforeseen. Smooth tax rates imply that these exceptional expenditures generate deficits, which are subsequently financed over long time periods. By way of example, the two World Wars increased public debt of the participating countries considerably. It then took many years to lower public debt to pre-war levels.

For most countries, the World Development Indicators provide data on military expenditures (relative to GDP) since 1988. To identify periods of abnormally high or low military expenditures, we calculate the deviation of military expenditures from their country-specific mean and use this variable in our empirical analysis. Because historical data on military expenditures is missing, in our long-run analysis we use a dummy variable for wars instead, which takes on the value one during World War I and World War II.

Interest rate: Interest rates on government bonds determine the cost of debt financing. For investors they convey information about the riskiness of the bonds; for issuers they are expected to work as automatic stabilizers: High interest rates limit spending of indebted countries whereas creditor countries are usually characterized by lower interest rates. Since high interest rates imply that a present deficit has to be balanced by larger future surpluses, it is less favorable to substitute future consumption by present one. Optimizing governments are expected to run higher budget balances.

The inclusion of interest rates as a determinant of public budget balances poses one major caveat: Interest rates are endogenous. They are determined by the level of government debt and the contemporaneous deficit (see Laubach, 2009). To circumvent the econometric problem of endogeneity, we use an instrumental variable approach in the regressions including interest rates.

Government orientation: Left-wing governments are ideologically in favor of a higher degree of public intervention. According to the partisan approach, they focus on economic growth and low unemployment while low inflation rates are a less important objective. Therefore, left-wing governments might be more prone to increase expenditures and generate deficits than right-wing governments.

Civil liberties/democracy: Countries with reliable institutions and a sound legal and political system are expected to attract private foreign capital flows, which facilitates the financing of public budget deficits. This effect works in addition to the impact of reserve currency status. We use an index of civil liberties, based on measures for personal freedom, human rights, rule of law and economic rights, to proxy for country risk. This measure is available from 1972 onward. For our historical analysis, we therefore rely on an index of democracy instead. Democratic governments are considered to be associated with lower country risk and larger capital inflows.

Financial deepening: The development of the domestic financial market is crucial for a government's ability to finance a budget deficit. In developed markets governments can more easily cover a deficit by the issuance of bonds and depend less on inflationary finance. Financial deepening is proxied by the ratio of M2 over GDP.

Market capitalization: An alternative measure of financial depth is provided by the size of the stock market relative to GDP. Large stock markets offer investment opportunities for foreign capital. This might be beneficial for the market for government bonds.

Financial center: We control for financial centers by the inclusion of a dummy variable. Countries whose gross positions of external assets and liabilities relative to GDP are both larger than their respective mean plus their standard deviation in the cross-section, are considered to be financial centers.[23] According to this definition the US is not identified as a financial center. To include countries that distinguish themselves by their developed financial markets, we additionally include countries listed as top ten in the Global Financial Centers Index, which evaluates the competitiveness of financial center cities. In particular, Hong Kong, Japan, Switzerland, the UK and the US are coded as financial centers over the entire period.[24]

Empirical approaches

We follow several complementary empirical approaches: First, we examine whether the accumulation of reserve currency bonds in the rest of the world directly affects public budget balances in reserve currency countries. To this end, we add the global demand for reserve assets to the standard set of explanatory variables explaining public budget balances. We present a time-series approach, which demonstrates the explanatory power of reserve demand for public balances in reserve currency countries.

Second, our main analysis follows the same strategy, but is based on a panel data set. Thanks to easy financing, reserve currency countries might react differently to changes in the control variables. The panel data approach has the merit to assume constant impact coefficients across countries, which allows to isolate the effect of reserve status in the reserve demand variable.

Our third approach controls for reserve status by the inclusion of a dummy variable for reserve currency countries. It tests whether the public budget balance of reserve currency countries behaves differently compared to peer countries and whether this difference is linked to reserve status.

We are aware that the global economy went through major changes during our time period spanning 120 years. The process of financial integration, the move to more

---

[23] By way of example, in 2005 the following countries are identified as financial centers: Belgium, Hong Kong, Ireland, the Netherlands, Singapore, Switzerland and the United Kingdom.

[24] While being in the top ten, Singapore's financial development is more recent. We therefore rely on the definition based on gross foreign assets and liabilities, according to which it has been a financial center since 1998.

flexible exchange rates after the breakdown of the Bretton Woods system, the rising reserve demand of emerging markets and China in particular and the introduction of the Euro are only some examples. We account for these effects by the inclusion of time effects in our regressions. We do not model these changes explicitly because we suspect that they do not change the fundamental determinants of the public budget balance. However, since we use the change in globally held reserves as a regressor, we control implicitly for changes in reserve demand, which are, in turn, related to changes in the international financial system.

4.4.2 Time-series analysis: US and UK

In a first step, we examine the determinants of the public budget balance for the US and the UK separately in a time-series analysis. This approach focuses on the question whether the demand for reserves is an important determinant of the budget balance in reserve currency countries. Importance is evaluated by the estimated magnitude of the effect and the marginal contribution of the reserve demand to R-squared. To make use of the richest data set (availability of additional controls), we concentrate on the more recent period (1970–2009).

Results are presented in Table 4.3. While the parsimonious model (columns (1)–(2) and (5)–(6)) is estimated by OLS, the remaining columns are based on an instrumental variable approach (2SLS). To control for potential endogeneity of interest rates, these are instrumented by the German interest rate, which is considered as a proxy for the world interest rate. Because of the small number of observations, findings should be interpreted with caution.

The results for the US (columns (1) to (4)) show that besides unemployment the demand for dollar reserves by the rest of the world significantly lowers the public budget balance: If the rest of the world accumulates dollar reserves equal to 1% of US GDP, the US public budget balance relative to GDP deceases by 0.75 to 1.1 percentage points. The inclusion of the demand for reserves raises the R-squared considerably (from 0.38 to 0.65 in the full specification).

Columns (5) to (8) show the results for the UK. Alike in the US, unemployment significantly lowers the public budget balance. The demand for sterling reserves by the rest of the world decreases the UK public budget balance considerably. The effect varies between 1.0 and 1.3 percentage points when the rest of the world accumulates sterling reserves equal to 1% of UK GDP. The consideration of reserve currency status positively affects the R-squared; this effect is especially strong in the parsimonious specification.

4.4.3 Analysis in a panel data set of industrialized countries

This section uses a panel data set to test directly whether the accumulation of reserve currency bonds in the rest of the world affects the public budget balance of reserve-providing countries. To this end, we regress the public budget balance relative to GDP on a set of possible determinants and add the demand for reserve-currency assets as

Table 4.3 Determinants of the public budget balance (1970–2009): Time-series analysis

	United States				United Kingdom			
	(1)	(2)	(3)	(4)	(5)	(6)	(7)	(8)
Inflation	0.0020	0.0007	0.0091	0.0048	0.0070**	0.0078***	0.0017	−0.0090
	(0.53)	(0.23)	(0.97)	(0.76)	(2.44)	(3.32)	(0.07)	(−0.59)
GDP growth	0.3311	0.2309	0.7451	0.4625	0.0637	0.0539	0.0516	0.0180
	(1.46)	(1.05)	(0.97)	(0.92)	(1.06)	(0.87)	(0.85)	(0.34)
Relative dependency ratio (old)	0.0075	−0.0028	0.0206	0.0015	0.0029	−0.0097	−0.0057	−0.0340
	(1.41)	(−0.40)	(1.03)	(0.16)	(0.21)	(−0.76)	(−0.15)	(−1.41)
Unemployment	−0.0145***	−0.0165***	−0.0078	−0.0130**	−0.0069**	−0.0081***	−0.0098	−0.0168**
	(−4.50)	(−6.13)	(−0.89)	(−2.37)	(−2.48)	(−2.92)	(−0.73)	(−2.07)
External shock	0.4165	0.1440	0.5485	0.1125	−0.8046	−0.8066	−0.5036	0.1407
	(0.69)	(0.23)	(0.78)	(0.18)	(−1.61)	(−1.46)	(−0.37)	(0.15)
Interest rate			−0.0092	−0.0061			0.0066	0.0209
			(−0.68)	(−0.63)			(0.23)	(1.14)
Δ global dollar reserves (relative to GDP)		−0.7517**		−1.0807*				
		(−2.43)		(−1.95)				
Δ global sterling reserves (relative to GDP)						−1.2571*		−0.9764*
						(−1.97)		(−1.65)
Observations	29	29	29	29	26	26	26	26
R-squared	0.66	0.73	0.38	0.65	0.39	0.47	0.43	0.44
Estimation	OLS	OLS	2SLS	2SLS	OLS	OLS	2SLS	2SLS

Notes: The dependent variable is the public budget balance to GDP ratio. Robust t-statistics are reported in parentheses. Standard errors are estimated robust to autocorrelation and heteroskedasticity. The symbols *, ** and *** denote statistical significance at the 10%, 5% and 1% levels, respectively. Interest rates are instrumented by the German rate in columns (3)–(4) and (7)–(8). The global change in reserves is measured relative to GDP.

an additional control variable. In particular, we estimate the following fixed-effects specification

$$\left(\frac{PubBudget}{GDP}\right)_{it} = \beta X_{it} + \gamma \left(\frac{\Delta IR^d}{GDP}\right)_{it} + c_i + d_t + \epsilon_{it} \qquad (4.6)$$

where $PubBudget/GDP$ is the ratio of the public budget balance to GDP, X is a vector of control variables, ΔIR^d measures the change in the demand for reserve assets of country i by foreign central banks,[25] c is a fixed country effect, d a fixed time effect and ϵ the error term. i denotes a specific country and t represents the time period. The slope parameters, represented by the vectors β and γ, are assumed to be constant across countries and time. We use the fixed effects estimator with a cluster-robust variance estimator.[26]

To control for the endogeneity of interest rates, we use an instrumental variable approach. We provide results for two different instruments: the lagged value of interest rates on government bonds and the world policy rate. Since interest rates may be characterized by autocorrelation, the world policy rate is our preferred instrument. The world policy rate is defined as the policy rate set by the Bank of England (1890–1935) and the US FED (1948–2009). The switch from the UK to the US accounts of the changing dominance in international finance. It is empirically required because data on US policy rates is only available after the FED was founded in 1913. For the UK and the US the German policy rate is used as world policy rate when the world policy rate as defined above would be their own domestic interest rate.

I use two different estimators, the instrumental variable two-stage least squares (IV-2SLS) and the two-step efficient generalized method of moments (GMM) estimators.[27] In the first step, both estimators create instruments by regressing interest rates on the instrumental variable. These instruments are then used to replace interest rates in the second-step regression.

Results spanning 120 years of history

The results for the entire time period (1890–2009) are presented in Table 4.4. While column (1) presents a parsimonious model only accounting for fundamental determinants of the budget balance (inflation, GDP growth and demographics), we add political and financial variables in subsequent columns.

Regarding our control variables, the following effects are found: Wars significantly decrease the budget balance. Countries with deep financial markets are characterized by lower budget balances. While not significant across all specifications, real GDP growth affects the public budget balance in the hypothesized direction: Real GDP growth positively affects the fiscal balance, which can be interpreted as evidence of countercyclical government spending. There is weak evidence that democratic governments are associated with larger public balances. When significant, higher inflation rates lower the public budget balance.

---

[25] ΔIR^d is zero for all countries besides those enjoying reserve currency status.

[26] The Hausman test rejects a random effects specification.

[27] Results are reported for 2SLS; those obtained with GMM may be provided upon request.

Table 4.4 Public budget balance (1890–2009): Panel data analysis

	(1)	(2)	(3)	(4)	(5)	(6)	(7)	(8)	(9)	(10)
Inflation	−0.0001	−0.0001	−0.0001	−0.0002	−0.0004**	−0.0003*	−0.0003*	−0.0005***	−0.0005***	−0.0005***
	(−0.78)	(−0.68)	(−0.63)	(−0.82)	(−2.22)	(−2.05)	(−2.03)	(−2.87)	(−2.88)	(−3.61)
Real GDP growth	0.0570	0.1147**	0.1065*	0.1109*	0.0101	−0.0176	−0.0257	−0.0476	−0.0473	−0.0392
	(0.81)	(2.11)	(1.77)	(1.97)	(0.21)	(−0.45)	(−0.62)	(−0.58)	(−0.58)	(−0.60)
Relative dependency ratio (old)	−0.0010	−0.0019	−0.0020*	−0.0016	−0.0014	−0.0008	−0.0009	−0.0012**	−0.0012**	−0.0000
	(−0.71)	(−1.62)	(−1.71)	(−1.25)	(−1.00)	(−0.81)	(−0.97)	(−2.08)	(−2.10)	(−0.01)
Wars				−0.1698*	−0.1110**	−0.1429***	−0.1496***	−0.1187***	−0.1183***	−0.1077***
				(−2.02)	(−2.44)	(−3.81)	(−3.76)	(−5.01)	(−4.99)	(−4.59)
Democracy					−0.0001	0.0003	0.0004	0.0013**	0.0013**	0.0013***
					(−0.11)	(0.59)	(0.68)	(2.51)	(2.50)	(2.60)
Financial deepening						−0.0003*	−0.0003*	−0.0003***	−0.0003***	−0.0002***
						(−1.88)	(−1.83)	(−3.48)	(−3.48)	(−3.44)
Interest rate								−0.0020***	−0.0021***	−0.0022***
								(−3.70)	(−3.76)	(−4.50)
Government debt										−0.0002***
										(−4.69)
Δ global dollar reserves * US dummy		−1.3412***	−1.3387***	−1.2828***	−1.2281***	−1.0226***	−1.0200***	−0.9892***	−0.9887***	−0.6988***
		(−4.50)	(−4.46)	(−3.87)	(−3.44)	(−4.68)	(−4.67)	(−5.39)	(−5.39)	(−3.88)
Δ global sterling reserves * UK dummy		−1.2537***	−1.2638***	−1.2433***	−1.1828***	−0.8314***	−0.8287***	−0.8379***	−0.8407***	−1.1545***
		(−6.22)	(−6.06)	(−5.52)	(−5.06)	(−5.01)	(−5.15)	(−2.72)	(−2.73)	(−2.99)
Δ global mark reserves * GER dummy			−0.1435				0.1367	0.0274	0.0296	0.0807
			(−0.83)				(0.81)	(0.11)	(0.12)	(0.33)
Δ global franc reserves * FRA dummy			−0.2421				0.3742	0.1193	0.1130	0.3102
			(−0.72)				(0.90)	(0.26)	(0.25)	(0.67)
Observations	1888	1821	1757	1716	1650	1436	1373	1164	1168	1146
R-squared	0.39	0.38	0.38	0.38	0.37	0.43	0.44	0.43	0.43	0.47
Number of countries	24	24	24	24	22	21	21	19	19	19

Notes: The dependent variable is the public budget balance to GDP ratio. Regressions include fixed country effects and time dummies. Estimation by OLS except columns (8) to (10) where 2SLS is used because interest rates are instrumented. Robust t-statistics are reported in parentheses. Standard errors are estimated robust to intragroup correlations. The symbols *, **, and *** denote statistical significance at the 10%, 5% and 1% levels, respectively. The global change in reserves is measured relative to GDP.

Columns (8) to (10) include the interest rate as additional variable and are estimated by IV-2SLS. Interest rates are instrumented by their lagged level (column (8)) or, alternatively, by the world policy rate (columns (9) and (10)). As expected higher interest rates and the existing level of government debt (column (10)) decrease the public budget balance. That is, the cost effect of higher interest payments dominates the disciplining effect.

Across all specifications, the public budget balances of the UK and the US are significantly affected by the demand for sterling and dollar reserve assets, respectively. If the rest of the world accumulates dollar reserves equivalent to 1% of US GDP, the US public budget balance decreases by 0.7–1.4 percentage points relative to GDP. For the UK, these numbers are comparable in magnitude. An increase in global sterling reserves by 1% of UK GDP lowers the UK public budget balance relative to GDP by 0.8–1.3 percentage points. While these results are in line with our hypothesis that reserve demand lowers the public budget balance, the magnitude of the effects is surprisingly large: Coefficients larger than one imply that the decrease in the public budget balance exceeds the financial resources provided by foreign official institutions. The official demand for reserve assets seems to attract an additional private demand for government bonds. Hence, the effect of reserve demand is multiplied. Foreign central banks do not crowd-out private investors on the market for government bonds. On the contrary, private agents follow central banks' investment strategy and increase their holdings of government bonds when central banks accumulate reserve assets.

Apart from sterling and dollar demand we also include the change in globally held franc and mark reserves (see columns (3), (7)–(10)). With respect to these secondary reserve currencies, we do not find significant effects.

The individual regressions presented in this table make use of all observations that are available in our sample. This implies that the numbers of observations and countries vary across specifications. To conclude that a change in a coefficient across specifications arises from different sets of control variables – and not from different samples – we would have to hold the numbers of countries and observations constant. Results for constant samples for all tables of this subsection are therefore reported in Appendix 4.D.

While this analysis over an extended time period benefits from the included amount of information, it may be plagued by structural breaks. We therefore proceed by splitting our sample into two sub-periods, namely the periods before and after World War II.

UK during sterling dominance

We replicate our fixed-effects regressions of Table 4.4 for the period from 1890 to 1935 excluding the period of World War I (1914–1919). The results in Table 4.5 show that most of the standard control variables do not significantly affect the public balance. We find some evidence that older societies are characterized by lower public balances. In two out of three specifications interest rates have a significant negative effect on the public budget balance. The demand for reserve assets, however, is significant: For

Table 4.5 Public budget balance (1890–1935): Panel data analysis

	(1)	(2)	(3)	(4)	(5)	(6)	(7)	(8)	(9)
Inflation	-0.0004	-0.0004	-0.0004	-0.0005	-0.0006	-0.0006	-0.0008	-0.0008	-0.0007
	(-0.83)	(-0.77)	(-0.83)	(-0.95)	(-1.15)	(-1.03)	(-1.19)	(-1.19)	(-1.00)
Real GDP growth	0.0336	0.0285	0.0336	0.0330	0.0320	0.0263	0.0103	0.0103	0.0272
	(0.61)	(0.45)	(0.61)	(0.59)	(0.55)	(0.39)	(0.14)	(0.14)	(0.39)
Relative dependency ratio (old)	-0.1527**	-0.1120	-0.1527**	-0.1678**	-0.1350*	-0.0966	-0.1007	-0.1007	-0.1193
	(-2.41)	(-1.38)	(-2.41)	(-2.56)	(-2.08)	(-1.15)	(-0.95)	(-0.95)	(-0.70)
Democracy				-0.0003	-0.0000	0.0004	0.0004	0.0004	0.0002
				(-0.47)	(-0.07)	(0.80)	(0.44)	(0.44)	(0.12)
Financial deepening					-0.0002	-0.0001	-0.0001	-0.0001	-0.0001
					(-1.42)	(-0.55)	(-0.50)	(-0.50)	(-0.66)
Interest rate							-0.0105*	-0.0105*	-0.0096
							(-1.95)	(-1.95)	(-1.54)
Government debt									-0.0002
									(-0.81)
Δ global dollar reserves * US dummy	1.5502***	1.4582***	1.5502***	1.5768***	1.6871***	1.6625***	1.2589***	1.2589***	0.9951*
	(3.65)	(3.10)	(3.65)	(3.85)	(4.88)	(4.69)	(2.73)	(2.73)	(1.88)
Δ global sterling reserves * UK dummy	-0.5811**	-0.5999**	-0.5811**	-0.5721**	-0.5378**	-0.5583*	-0.6805**	-0.6805**	-0.9378*
	(-2.50)	(-2.36)	(-2.50)	(-2.30)	(-2.16)	(-2.07)	(-2.16)	(-2.16)	(-1.90)
Δ global mark reserves * GER dummy		-0.2486				-0.2247	-0.7944	-0.7944	-0.9045
		(-0.63)				(-0.50)	(-1.28)	(-1.28)	(-0.90)
Δ global franc reserves * FRA dummy		0.5279*				0.6083*	0.1987	0.1987	0.8413
		(1.92)				(2.06)	(0.83)	(0.83)	(1.58)
Observations	426	396	426	402	374	344	268	268	256
R-squared	0.31	0.32	0.31	0.31	0.33	0.33	0.38	0.38	0.39
Number of countries	14	14	14	14	13	13	10	10	10

Notes: The dependent variable is the public budget balance to GDP ratio. The global change in reserves is measured relative to GDP. Regressions include fixed country and time effects. Estimation by OLS. Instrumental variable 2SLS is used in specifications including the interest rate. In columns (7) and (9) the interest rate is instrumented by its lagged value, in column (8) by the world policy rate. Robust t-statistics are reported in parentheses. Standard errors are estimated robust to intragroup correlations. The symbols *, ** and *** denote statistical significance at the 10%, 5% and 1% levels, respectively.

the UK, sterling demand lowers the public budget balance albeit its effect is economically somewhat smaller compared to the entire period. An increase in global sterling reserves by 1% of UK GDP lowers its public balance relative to GDP by 0.6–0.9 percentage points. The demand for dollar assets significantly increases the US public balance. This unexpected result may have various explanations: First, before World War I, the dollar's role in foreign exchange reserves was marginal. More importantly, relative to US GDP, dollar reserve demand was relatively low during the entire period up to 1935 (see Figure 4.4). Hence, its effect on the public budget balance was economically small. Second, before World War II the US has actively promoted the rise of the dollar as reserve currency. This might explain the positive coefficient implying that fiscal policy was more restrictive when dollar reserves were accumulated in the rest of the world. This is consistent with the observation that the US accumulated gold during that period.

US during dollar dominance

For the dollar dominance since World War II (see Table 4.6) real GDP growth has a robust positive effect on the public budget balance confirming the tax- and consumption-smoothing hypothesis. Interest rates and government debt decrease the public balance significantly. For both the UK and the US the demand for reserve assets significantly lowers the respective public budget balances. This effect holds for the French franc in two out of five specifications, while the demand for mark reserves has the expected sign, but is only significant in one out of five specifications. An increase in global dollar reserves by 1% of US GDP lowers the US public balance relative to GDP by 0.6–1.2 percentage points. The corresponding effect for the UK amounts to 1.0–1.4 percentage points.

For the more recent period beginning in 1970, data availability allows us to use a richer data set. In particular, besides the variables used before, we have data on the rate of unemployment, external shocks, military expenditures, government orientation and market capitalization. The results are presented in Table 4.7. For the following variables we find significant and robust results: The public budget balance increases in real GDP growth, while it is negatively correlated with the rate of unemployment. When military expenditures exceed their country average, public budget balances are lower. Financial centers, characterized by easy access to private external financial resources, run lower public balances. Interest rates and government debt negatively affect the fiscal balance.

The global demand for official reserves lowers the public budget balance of the dominant reserve-providing countries. Across all specifications we find significant negative effects for the US and the UK. While the magnitude of the effect in the US is comparable to that found in Tables 4.4 and 4.6, the estimated impact on the UK balances is now larger ranging between 1.2 and 2.2 percentage points of GDP. New is the finding of a robust and large effect of the demand for official franc reserves on the French public balance. This shows that France only recently used its reserve status to finance additional government spending.

In sum, the demand for reserve assets affects public balances of the dominant reserve currencies. When reserves are accumulated by the rest of the world, public

Table 4.6 Public budget balance (1950–2009): Panel data analysis

	(1)	(2)	(3)	(4)	(5)	(6)	(7)	(8)	(9)
Inflation	0.0000	0.0000	−0.0002	−0.0001	−0.0006	−0.0005	0.0006	0.0006	0.0007
	(0.16)	(0.33)	(−0.48)	(−0.13)	(−1.07)	(−0.89)	(1.37)	(1.36)	(1.52)
Real GDP growth	0.1426**	0.1465**	0.1299**	0.1201**	0.0750*	0.0826*	0.0787	0.0749	0.0170
	(2.48)	(2.41)	(2.42)	(2.19)	(1.73)	(1.74)	(1.63)	(1.57)	(0.37)
Relative dependency ratio (old)	−0.0014	−0.0016	−0.0010	−0.0010	−0.0001	−0.0004	−0.0005	−0.0005	0.0025***
	(−1.06)	(−1.16)	(−0.64)	(−0.61)	(−0.05)	(−0.26)	(−0.77)	(−0.75)	(3.56)
Democracy				−0.0007	−0.0006	−0.0005	−0.0003	−0.0003	−0.0007**
				(−1.34)	(−1.03)	(−0.71)	(−0.88)	(−0.86)	(−2.06)
Financial deepening					−0.0002	−0.0001	−0.0001**	−0.0002**	−0.0002***
					(−1.15)	(−0.87)	(−2.27)	(−2.32)	(−3.65)
Interest rate							−0.0014**	−0.0014**	−0.0022***
							(−2.15)	(−2.18)	(−3.77)
Government debt									−0.0005***
									(−6.74)
Δ global dollar reserves * US dummy	−1.1765***	−1.1634***	−1.0854***	−1.1255***	−0.8883***	−0.8732***	−0.8657***	−0.8662***	−0.5713***
	(−4.16)	(−4.03)	(−3.23)	(−3.16)	(−4.39)	(−4.36)	(−5.04)	(−5.04)	(−3.49)
Δ global sterling reserves * UK dummy	−1.3769***	−1.3990***	−1.3489***	−1.3631***	−1.0437***	−1.0731***	−0.9717***	−0.9691***	−1.2968***
	(−5.40)	(−5.39)	(−4.62)	(−4.48)	(−5.30)	(−5.57)	(−2.62)	(−2.62)	(−2.71)
Δ global mark reserves * GER dummy		−0.5142***				−0.1583	−0.1132	−0.1153	−0.1568
		(−3.89)				(−1.71)	(−0.45)	(−0.46)	(−0.66)
Δ global franc reserves * FRA dummy		−1.4356***				−0.2387**	−0.2707	−0.2668	−0.3516
		(−5.38)				(−2.60)	(−0.47)	(−0.46)	(−0.47)
Observations	1225	1195	1120	1092	918	888	795	798	796
R-squared	0.36	0.37	0.36	0.36	0.35	0.37	0.36	0.36	0.42
Number of countries	24	24	24	22	21	21	19	19	19

Notes: The dependent variable is the public budget balance to GDP ratio. The global change in reserves is measured relative to GDP. Regressions include fixed country and time effects. Estimation by OLS. Instrumental variable 2SLS is used in specifications including the interest rate. In columns (7) and (9) the interest rate is instrumented y its lagged value, in column (8) by the world policy rate. Robust t-statistics are reported in parentheses. Standard errors are estimated robust to intragroup correlations. The symbols *, ** and *** denote statistical significance at the 10%, 5% and 1% levels, respectively.

Table 4.7 Public budget balance (1970–2009): Panel data analysis

	(1)	(2)	(3)	(4)	(5)	(6)	(7)	(8)	(9)	(10)	(11)	(12)
Inflation	0.0000	−0.0008	−0.0008	−0.0010	−0.0010	0.0037**	−0.0013	−0.0014	−0.0008	0.0053***	0.0053***	0.0051***
	(0.27)	(−1.01)	(−1.02)	(−0.46)	(−0.47)	(2.75)	(−0.70)	(−0.73)	(−0.36)	(4.84)	(4.86)	(4.55)
Real GDP growth	0.0732***	0.0492**	0.0489**	0.0600**	0.0630**	0.0481	0.0506**	0.0504**	0.0557*	0.0444**	0.0446**	0.0461**
	(4.89)	(2.19)	(2.17)	(2.38)	(2.47)	(1.62)	(2.15)	(2.11)	(2.06)	(2.18)	(2.19)	(2.25)
Relative dependency ratio (old)	−0.0019	−0.0021	−0.0022	−0.0027	−0.0028	−0.0030*	−0.0030	−0.0032	−0.0022	−0.0035***	−0.0035***	−0.0017
	(−1.05)	(−0.85)	(−0.88)	(−1.01)	(−1.04)	(−3.09)	(−1.17)	(−1.23)	(−0.82)	(−3.48)	(−3.47)	(−1.06)
Unemployment		−0.0051***	−0.0051***	−0.0050***	−0.0049***	−0.0058*	−0.0046***	−0.0048***	−0.0049***	−0.0044***	−0.0043***	−0.0035***
		(−4.29)	(−4.31)	(−3.05)	(−3.04)	(−2.16)	(−2.89)	(−2.94)	(−2.66)	(−5.49)	(−5.49)	(−4.34)
External shock		0.0624	0.0633	0.0959	0.0903	−0.0497	0.0947	0.0986	0.1023	−0.1452**	−0.1440**	−0.1383**
		(1.16)	(1.17)	(1.01)	(0.94)	(−0.95)	(1.10)	(1.13)	(1.09)	(−2.24)	(−2.22)	(−2.05)
Relative income		−0.0079	−0.0086	−0.0271	−0.0278	−0.0003	−0.0078	−0.0096	−0.0043	−0.0278***	−0.0273***	−0.0276***
		(−0.46)	(−0.50)	(−1.26)	(−1.30)	(−0.01)	(−0.41)	(−0.51)	(−0.19)	(−2.77)	(−2.77)	(−2.81)
Military expenditure (deviation from mean)				−0.0194*	−0.0194*	−0.0250*	−0.0186	−0.0187*	−0.0142	−0.0235***	−0.0236***	−0.0246***
				(−1.77)	(−1.80)	(−2.23)	(−1.72)	(−1.73)	(−1.37)	(−4.68)	(−4.71)	(−5.16)
Democracy					0.0065		0.0073	0.0076	0.0055	0.0050*	0.0050*	0.0058*
					(1.39)		(1.57)	(1.64)	(1.16)	(1.68)	(1.68)	(1.95)
Left government					−0.0000	−0.0002**	−0.0000	−0.0000	−0.0000	−0.0000	−0.0000	−0.0000
					(−0.28)	(−3.03)	(−0.16)	(−0.26)	(−0.14)	(−0.16)	(−0.19)	(−0.18)
Financial deepening						−0.0001						
						(−0.29)						
Financial center (dummy)							−0.0591***	−0.0592***		−0.0272**	−0.0276**	−0.0292**
							(−3.11)	(−3.13)		(−2.19)	(−2.22)	(−2.33)
Market capitalization									0.0002			
									(1.67)			
Interest rate										−0.0064***	−0.0065***	−0.0063***
										(−6.56)	(−6.56)	(−6.32)
Government debt												−0.0003**
												(−2.21)

Table 4.7 (continued)

	(1)	(2)	(3)	(4)	(5)	(6)	(7)	(8)	(9)	(10)	(11)	(12)
Δ global dollar reserves	−0.8977***	−1.0079***	−1.0164***	−1.0373***	−1.0452***	−1.0498***	−1.1201***	−1.1319***	−1.0470**	−1.1399***	−1.1371***	−0.9855***
* US dummy	(−4.42)	(−3.62)	(−3.64)	(−2.86)	(−2.87)	(−4.97)	(−3.15)	(−3.19)	(−2.77)	(−4.64)	(−4.63)	(−3.78)
Δ global sterling reserves	−1.2505***	−2.1947***	−2.2106***	−1.9025***	−1.8655***	−1.3970***	−2.1138***	−2.1242***	−1.6673**	−1.7893***	−1.7909***	−1.5285***
* UK dummy	(−3.78)	(−5.61)	(−5.63)	(−3.60)	(−3.36)	(−3.66)	(−3.74)	(−3.75)	(−2.81)	(−4.00)	(−4.00)	(−3.33)
Δ global mark reserves			0.2080					0.2032				0.2557
* GER dummy			(0.96)					(1.18)				(1.16)
Δ global franc reserves			−2.5635***					−3.3088***				−2.2646*
* FRA dummy			(−3.21)					(−3.73)				(−1.69)
Observations	861	531	531	420	418	204	418	418	411	408	409	409
R-squared	0.38	0.54	0.54	0.56	0.56	0.70	0.58	0.59	0.58	0.65	0.65	0.65
Number of countries	24	21	21	21	20	12	20	20	20	20	20	20

Notes: The dependent variable is the public budget balance to GDP ratio. The global change in reserves is measured relative to GDP. Regressions include fixed country and time effects. Estimation by OLS except columns (10) to (12) where an instrumental variable approach is used (2SLS). Robust t-statistics are reported in parentheses. Standard errors are estimated robust to intragroup correlations. The symbols *, ** and *** denote statistical significance at the 10%, 5% and 1% levels, respectively.

budget balances of the US and the UK decrease. They increase when global reserve holdings are reduced.

4.4.4 Alternative identification: Are reserve currency countries outliers?

While the previous section has shown that reserve currency status affects the public budget balance, we have not determined whether this effect is positive or negative on average.[28] As an alternative econometric approach we show in a dummy variable analysis that public budget balances of reserve currency countries are outliers. In a subsequent step, we provide evidence that the outlier status disappears once we account for reserve currency status.

We apply the pooled regression model using a variance estimator robust to within-country correlations. To account for the effect of reserve currency status we add an indicator variable that takes on the value one for reserve currency countries. While the main analysis focuses on the UK and the US, we add specifications that include dummy variables for France and Germany as well. It tests the hypothesis that reserve currency status relaxes the public budget constraint and, therefore, induces the government to save less. In particular, the following relationship is estimated:

$$\left(\frac{PubBudget}{GDP}\right)_{it} = \beta X_{ti} + \gamma RCD_i + d_t + \epsilon_{it} \tag{4.7}$$

which corresponds to equation (4.6) with the difference that we use the pooled model with a reserve currency dummy (RCD) and with time effects but without fixed country effects. RCD equals one for reserve currency countries and zero otherwise. As in the previous section, the periods before and after World War II are considered separately.

UK under sterling dominance

For the period 1890–1935 we include the same set of control variables as in the fixed-effects analysis of Section 4.4.3. The results, which are presented in Table 4.8, confirm previous findings: Most control variables are insignificant. Democracy is positively linked to public balances. Wars significantly lower budget balances.[29] The dummy for the UK is negative and significant in 5 of 7 specifications. This confirms our hypothesis that the UK is different. In comparison to other industrialized countries, the set of economic and demographic determinants cannot explain the UK public budget balance. Depending on the specification, the ratio of public budget balance to GDP is 1.6 to 2.2 percentage points lower than in a country with the same characteristics. This effect is economically significant.

---

[28] The sign of the effect may be derived from Figure 4.4, which shows that the demand for reserve assets has been positive on average for most currencies across different time periods. Hence, reserve currency status has lowered the public budget balance on average.

[29] Wars were not included in the corresponding panel analysis of Table 4.5 because the relevant years between 1914 and 1919 were dropped. The reason for this is that currency shares in foreign exchange reserves were pivotal in the fixed-effects analysis. However, this data is unavailable between 1914 and 1919.

Table 4.8 Public budget balance (1890–1935): Outlier analysis

	(1)	(2)	(3)	(4)	(5)	(6)	(7)
Dependent variable: Reported public budget balance							
Inflation	−0.0002	−0.0002	−0.0001	−0.0001	−0.0018**	−0.0001	−0.0019**
	(−0.53)	(−0.53)	(−0.49)	(−0.47)	(−2.43)	(−0.54)	(−2.48)
Real GDP growth	−0.0402	−0.0402	−0.0368	−0.0560	−0.0226	−0.0422	−0.0209
	(−0.38)	(−0.38)	(−0.35)	(−0.52)	(−0.19)	(−0.40)	(−0.17)
Relative dependency ratio (old)	−0.0302	−0.0302	0.0440	0.0484	0.0252	−0.0796	−0.0364
	(−0.48)	(−0.48)	(0.70)	(0.66)	(0.58)	(−0.77)	(−0.48)
Wars		−0.1087**	−0.1295**	−0.1304**	−0.1019*	−0.1151**	−0.1064*
		(−2.36)	(−2.66)	(−2.57)	(−1.89)	(−2.46)	(−1.95)
Democracy			0.0025**	0.0024*	0.0030***		0.0027***
			(2.43)	(2.05)	(4.00)		(3.16)
Financial deepening				0.0001	0.0003**		0.0003**
				(0.39)	(2.56)		(2.35)
Interest rate					0.0047		0.0059
					(1.40)		(1.46)
Dummy UK	−0.0163**	−0.0163**	−0.0216***	−0.0213***	−0.0166	−0.0208**	−0.0201
	(−2.83)	(−2.83)	(−4.51)	(−4.33)	(−1.25)	(−2.76)	(−1.42)
Dummy US						0.0128	0.0061
						(1.65)	(0.79)
Dummy GER						−0.0255***	−0.0193***
						(−5.84)	(−4.27)
Dummy FRA						−0.0148	−0.0149
						(−0.97)	(−1.49)

(continued on next page)

Table 4.8 (*continued*)

Dependent variable: Adjusted public budget balance

	(1)	(2)	(3)	(4)	(5)	(6)	(7)
Dummy UK	0.0188***	0.0188***	0.0150**	0.0156**	0.0174***	0.0161*	0.0158**
	(3.84)	(3.84)	(2.94)	(2.59)	(3.12)	(2.02)	(2.16)
Dummy US						0.0189**	0.0142
						(2.51)	(1.61)
Dummy GER						−0.0267***	−0.0236***
						(−9.03)	(−5.95)
Dummy FRA						−0.0096	−0.0056
						(−0.65)	(−0.57)
Observations	513	513	486	457	366	513	366
R-squared	0.24	0.24	0.29	0.29	0.39	0.26	0.40
Number of countries	14	14	14	13	10	14	10

Notes: The dependent variable is the public budget balance to GDP ratio. Interest rates are instrumented by the world policy rate. Estimation by pooled OLS with the exception of columns including the interest rate, where 2SLS is used. Robust t-statistics are reported in parentheses. Standard errors are estimated robust to intragroup correlations. The symbols *, **, and *** denote statistical significance at the 10%, 5% and 1% levels, respectively.

This result highlights two anomalies with respect to supply of and demand for government bonds: First, the UK government saves less than governments in comparable countries. Second, investors provide more funds to the UK government than to governments characterized by similar fundamentals.

The funds to cover the UK budget deficit might be provided by domestic or foreign creditors, where the latter can be divided in private and official ones. Since only the demand by foreign official institutions is directly linked to the reserve currency status of the UK we have not yet identified the effect of reserve status.

To isolate the effect of foreign central banks on the UK public balance, we construct a hypothetical UK public budget balance for the case that sterling is not used as reserve currency: We set the foreign official demand for UK government bonds equal to zero. In other words, we calculate an adjusted public budget balance where net foreign official purchases of government bonds are added to the reported balance.[30]

We then re-run the regressions of Table 4.8 using the adjusted public budget balance as dependent variable. Since the effects of the set of control variables are basically unaffected from this change, we only report the coefficients for the reserve country dummies in the bottom of Table 4.8. The dummy for the UK becomes significant and positive in all specifications. This provides additional evidence that reserve currency status is linked to the lower UK budget balance. In the absence of the demand for UK government bonds by foreign official institutions, the UK budget balance would have been significantly larger than suggested by its fundamentals. The positive dummy for the UK may be due to the fact that our adjusted public budget balance overstates the actual effect of reserve demand. Our proxy assumes that (1) all sterling reserves are held in UK government bonds and (2) that the official demand for government bonds does not affect the private demand (no crowding-out). If these assumptions are not met, our adjustment of the budget balance is too strong. Notwithstanding, we can conclude that reserve currency status significantly lowers the UK public balance because after controlling for it, the UK dummy turns from a significant negative to a significant positive value. With respect to secondary reserve currencies the only qualitative difference can be observed for the US dummy, which turns from insignificant to significantly positive. This is in line with the growing importance of the dollar as reserve currency during that period.

US during dollar dominance

We repeat the analysis as described in the previous section for the more recent period of dollar dominance. While we stick to our approach to account for reserve status by a dummy variable, thanks to data availability we make use of the richer data set that was deployed for the regressions of Table 4.7. In addition to the control variables used in the previous analysis, we include the rate of unemployment, external shocks, government ideology and income relative to the sample average in a given year. The dummy variable for wars is replaced by military expenditure, which is expected to

---

[30] This is an extreme method because part of the decline in official demand might be substituted by an increase in private investors' demand. Nevertheless, while the UK might still be able to finance its public budget deficit without reserve currency status, the costs would increase due to higher interest rates.

account more precisely for temporary increases in the military budget. Results are presented in Table 4.9.

We first concentrate on columns (1) to (4), which present the results for regressions that include the standard set of control variables. We find evidence for countercyclical fiscal policies: Periods of higher GDP growth are correlated with larger public budget balances. The US dummy variable shows up negative and significant across all specifications. The US public budget balance (relative to GDP) is 1 to 5 percentage points lower than that of its peers with identical fundamentals.

This result, however, does not allow to conclude that the outlier status of the US is caused by its reserve currency function. The lower US public balance may be due to private capital flows, which result from its status as financial center. To disentangle the effects of private and official capital flows we include three additional variables that control for the development of financial markets: money relative to GDP as a measure for financial deepening, a dummy for financial centers and a measure of stock market capitalization.[31]

The results, presented in columns (5) to (7), coincide in the finding that financial centers impose a negative effect on the public budget balance. Thanks to private capital flows the government sector can more easily finance budget deficits. More importantly, the US dummy remains negative and significant even after controlling for financial center status.

Column (8) includes additionally the world interest rate and government debt. Both decrease the public balance. Columns (9) to (11) add dummy variables for secondary reserve currency countries, namely the UK, France and Germany. In contrast to the period before World War II we find an insignificant or positive effect for the UK. This is evidence for the demise of the UK as reserve country. Global sterling reserves were reduced. Moreover, this finding points to a change in UK fiscal policies: After the loss of its role as predominant reserve country, UK fiscal policies have become more restrictive. The dummy variables for Germany and France are negative, albeit not always significant. In the full specification (column (11)) the German public budget balance relative to GDP is 4.6 percentage points lower and that of France 3.1 percentage points below that of their peers.

Analogously to the analysis for the period before World War II, we proceed by accounting for reserve currency status by an adjusted public budget balance for reserve-providing countries. This hypothetical public budget balance is defined as the reported balance plus net foreign official purchases of reserves. The results for the dummy variables are presented in the bottom part of Table 4.9.

The dummy variable for the US turns insignificant across all specifications with one exception where it becomes positive and significant. We read this as evidence in favor of the hypothesis that the lower US public budget balance can be explained by its reserve status. The dummy for the UK is still positive. The impact on public balances in Germany and France remains negative, albeit smaller in absolute magnitude.

---

[31] Data for these variables is not available for the period before World War II. That is why we do not include them in the regressions for the period of sterling dominance (see Table 4.8).

Table 4.9 Public budget balance (1970–2009): Outlier analysis

	(1)	(2)	(3)	(4)	(5)	(6)	(7)	(8)	(9)	(10)	(11)
Dependent variable: Reported public budget balance											
Inflation	−0.0000	−0.0007	−0.0007	−0.0006	0.0004	−0.0019	−0.0005	0.0079*	−0.0007	−0.0025	0.0063*
	(−0.17)	(−0.42)	(−0.27)	(−0.23)	(0.18)	(−0.80)	(−0.19)	(1.88)	(−0.47)	(−1.11)	(1.71)
GDP growth	0.0774***	0.0674***	0.0776***	0.0747***	0.0515*	0.0704***	0.0707***	0.0339	0.0671**	0.0695***	0.0339
	(4.29)	(2.86)	(4.29)	(3.10)	(1.95)	(2.98)	(3.20)	(1.28)	(2.84)	(2.95)	(1.35)
Relative dependency ratio (old)	−0.0012	−0.0011	−0.0019	−0.0022	−0.0020**	−0.0018	−0.0021	−0.0002	−0.0008	−0.0016	0.0010*
	(−1.16)	(−0.88)	(−1.34)	(−1.72)	(−2.71)	(−1.56)	(−1.48)	(−0.34)	(−0.62)	(−1.36)	(1.95)
Unemployment		−0.0023	−0.0017	−0.0017	−0.0085***	−0.0029*	−0.0022	−0.0025***	−0.0022	−0.0030*	−0.0022***
		(−1.49)	(−1.11)	(−1.24)	(−3.80)	(−1.98)	(−1.45)	(−5.12)	(−1.42)	(−1.91)	(−4.50)
External shock		0.1172*	0.1604*	0.1362	0.1250	0.1601*	0.1321	−0.1764	0.1173*	0.1715*	−0.1382
		(1.87)	(1.74)	(1.32)	(1.52)	(1.75)	(1.28)	(−1.11)	(1.87)	(1.93)	(−0.96)
Relative income		0.0323	0.0296	0.0302	0.0085	0.0301*	0.0321*	0.0120*	0.0328	0.0307**	0.0112*
		(1.64)	(1.49)	(1.61)	(0.49)	(2.03)	(1.80)	(1.79)	(1.69)	(2.15)	(1.78)
Military expenditure (deviation from mean)			−0.0168	−0.0154	−0.0131	−0.0173	−0.0150	−0.0236***		−0.0194	−0.0285***
			(−1.31)	(−1.17)	(−1.12)	(−1.21)	(−1.06)	(−3.24)		(−1.29)	(−3.99)
Democracy				0.0081	−0.0064	0.0127*	0.0074	0.0129***		0.0092	−0.0000
				(1.57)	(−0.67)	(2.08)	(1.30)	(2.92)		(1.56)	(−0.01)
Left government				0.0001	−0.0001	0.0001*	0.0002	0.0001		0.0001	0.0000
				(1.65)	(−1.03)	(1.73)	(1.69)	(1.59)		(1.25)	(1.08)
Financial deepening					−0.0004***						
					(−4.33)						
Financial center (dummy)						−0.0321***		−0.0459***		−0.0414***	−0.0562***
						(−3.05)		(−4.95)		(−3.23)	(−4.73)
Market capitalization							−0.0001				
							(−0.66)				
Interest rate								−0.0135**			−0.0141**
								(−2.04)			(−2.29)
Government debt								−0.0005***			−0.0007***
								(−7.68)			(−8.80)

(continued on next page)

Table 4.9 (continued)

	(1)	(2)	(3)	(4)	(5)	(6)	(7)	(8)	(9)	(10)	(11)
Dummy US	−0.0095* (−1.80)	−0.0473** (−2.53)	−0.0494** (−2.62)	−0.0463** (−2.59)	−0.0472*** (−3.38)	−0.0547*** (−3.19)	−0.0450*** (−2.92)	−0.0389*** (−5.63)	−0.0481** (−2.57)	−0.0575*** (−3.24)	−0.0382*** (−5.64)
Dummy UK									−0.0092 (−1.12)	0.0197* (1.88)	0.0101 (1.15)
Dummy GER									−0.0094 (−1.09)	−0.0172** (−2.12)	−0.0458*** (−7.21)
Dummy FRA									−0.0126 (−1.70)	−0.0088 (−1.32)	−0.0309*** (−6.43)
Dependent variable: Adjusted public budget balance											
Dummy US	0.0199*** (3.79)	−0.0160 (−0.87)	−0.0223 (−1.20)	−0.0188 (−1.09)	−0.0233 (−1.65)	−0.0265 (−1.59)	−0.0174 (−1.17)	−0.0094 (−0.56)	−0.0160 (−0.85)	−0.0288 (−1.63)	−0.0105 (−1.42)
Dummy UK									−0.0024 (−0.29)	0.0261** (2.52)	0.0191* (1.81)
Dummy GER									0.0062 (0.71)	−0.0000 (−0.00)	−0.0285*** (−3.22)
Dummy FRA									−0.0102 (−1.39)	−0.0042 (−0.64)	−0.0265*** (−4.35)
Observations	861	531	420	418	204	418	411	409	531	418	409
R-squared	0.24	0.47	0.48	0.50	0.69	0.55	0.51	0.58	0.47	0.56	0.62
Number of countries	24	21	21	20	12	20	20	20	21	20	20

Notes: The dependent variable is the public budget balance to GDP ratio. Estimation by pooled OLS except specifications including the interest rate where an instrumental variable approach (2SLS) is used. Robust t-statistics are reported in parentheses. Standard errors are estimated robust to intragroup correlations. The symbols *, **, and *** denote statistical significance at the 10%, 5% and 1% levels, respectively.

4.4.5   Robustness checks

In this section we check whether our results are robust with respect to an alternative sample of countries and to different measures for our main variables. Due to limited space, we do not include the tables of the robustness analyses but these may be obtained upon request.

Alternative sample: Our sample is restricted to 24 industrialized countries, for which historical data before World War II is available. For the more recent period data can be obtained for a much broader set of countries. We check the robustness of our results for a sample of up to 125 nations, including industrialized, emerging and developing countries for the period 1970–2009. While the explanatory power of the regressions is low, a negative effect of the official demand for dollars on the US public balance is confirmed.

Means over 5-year-periods: We replicate our analysis over the entire time period (1890–2009) from Table 4.5 using 5-year averages of the data. This allows to abstract from cyclical shifts in the public budget balance and to concentrate on structural effects. The effect of the global demand for reserves on national budget balances is confirmed.

Alternative measure for foreign official reserve demand: Since currency shares in foreign exchange reserves are not known for all countries, we use estimates for the demand for reserve assets denominated in a certain currency. Moreover, data availability makes it impossible to distinguish between the demand for reserve assets and the demand for government bonds. The demand for reserve assets provides an upper bound of the official demand for government bonds because reserve assets might be invested in assets other than government bonds.

The only exception is the US. It reports the amount of Treasuries held by foreign official institutions in its Flow of Funds statistics. We use this information for more accurate estimates. Accordingly, we replace the demand for reserve assets by the change in Treasuries held by foreign official institutions as explanatory variable in our fixed-effects regressions. By and large, previous findings are qualitatively confirmed.

Data on public deficits: Data on public budget balances are known to be imprecise, subject to revisions and may be manipulated for political reasons. This might be even more true for historical data. We therefore repeat our analysis using Accominotti et al. (2011) as an alternative data source for historical values of our dependent variable. The main results are robust to this change.

4.5   Conclusions

Reserve currency status entails benefits and costs. It may affect decisions taken by individuals and the government of the reserve-providing country. While there exists a vast literature examining the effects of reserve currency status on interest rates, this study is the first to consider the impact on the public budget balance.

Reserve currency status eases the public budget constraint and enables the center country to run a lower public budget balance. Foreign central banks finance the budget deficit of the center's government by their purchase of reserves in the form of Treasury bonds. The government decision to run lower public budget balances is the optimal response to the increased demand for government bonds and their lower interest rate. As long as reserve status is retained, a higher level of debt is compatible with standard criteria for sustainability.

We provide empirical evidence that reserve currency status decreases the public budget balance of center countries by 1 to 5 percentage points (relative to GDP). Any dollar of reserve assets purchased by official institutions in the rest of the world decreases the budget balance of the center by 0.6–1.4 dollars depending on time period and specific country. These numbers are economically significant. Expressed in absolute terms they are outstanding.

Besides reserve status, we identify wars, high interest rates and the level of government debt as robust factors that have negatively affected the public budget balance over the last 120 years. For the more recent period since 1970, unemployment, deep financial markets and low GDP growth have contributed to low public balances.

This study distinguishes itself by covering 120 years of history and including two episodes of dominant reserve currencies: the sterling period until the interwar years and the dollar dominance since World War II. While we examine both periods separately, we derive surprisingly resembling results for US and UK public budget balances. This provides further evidence in favor of our hypothesis: The lower public budget balance is not peculiar to a specific country. On the contrary, our study over a historical time span allows to conclude that lower public budget balances are a phenomenon akin to reserve currency countries. This phenomenon persists independently of the time period, national policies or the provision of alternative reserve assets. More importantly, the presented facts may not be interpreted as evidence that the UK or US have abused their privilege as reserve currency country. The problem is a more fundamental one: It lies in the fact that a national currency is used as global reserve currency. For secondary reserve currencies like the French Franc and the German Mark we do not find robust effects.

The flip side of this easy financing is an increasing level of sovereign (external) debt. Persistent government deficits may question the sustainability of public debt, which, in turn, undermines the stability of the reserve currency. The theoretical and empirical literature concur that the probability of a sovereign debt crisis increases with the level of public debt (see Reinhart and Rogoff, 2011). In conjunction with a decreasing US share in global economic activity and rising alternative reserve currencies this process might prove to be unsustainable in the long run. Moreover, the US may be tempted to erode the real value of its debt by inflation (Aizenman and Marion, 2011).

The importance of these facts is highlighted by the ongoing sovereign debt crisis in European countries. While in the past sovereign debt crises have been mostly a feature of developing countries, the recent European crisis shows that advanced countries may be affected by a loss of confidence and capital outflows alike. When sovereign debt exceeds a sustainable threshold, a crisis emerges.

To some extent, the European debt crisis has diverted attention from US debt levels. "But then began the eurozone phase of the global financial crisis. This has provided the U.S. government with a timely respite from both domestic forces and Triffin's endgame. U.S. policymakers need to understand that this is not a reset, not a new beginning; it is a lucky break" (Warnock, 2010, p. 2). A loss of confidence in the dollar might cause central bank runs, characterized by central banks substituting alternative safe assets for their dollar reserves. An uncoordinated shift of reserve status to other currencies, however, would entail major global disruptions.

Appendix 4.A List of variables and data sources

Variable	Source	Definition
Public (government) budget balance (relative to GDP)	WEO, GFS, WDI; complemented by Bordo et al. (2001)	Data equals the variable general government net lending/borrowing provided in the WEO database, which is calculated as revenue minus total expenditure. Missing values are filled – where possible – by the variable *government cash surplus/deficit* of the GFS database (years from 1990 onward) and *overall deficit/surplus of consolidated central government* from the historical GFS database (for years prior to 1989). Data are converted to dollars by end of period exchange rates and divided by current GDP.
Inflation	WDI	Inflation is measured as the growth rate of the GDP implicit deflator (annual %)
	Bordo et al. (2001)	Change in CPI
Real GDP	WDI	GDP is measured as gross domestic product in constant international dollars with the year 2005 as base. An international dollar has the same purchasing power over GDP as the US dollar has in the United States.
	Comin and Hobijn (2009)	
Relative dependency ratio (old)	WDI; Mitchell (2007); for US: U.S. Census Bureau (2003)	Ratio of old (65+ years) to working (15–65 years) population measured as deviation from world average
Wars		Dummy that takes the value one between 1914 and 1919 and 1940 and 1944; 0 otherwise.

(continued on next page)

Variable	Source	Definition
Interest rate	Armingeon et al. (2011); Bordo et al. (2001)	Long term (in most cases 10 years) interest rate on government bonds. Missings filled with data on government bonds as provided in the IFS if at least 10 data points could be added for a given country. Historical data (based on Bordo) use long-term interest rates, mostly for government securities or high grad bonds.
Policy rate	Center for Financial Stability, ECB	Interest rate set by the central bank
Democracy	Marshall and Jaggers (2011)	Democracy is measured by a score which combines the information contained in indicators of democracy and autocracy (POLITY2 variable). It ranges from +10 (strongly democratic) to −10 (strongly autocratic).
Financial deepening	WDI	Money and quasi-money (M2) as a percentage of GDP. Complemented by data for the UK based on Bank of England (2012), Series LPMVWYH.
	Bordo et al. (2001)	Money as a percentage of GDP, where money is M1, M2 or M3 depending on the country and data availability.
Unemployment rate	WDI	Percentage of unemployed out of total labor force
External shock	WDI, own calculation	Growth rate of terms of trade multiplied by trade openness. Trade openness is defined as the ratio of exports plus imports over GDP.
Civil liberties	Freedom House	Index of civil liberties, which is based on ratings with respect to the freedom of expression, right of assembly, rule of law and individual rights. The ratings lie between 1 and 7 with 1 representing the highest degree of freedom.
Military spending	WDI	Deviation of military expenditure (expressed as % of GDP) from its country-specific mean over the period under consideration

Variable	Source	Definition
Financial center, dummy	Own calculations based on Lane and Milesi-Ferretti (2007) and update, and GFCI	The dummy takes on the value one in a country year where the country is identified as a financial center. A financial center is defined as having both a ratio of foreign assets to GDP and of foreign liabilities to GDP that exceed the mean plus one standard deviation of the respective variables in a given year where mean and standard deviation are calculated over the whole sample. Based on information provided by the Global Financial Centres index the following countries are labeled financial centers over the whole period: Hong Kong, Japan, Switzerland, the United Kingdom and the United States.
Market capitalization	Standard & Poor's and WDI	Market capitalization is the market value (share price times the number of shares outstanding) of domestic companies listed on the country's stock exchanges. Investment companies, mutual funds or other collective investment vehicles are not included.
Net change in Treasury bonds held by foreign official institutions	Federal Reserve	Difference of Treasury securities held by non-US official institutions (Flow of Funds, Table L.107, line 11) between two consecutive years
World foreign exchange reserves	IFS, Lindert (1969)	Central banks' reserves of foreign exchange, converted in US$
World official gold reserves	IFS, Lindert (1969)	Total amount of gold at historical prices (35 US$ per ounce) held at central banks

Notes: Since the data set combines data from various sources, in some cases the table provides two definitions for the same variable: The first refers to more recent data running until 2009 and the second definition corresponds to the historical data.

Sources: GFCI: Global Financial Centres Index provided by Z/Yen; GFS: Government Finance Statistics (online and historical database); IFS: International Financial Statistics; WEO: World Economic Outlook Database; WDI: World Development Indicators.

Appendix 4.B   Sample of countries

Australia	Denmark	Greece	Japan	Norway	Sweden
Austria	Finland	Iceland	Luxembourg	Portugal	Switzerland
Belgium	France	Ireland	Netherlands	Russia	United Kingdom
Canada	Germany	Italy	New Zealand	Spain	United States

Appendix 4.C   Data sources: Shares of reserve currencies in total foreign exchange reserves

1899 & 1913	Lindert (1969) [used in Figure 4.2]
1890–1913	Lindert (1967) via Troutman (2010) [used in regression analysis]
1920–1936	Eichengreen and Flandreau (2009) via Troutman (2010)
1953–1994	IMF Annual Report, various years
1995–2010	IMF, COFER Database

Appendix 4.D   Regression results: Robustness using fixed sample sizes

For completeness the following tables reproduce the results presented in Section 4.4.3 with the difference that the estimations within one table are based on fixed numbers of countries and observations. In particular, we use the lowest common sample size across the featured specifications. Changes in coefficients are hence due to the added control variables and not to a modified sample.

Table 4.D.1 Public budget balance (1890–2009): Panel data with fixed number of observations

	(1)	(2)	(3)	(4)	(5)	(6)	(7)	(8)	(9)	(10)
Inflation	-0.0006*** (-6.49)	-0.0006*** (-6.55)	-0.0006*** (-6.53)	-0.0006*** (-6.55)	-0.0005*** (-6.63)	-0.0006*** (-6.74)	-0.0006*** (-6.73)	-0.0005*** (-3.50)	-0.0005*** (-3.50)	-0.0005*** (-3.61)
Real GDP growth	-0.0376 (-0.68)	-0.0353 (-0.64)	-0.0347 (-0.63)	-0.0353 (-0.64)	-0.0347 (-0.68)	-0.0408 (-0.84)	-0.0403 (-0.83)	-0.0417 (-0.59)	-0.0417 (-0.59)	-0.0395 (-0.60)
Relative dependency ratio (old)	-0.0012 (-0.91)	-0.0017 (-1.50)	-0.0017 (-1.49)	-0.0017 (-1.50)	-0.0018 (-1.55)	-0.0014 (-1.30)	-0.0014 (-1.29)	-0.0012** (-1.99)	-0.0012** (-1.99)	-0.0000 (-0.00)
Wars				-0.1659*** (-3.77)	-0.1752*** (-4.52)	-0.1717*** (-4.52)	-0.1717*** (-4.50)	-0.1160*** (-5.00)	-0.1160*** (-5.00)	-0.1081*** (-4.60)
Democracy					0.0013** (2.46)	0.0012* (2.03)	0.0012* (2.02)	0.0014*** (2.77)	0.0014*** (2.77)	0.0013*** (2.60)
Financial deepening						-0.0001 (-1.39)	-0.0001 (-1.38)	-0.0002*** (-2.90)	-0.0002*** (-2.90)	-0.0002*** (-3.43)
Interest rate								-0.0018*** (-3.48)	-0.0018*** (-3.48)	-0.0022*** (-4.45)
Government debt										-0.0002*** (-4.69)
Δ global dollar reserves *US dummy		-1.0105*** (-4.28)	-1.0098*** (-4.26)	-1.0105*** (-4.28)	-1.0008*** (-4.12)	-1.0151*** (-4.51)	-1.0146*** (-4.49)	-0.9615*** (-5.29)	-0.9615*** (-5.29)	-0.6994*** (-3.88)
Δ global sterling reserves *UK dummy		-1.0108*** (-5.91)	-1.0092*** (-5.91)	-1.0108*** (-5.91)	-1.0188*** (-5.89)	-0.9376*** (-5.22)	-0.9368*** (-5.22)	-0.9172*** (-2.89)	-0.9172*** (-2.89)	-1.1517*** (-2.98)
Δ global mark reserves *GER dummy			0.3400* (1.98)				0.2370 (1.39)	0.1037 (0.42)	0.1037 (0.42)	0.0786 (0.33)
Δ global franc reserves *FRA dummy			0.2249 (0.79)				0.2092 (0.64)	0.1255 (0.24)	0.1255 (0.24)	0.3170 (0.69)
Observations	1142	1142	1142	1142	1142	1142	1142	1142	1142	1142
R-squared	0.43	0.44	0.44	0.44	0.45	0.45	0.45	0.45	0.45	0.47
Number of countries	19	19	19	19	19	19	19	19	19	19

Notes: The dependent variable is the public budget balance to GDP ratio. Regressions include fixed country effects and time dummies. Estimation by OLS except columns (8) to (10) where 2SLS is used because interest rates are instrumented. Robust t-statistics are reported in parentheses. Standard errors are estimated robust to intragroup correlations. The symbols *, **, and *** denote statistical significance at the 10%, 5% and 1% levels, respectively. The global change in reserves is measured relative to GDP.

Table 4.D.2 Public budget balance (1890–1935): Panel data with fixed number of observations

	(1)	(2)	(3)	(4)	(5)	(6)	(7)	(8)	(9)
Inflation	−0.0010	−0.0010	−0.0010	−0.0009	−0.0009	−0.0009	−0.0008	−0.0008	−0.0007
	(−1.57)	(−1.52)	(−1.57)	(−1.36)	(−1.22)	(−1.22)	(−1.09)	(−1.09)	(−1.00)
Real GDP growth	0.0299	0.0388	0.0299	0.0289	0.0318	0.0389	0.0249	0.0249	0.0272
	(0.36)	(0.49)	(0.36)	(0.36)	(0.40)	(0.50)	(0.34)	(0.34)	(0.39)
Relative dependency ratio (old)	−0.1583	−0.1560	−0.1583	−0.0434	−0.0367	−0.0386	−0.0922	−0.0922	−0.1193
	(−1.14)	(−1.11)	(−1.14)	(−0.22)	(−0.18)	(−0.19)	(−0.54)	(−0.54)	(−0.70)
Democracy				0.0010	0.0011	0.0011	0.0004	0.0004	0.0002
				(0.85)	(0.87)	(0.82)	(0.36)	(0.36)	(0.12)
Financial deepening					0.0001	0.0000	−0.0000	−0.0000	−0.0001
					(0.22)	(0.14)	(−0.16)	(−0.16)	(−0.66)
Interest rate							−0.0103*	−0.0103*	−0.0096
							(−1.80)	(−1.80)	(−1.54)
Government debt									−0.0002
									(−0.81)
Δ global dollar reserves	1.5761**	1.4423**	1.5761**	1.5305**	1.5413**	1.4153**	1.0896**	1.0896**	0.9951*
	(3.16)	(2.66)	(3.16)	(3.21)	(3.18)	(2.61)	(2.01)	(2.01)	(1.88)
* US dummy	−0.7437*	−0.7434*	−0.7437*	−0.8133*	−0.8292*	−0.8266	−0.7875**	−0.7875**	−0.9378*
	(−1.94)	(−1.94)	(−1.94)	(−1.95)	(−1.87)	(−1.83)	(−2.06)	(−2.06)	(−1.90)
Δ global sterling reserves									
* UK dummy									
Δ global mark reserves		0.0030				−0.5339	−0.6581	−0.6581	−0.9045
		(0.00)				(−0.53)	(−0.74)	(−0.74)	(−0.90)
* GER dummy		1.4528***				1.3162*	0.9864**	0.9864**	0.8413
		(3.71)				(2.09)	(2.04)	(2.04)	(1.58)
Δ global franc reserves									
* FRA dummy									
Observations	256	256	256	256	256	256	256	256	256
R-squared	0.35	0.36	0.35	0.36	0.36	0.36	0.38	0.38	0.39
Number of countries	10	10	10	10	10	10	10	10	10

Notes: The dependent variable is the public budget balance to GDP ratio. The global change in reserves is measured relative to GDP. Regressions include fixed country and time effects. Estimation by OLS. Instrumental variable 2SLS is used in specifications including the interest rate. In columns (7) and (9) the interest rate is instrumented by its lagged value, in column (8) by the world policy rate. Robust t-statistics are reported in parentheses. Standard errors are estimated robust to intragroup correlations. The symbols *, ** and *** denote statistical significance at the 10%, 5% and 1% levels, respectively.

Table 4.D.3 Public budget balance (1950–2009): Panel data with fixed number of observations

	(1)	(2)	(3)	(4)	(5)	(6)	(7)	(8)	(9)
Inflation	0.0002	0.0002	0.0002	0.0003	0.0002	0.0002	0.0006	0.0006	0.0007
	(0.24)	(0.24)	(0.24)	(0.28)	(0.24)	(0.23)	(1.32)	(1.32)	(1.53)
Real GDP growth	0.1059	0.1057	0.1059	0.1018	0.0799	0.0796	0.0773	0.0773	0.0196
	(1.61)	(1.60)	(1.61)	(1.56)	(1.19)	(1.18)	(1.60)	(1.60)	(0.43)
Relative dependency ratio (old)	−0.0011	−0.0011	−0.0011	−0.0011	−0.0007	−0.0007	−0.0005	−0.0005	0.0025***
	(−0.80)	(−0.80)	(−0.80)	(−0.77)	(−0.42)	(−0.42)	(−0.80)	(−0.80)	(3.53)
Democracy				−0.0003	−0.0005	−0.0005	−0.0003	−0.0003	−0.0007**
				(−0.50)	(−0.67)	(−0.68)	(−0.92)	(−0.92)	(−2.05)
Financial deepening					−0.0001	−0.0001	−0.0001**	−0.0001**	−0.0002***
					(−0.73)	(−0.73)	(−2.26)	(−2.26)	(−3.60)
Interest rate							−0.0013**	−0.0013**	−0.0022***
							(−1.99)	(−1.99)	(−3.75)
Government debt									−0.0005***
									(−6.73)
Δ global dollar reserves * US dummy	−0.8750***	−0.8748***	−0.8750***	−0.8729***	−0.9022***	−0.9021***	−0.8731***	−0.8731***	−0.5714***
	(−4.21)	(−4.21)	(−4.21)	(−4.24)	(−4.53)	(−4.52)	(−5.07)	(−5.07)	(−3.49)
Δ global sterling reserves * UK dummy	−1.1047***	−1.1062***	−1.1047***	−1.0965***	−1.0087***	−1.0100***	−0.9768***	−0.9768***	−1.2985***
	(−6.59)	(−6.60)	(−6.59)	(−6.58)	(−4.78)	(−4.78)	(−2.63)	(−2.63)	(−2.71)
Δ global mark reserves * GER dummy		−0.0586				−0.0907		−0.1158	−0.1553
		(−0.60)				(−0.94)		(−0.46)	(−0.65)
Δ global franc reserves * FRA dummy		−0.2315*				−0.2609***		−0.2782	−0.3556
		(−2.08)				(−2.93)		(−0.47)	(−0.48)
Observations	793	793	793	793	793	793	793	793	793
R-squared	0.36	0.36	0.36	0.36	0.36	0.36	0.36	0.36	0.42
Number of countries	19	19	19	19	19	19	19	19	19

Notes: The dependent variable is the public budget balance to GDP ratio. The global change in reserves is measured relative to GDP. Regressions include fixed country and time effects. Estimation by OLS. Instrumental variable 2SLS is used in specifications including the interest rate. In columns (7) and (9) the interest rate is instrumented by its lagged value, in column (8) by the world policy rate. Robust t-statistics are reported in parentheses. Standard errors are estimated robust to intragroup correlations. The symbols *, **, and *** denote statistical significance at the 10%, 5% and 1% levels, respectively.

Table 4.D.4 Public budget balance (1970–2009): Panel data with fixed number of observations

	(1)	(2)	(3)	(4)	(5)	(6)	(7)	(8)	(9)	(10)	(11)	(12)
Inflation	0.0036***	0.0032	0.0031	0.0028	0.0028	0.0037***	0.0021	0.0020	0.0027	0.0054***	0.0054***	0.0052***
	(3.16)	(1.40)	(1.36)	(1.27)	(1.23)	(2.75)	(1.06)	(1.00)	(1.16)	(4.81)	(4.81)	(4.51)
Real GDP growth	0.0691***	0.0540**	0.0540**	0.0474*	0.0481*	0.0481	0.0412	0.0412	0.0442*	0.0428**	0.0428**	0.0445**
	(3.28)	(2.33)	(2.31)	(2.01)	(1.98)	(1.62)	(1.71)	(1.69)	(1.80)	(2.06)	(2.06)	(2.14)
Relative dependency ratio (old)	−0.0043	−0.0041	−0.0043	−0.0030	−0.0031	−0.0030***	−0.0032	−0.0033	−0.0025	−0.0034***	−0.0034***	−0.0016
	(−1.41)	(−1.44)	(−1.52)	(−1.19)	(−1.20)	(−3.09)	(−1.27)	(−1.35)	(−0.96)	(−3.41)	(−3.41)	(−1.01)
Unemployment		−0.0048**	−0.0049***	−0.0046**	−0.0046***	−0.0058**	−0.0044**	−0.0045**	−0.0045**	−0.0043***	−0.0043***	−0.0035***
		(−2.83)	(−2.90)	(−2.89)	(−2.92)	(−2.16)	(−2.77)	(−2.84)	(−2.66)	(−5.44)	(−5.44)	(−4.25)
External shock		−0.0680	−0.0641	−0.0587	−0.0541	−0.0497	−0.0348	−0.0303	−0.0329	−0.1457**	−0.1457**	−0.1402**
		(−0.82)	(−0.77)	(−0.71)	(−0.64)	(−0.95)	(−0.47)	(−0.40)	(−0.37)	(−2.24)	(−2.24)	(−2.07)
Relative income		−0.0126	−0.0140	−0.0141	−0.0150	−0.0003	−0.0022	−0.0040	−0.0071	−0.0200*	−0.0200**	−0.0189
		(−0.56)	(−0.62)	(−0.62)	(−0.65)	(−0.01)	(−0.10)	(−0.19)	(−0.30)	(−1.71)	(−1.71)	(−1.61)
Military expenditure (deviation from mean)				−0.0176*	−0.0178*	−0.0250**	−0.0178*	−0.0179*	−0.0157	−0.0225***	−0.0225**	−0.0231***
				(−1.80)	(−1.84)	(−2.23)	(−1.80)	(−1.82)	(−1.67)	(−4.26)	(−4.26)	(−4.56)
Democracy					0.0055		0.0062	0.0065	0.0050	0.0048	0.0048	0.0055*
					(1.33)		(1.48)	(1.57)	(1.18)	(1.61)	(1.61)	(1.86)
Left government					−0.0000	−0.0002**	−0.0000	−0.0000	−0.0000	−0.0000	−0.0000	−0.0000
					(−0.27)	(−3.03)	(−0.24)	(−0.36)	(−0.22)	(−0.18)	(−0.18)	(−0.16)
Financial deepening						−0.0001						
						(−0.29)						
Financial center (dummy)							−0.0432**	−0.0434**		−0.0238**	−0.0238**	−0.0253**
							(−2.65)	(−2.65)		(−2.00)	(−2.00)	(−2.11)
Market capitalization									0.0001			
									(1.47)			
Interest rate										−0.0063***	−0.0063***	−0.0062***
										(−6.36)	(−6.36)	(−6.11)
Government debt												−0.0003**
												(−2.25)

Table 4.D.4 (continued)

	(1)	(2)	(3)	(4)	(5)	(6)	(7)	(8)	(9)	(10)	(11)	(12)
Δ global dollar reserves	-1.4673***	-1.3566***	-1.3626***	-1.2395***	-1.2408***	-1.0498***	-1.2657***	-1.2748***	-1.2143***	-1.1473***	-1.1473***	-0.9937***
* US dummy	(-5.02)	(-3.48)	(-3.53)	(-3.46)	(-3.42)	(-4.97)	(-3.54)	(-3.58)	(-3.22)	(-4.64)	(-4.64)	(-3.79)
Δ global sterling reserves	-1.7848***	-1.8129***	-1.8251***	-1.9002***	-1.8755***	-1.3970***	-2.0493***	-2.0516***	-1.6605***	-1.8092***	-1.8092***	-1.5436***
* UK dummy	(-4.03)	(-3.83)	(-3.86)	(-3.89)	(-3.56)	(-3.66)	(-3.84)	(-3.83)	(-3.05)	(-3.99)	(-3.99)	(-3.34)
Δ global mark reserves			0.4055*					0.2774				0.2780
* GER dummy			(1.96)					(1.59)				(1.26)
Δ global franc reserves			-2.4712***					-3.0897***				-2.1305
* FRA dummy			(-3.33)					(-4.00)				(-1.60)
Observations	401	401	401	401	401	204	401	401	401	401	401	401
R-squared	0.53	0.59	0.59	0.60	0.60	0.70	0.61	0.62	0.61	0.65	0.65	0.66
Number of countries	20	20	20	20	20	12	20	20	20	20	20	20

Notes: All regressions except that of column (6) are based on the same set of observations. We prefer not to reduce the common sample size to that of column (6) because the low number of observations is specific to this particular specification and arises from the unavailability of data on financial deepening. The dependent variable is the public budget balance to GDP ratio. The global change in reserves is measured relative to GDP. Regressions include fixed country and time effects. Estimation by OLS except columns (10) to (12) where an instrumental variable approach is used (2SLS). Robust t-statistics are reported in parentheses. Standard errors are estimated robust to intragroup correlations. The symbols *, ** and *** denote statistical significance at the 10%, 5% and 1% levels, respectively.

Reserve Accumulation and Financial Crises: From Individual Protection to Systemic Risk[1]

Contents

5.1 Introduction 119
5.2 Reserves and crises: The links 121
   5.2.1 Reserves and domestic crises 122
   5.2.2 Reserves and crises in the reserve currency country 123
   5.2.3 Reserves and global crises 126
5.3 The optimal amount of reserves 127
   5.3.1 The benchmark model 128
   5.3.2 Modeling the behavior of the reserve currency country 131
   5.3.3 Optimal reserve level in the presence of local and global crises 132
   5.3.4 Optimal reserve level in the presence of a global social planner 134
   5.3.5 How can the socially optimal level of reserves be implemented? 135
   5.3.6 Robustness analysis 136
5.4 Quantitative implications of the model – a calibration analysis 140
5.5 Conclusions 151
Appendix 5.A Uses of reserve income: Investment vs. consumption 151
Appendix 5.B Probit analysis of financial crises 154

5.1 Introduction

Central banks' hoardings of international reserves are considered as a form of self-protection against financial crises. They enable central banks to intervene in the foreign exchange market and help to cushion the economy from external shocks. This chapter turns the tables and shows that the accumulation of reserves might also have a flip-side: Whereas large reserve holdings may indeed protect a country from domestic crises, their accumulation increases the instability of the international financial system and might cause a global crisis emanating from the reserve currency country. In the end, central banks' attempt to insure against financial crises via the accumulation of reserves may be counterproductive. Good intentions may result in bad outcomes.

The idea is motivated by the global financial crisis that began as the US subprime crisis in 2007 and affected the rest of the world through trade and financial linkages. In this regard it has been noted that global imbalances have increased the vulnerability of the US (e.g. Aizenman, 2010; Ferguson and Schularick, 2011; IMF, 2009a;

---

[1] This is an extended and updated version of Steiner (2014b). Publication with permission from Elsevier. Differences in the quantitative results may arise from revised data.

Global Imbalances, Financial Crises, and Central Bank Policies
Copyright © 2016 Elsevier Inc. All rights reserved.

Obstfeld and Rogoff, 2010; Portes, 2009). Global imbalances, in turn, have been partly sustained by central banks' accumulation of reserves, especially in Asian emerging markets (see Chapter 3). Moreover, reserve accumulation has lowered US interest rates (see Warnock and Cacdac Warnock, 2009). Low interest rates, in turn, were a driving force of the US housing bubble. By implication, the accumulation of reserves has contributed to developments in the US, that eventually turned into a global crisis.

The recurrence of financial crises in the recent past questioned the benefits of the increasing international financial integration and challenged countries to find ways how to protect the domestic economy from the downside risks of financial openness. Many countries faced this challenge by the accumulation of foreign reserves. Since the East Asian financial crisis of 1997–98 the worldwide level of real reserves has more than tripled. Reserves are considered as a precautionary cushion against the risks of financial openness, namely sudden stops of capital flows and contagious financial crises. Their function includes both crisis prevention and crisis management (see Aizenman and Lee, 2007; Obstfeld et al., 2010).[2]

This unprecedented increase in international reserves also reflects previous advice given to emerging and developing countries by various sources. In the aftermath of the East Asian financial crisis the IMF emphasized the importance of reserves as a means of crisis prevention and proposed new measures to evaluate their adequacy (IMF, 2000). Feldstein (1999) advised emerging markets to rely on large foreign exchange reserves as a form of self-protection and to count less on assistance by the IMF. Finally, the burdensome conditionality and unpredictability of IMF assistance may explain why many countries prefer to self-insure (see Bird and Mandilaras, 2011).

The accumulation of reserves, however, contains costs that have been neglected so far: While reserves might effectively protect the domestic economy from external shocks, their global and continuous accumulation might create systemic risks. Since the accumulation of net reserves constitutes a capital inflow to the reserve currency country, it increases its external indebtedness. As a matter of fact, holdings of foreign reserves by global central banks are an important source of US external debt: In 2010, 36% of outstanding Treasuries and 15% of total US foreign liabilities were held by foreign official institutions. Between 1998 and 2010, despite the Fed's policy of quantitative easing, 49% of the increase in outstanding Treasuries were purchased by foreign official institutions.[3]

The rising external indebtedness may create the macroeconomic backdrop for a financial crisis. The accumulation of reserves might induce two types of crises: First, it might lead to overborrowing and overinvestment in the reserve currency country and cause a financial crisis when expectations worsen or the reserve accumulation ends. Second, by steadily worsening the net foreign asset position of the reserve currency

---

[2] There exist other reasons why countries hoard reserves. The mercantilist approach, for example, argues that the accumulation of reserves is the by-product of an export-led growth strategy (see, among others, Dooley et al., 2003). This chapter, however, focuses on the relationship between reserves and crises.

[3] Data based on Flow of Funds, Federal Reserve, Table L.106 (lines 11 and 12) and Table L.209 (line 1), and Lane and Milesi-Ferretti (2007) and update.

country, it might result in a currency crisis where the reserve currency country deliberately decides to devalue its currency. Whereas the first type of crisis follows the lines of the financial crisis of 2008–10, the second type also has its precedent, namely the breakdown of the Bretton Woods system.

A crisis in the center country could destabilize the international financial system. Since the reserve currency country is per definition at the center of the international financial system, a crisis originating there spreads to other countries and causes a global downturn. This crisis affects accumulating and non-accumulating countries alike. Hence, the accumulation of reserves has a negative externality.

A dilemma arises: On the one hand, the recent reserve accumulation is partly due to concerns for financial stability in a financially globalized world (see Obstfeld et al., 2010). On the other, policies of reserve accumulation expose the system to additional risks and shocks. Hence, the blessing attributed to the accumulation of reserves might become a curse.[4]

The relationship between reserve accumulation and systemic risk creation has been identified only recently (see Ferguson and Schularick, 2011; Gourinchas et al., 2010; IMF, 2010a; Obstfeld and Rogoff, 2010; Taylor, 2013). This chapter extends the preceding literature in several dimensions: First, the line of causality from reserve accumulation to a global financial crisis is traced both on empirical and theoretical grounds. Second, this chapter integrates the idea of negative feedback in a model of the demand for reserves and formalizes the difference between local and global optimality. It solves for the first best policy chosen by a social planner that internalizes the externality associated with local optimality. A calibration analysis quantifies these effects.

This chapter is organized as follows. The next section elaborates on the link between reserves and financial crises, both on theoretical and empirical grounds. The model and its solution are presented in Section 5.3. Section 5.4 provides a calibration analysis that quantifies the difference between local and global optimum. Concluding remarks are offered in Section 5.5.

5.2   Reserves and crises: The links

This section illustrates the links between central banks' international reserve holdings and the probability of financial crises. In this context it is important to distinguish between domestic and global crises. A global crisis is defined here as a crisis that originates in one country and spreads to a number of countries due to their real and financial linkages with the crisis country. As will be shown later, the reserve currency country could trigger such a global financial crisis.

---

[4] This is an example of the law of unintended consequences, which was popularized by Robert K. Merton: Any intervention – in our case a central bank intervention – creates unanticipated and undesired outcomes. In the end, the intended solution may aggravate the problem.

5.2.1 Reserves and domestic crises

Theoretical models and empirical findings with respect to the link between the level of international reserves and currency crises show that reserves reduce both the probability and severity of domestic financial crises.

In the first generation of currency crisis models inconsistent policies lead to a continuous loss of reserves and, consequently, to a devaluation crisis when reserves have fallen below some critical value (e.g. Krugman, 1979; Flood and Garber, 1984). Hence, reserves can avoid a crisis when the policy inconsistency is transitory. Otherwise, reserves can postpone the occurrence of a crisis and provide a time buffer within which domestic policies can be reconciled with the exchange rate commitment. Models of the second generation emphasize that crisis expectations might become self-fulfilling. Reserves may signal a government's ability and willingness to defend the exchange rate and prevent a speculative attack. Another strand of the crisis literature stresses the fragility of balance sheets in the presence of currency mismatches. Reserves reduce these mismatches at the country level and might be used to support the banking and corporate sector during balance sheet crises.

Accordingly, the literature traditionally derives central banks' demand for reserves from the benefits they provide in the face of shocks: Reserves might be used to smooth economic adjustment processes in the face of external shocks (Heller, 1966) and to prevent financial and sovereign crises (Ben-Bassat and Gottlieb, 1992). Theoretical models show that reserves help to smooth consumption intertemporally in the presence of productivity shocks (Aizenman and Marion, 2004) and mitigate the output effects of liquidity shock (Aizenman and Lee, 2007). Li and Rajan (2009) show in a theoretical model that high reserves may offset the negative impact of moderately weak fundamentals and prevent speculative attacks on the currency. According to Jeanne and Rancière (2011) the optimal amount of reserves for a small open economy increases with the probability and potential size of a sudden stop in capital flows.

Although these models differ considerably, they coincide in the view that reserves might reduce the incidence and the cost of financial crises. These theoretical results are confirmed by a series of empirical papers.

In a meta-analysis Frankel and Saravelos (2012) review more than 80 papers of the literature on early warning systems for currency crises. They find low central banks' reserves to be the most reliable warning indicator including the crisis of 2008–10. Concerning the depth of a crisis once it materializes, De Gregorio and Lee (2004) and Aizenman et al. (2012) demonstrate that reserves reduce the output costs of a crisis. Obstfeld et al. (2009) and Fratzscher (2009) note that low reserves are associated with larger depreciations during the crisis of 2008–10.[5]

Based on these theoretical and empirical findings and in line with the literature (see Aizenman and Marion, 2004 and Jeanne, 2007) we assume that the probability of a

---

[5] Frankel and Saravelos (2012, p. 230) conclude that "to the extent that a low level of reserves is a cause, rather than just an indicator of country vulnerability to external shocks, [...] the large accumulation of reserves by many developing countries prior to 2008 may have played an important role in reducing their vulnerability during the latest crisis." Alike, Obstfeld et al. (2009, p. 483) state that "international reserves did provide effective insurance against currency instability, for advanced and emerging countries alike."

local output-reducing crisis (p^L) in country i decreases in the level of reserves (R). Reserves may prevent financial crises or help to cushion terms-of-trade shocks. Since the effect of reserves depends on the potential volume of capital flight, reserves are scaled by the level of external debt (B)[6]:

$$p_i^L = \phi_i^L + \alpha_i \frac{B_i}{R_i}, \qquad \alpha_i > 0, \quad 0 < p^L < 1 \tag{5.1}$$

where the index i indicates that all variables and coefficients may be country-specific. ϕ captures all other factors that influence the probability of a crisis and which, for the sake of simplicity, are taken as constant in our analysis. A crisis is defined in general terms as a fall in output caused by a currency, banking or sovereign debt crisis.[7] All three crisis types have been discussed in relation to reserves in the existing literature (see Obstfeld et al., 2010 for banking crises, Flood and Garber, 1984 and Jeanne and Rancière, 2011 for currency crises, and Aizenman and Marion, 2004 for sovereign debt crises).

5.2.2   Reserves and crises in the reserve currency country

This section discusses the argument that the virtue of being the provider of the world's reserve currency – often referred to as an exorbitant privilege[8] – may destabilize the economy of the reserve currency country.

Changes in reserve hoardings in the rest of the world induce a counter entry in the balance of payments of the reserve currency country: Any net dollar accumulated by the rest of the world represents external debt of the reserve currency country. Our empirical analyses of Chapters 3 and 4 have shown that the provision of reserves lowers both its current account balance and its public budget balance. If, however, the accumulation of reserves implies an increasing level of external debt of the reserve provider, it might endanger its financial stability. This section examines this concern.

Based on balance-of-payments accounting, Section 3.2.3 has shown that the accumulation of reserves in the rest of the world may be financed by a current account deficit or a deficit in the capital account. However, if reserves are accumulated via a deficit in the capital account (private capital outflows), external net positions of center and periphery countries are unaffected. Hence, this form of reserve accumulation might be ineffective in reducing country vulnerability in countries of the periphery. Consequently, it is true that the reserve-providing country has to run a current account

---

[6] Besides the level of external debt, its maturity composition is found to be an important crisis indicator with a high level of short-term debt being considered to be harmful. Since our model focuses on one period, we do not make a distinction between long-term and short-term external debt in the core analysis. We do, however, account for the maturity structure in the extensions provided in Section 5.3.6.

[7] The output drop in a crisis may be explained by the costly liquidation of investment projects (see Chang and Velasco, 2000). For empirical evidence refer to Cerra and Chaman Saxena (2008) among others.

[8] Gourinchas et al. (2010) note that this privilege comes at the cost of an exorbitant duty: The US provides insurance to the rest of the world during crisis episodes. This insurance comes in the form of a transfer of wealth since the US suffers valuation losses in its assets during crises. The costs we analyze in this chapter, however, are of a different nature.

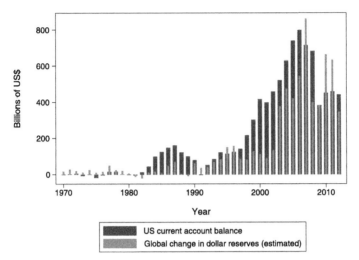

Figure 5.1 US current account deficit and global dollar reserve accumulation. *Notes:* A positive number indicated by the light grey (green in the web version) bars corresponds to a current account deficit, whereas a negative number is defined as a surplus.
Data source: World Bank (2013) and own calculations based on the COFER database.

deficit when the rest of the world accumulates *net* reserve assets. A current account deficit, however, corresponds to an equal increase in external debt.

Empirically, the current account deficit of the US – the center of the current international monetary system – has been persistent and accounted for 47% (51%) of the global deficit over the period 1970–2012 (1995–2012). Moreover, Figure 5.1 shows that a substantial part of its current account deficit has been financed through the purchase of reserves by foreign central banks.[9]

The reserve currency country faces the exceptional situation that its external debt is not only held by private agents but also by foreign central banks. Accordingly, if the rest of the world accumulates net reserves, the level of net external debt of the reserve currency country, which is denoted by the index C, increases:

$$\Delta B_C = \Delta B_C^{pr} + \Delta R_{ROW} \tag{5.2}$$

where B_C^{pr} denotes privately held external debt of the reserve currency country (outside the central bank) and ΔR_{ROW} is the increase in reserves in the rest of the world. As emphasized before we do not allow that any increased supply of reserve assets be

---

[9] Given that not all reserves are denoted in US dollars and that central banks disclose their reserve composition on a voluntary basis, the change in dollar reserves is estimated on the basis of data taken from the COFER database of the IMF. For a given year the amount of reserves denominated in dollars is calculated as the worldwide level of reserves excluding the US multiplied by that year's dollar share in reserves. The change in this variable between two consecutive years is the change in dollar reserves.

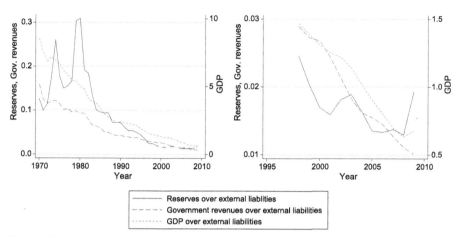

Figure 5.2 US collateral relative to external liabilities. *Notes:* The graph visualizes the evolution of different measures that might be linked to the confidence put in the dollar. While the left-hand panel covers the period 1970–2010, the right-hand panel zooms in the recent period of reserve accumulation since the East Asian financial crisis. The scale on the left axis corresponds to the ratio of reserves to external liabilities and federal government receipts relative to external liabilities. For GDP over foreign liabilities the right axis applies.
Data sources: Reserves and GDP: World Bank (2012); government receipts: US Office of Management and Budget, Historical Tables, Table 1.3; total liabilities: Lane and Milesi-Ferretti (2007) and update.

offset by a decrease in B_C^{pr} because we examine the case of a demand for *net* reserves. Hence, B_C^{pr} can be set constant.

The probability of a local financial crisis in the reserve currency country depends on the same fundamental relationship as in the rest of the world (see equation (5.1)). Confidence in the reserve currency is linked to the amount of foreign liabilities relative to collateral in the form of reserves held by the reserve currency country. Alternatively, one may argue that the reserve currency is backed by GDP or the fiscal capacity of its issuer. Figure 5.2 shows for the US how these measures have deteriorated over time. A loss of confidence may restrict the reserve currency country's access to external credit, cause capital flight and end in a crisis in the center country. Kenen (1960) shows in a theoretical model that a decreasing ratio of reserves to foreign liabilities may erode confidence in the dollar, cause countries to sell their dollar reserves and bring about global instability. At a certain threshold the international monetary system enters a "crisis zone", where central banks switch to alternative reserve assets (Officer and Willett, 1969). It is true that the reserve currency country suffers less from a currency mismatch because part of its foreign liabilities are denoted in its own currency. An inflationary policy could reduce the real burden of these liabilities. While this might prevent a crisis in the US, a fall of the value of the dollar would lead to a recession in the rest of the world. Hence, this scenario is also consistent with our assumption that increasing external debt in the center raises the crisis probability in the rest of the world.

After expressing (5.2) in levels and then substituting B_C in (5.1), the crisis probability in the reserve currency country can be expressed as:

$$p_C^L = \phi_C^L + \alpha_C \frac{B_C^{pr} + R_{ROW}}{R_C} \tag{5.3}$$

As a result, the fragility of the reserve currency country is a positive function of the level of reserves in the rest of the world.

Besides this direct effect, there exist additional arguments explaining why the accumulation of reserves may increase instabilities in the reserve currency country. Although these are not integrated explicitly in our model, we summarize them next.

Instability due to lower interest rates. As has been described before (see Section 4.3.1), reserve currency status causes an additional demand for assets and lowers interest rates in the reserve currency country. Low interest rates, in turn, create incentives for higher deficits and debt. This holds for government finances in the first place because central banks invest predominantly in sovereign bonds of the reserve country (see Chapter 4). Policy discipline is weakened and instabilities may result (see Daniel, 2001). If low interest rates are transmitted to the private sector, households might save less.

Instability due to the relaxation of the sovereign credit ceiling. The accumulation of international reserves in the form of Treasury bonds is basically a form of lending to the sovereign of a foreign country.[10] In order to make repayment incentive compatible maximal lending is constrained by a credit ceiling. This ceiling, however, might be more flexible for reserve-providing countries. First, lenders might disregard the ceiling because they hold reserves as an insurance rather than to generate interest income. This behavior is corroborated by the observation that the hoarding of reserves is insensitive to their return (see Krishnamurthy and Vissing-Jorgensen, 2012). Second, sequential lending from multiple sources involves the danger of overlending. Since countries continuously adjust their level of international reserves, lending leads to the dilution of the value of existing debt. Since this negative externality is not internalized in the price of debt, a social planner would restrict lending to lower levels.

Instability due to a risk mismatch. Caballero and Krishnamurthy (2009) stress that global imbalances can be interpreted as the result of an imbalance in the supply of safe assets: Capital inflows to the US have been sustained by the rest of the world's demand for a safe store of value. This not only contributes to global imbalances, but also leads to a concentration of risky assets in the US.[11]

5.2.3   Reserves and global crises

The previous section has shown that central banks' desire for larger stocks of reserves increases the risk of a financial crisis in the reserve currency country. Due to

---

[10] The share of foreign official holdings in total Treasury debt securities outstanding has risen from 6% in 1970 to an unprecedented value of 38% in 2008. Due to unconventional monetary policies including quantitative easing it has fallen to 35% in 2012 (see Figure 4.3).

[11] See also Gourinchas and Rey (2007).

international business cycle correlation and contagion (see Eichengreen et al., 1996; Kose et al., 2003), a crisis in the center country, in turn, increases the crisis probability in the countries of the periphery.[12] We assume that a crisis in the center is transmitted to the periphery with an impact coefficient of λ with $0 < \lambda < 1$. Hence, the probability of both a local or globally transmitted crisis p^{LG} in country i is given by

$$p_i^{LG} = p_i^L + \lambda p_C^L = \phi_i^{LG} + \alpha_i \frac{B_i}{R_i}, \tag{5.4}$$

where $\phi_i^{LG} = \phi_i^L + \lambda\left(\phi_C^L + \alpha_C \frac{B_C}{R_C}\right)$. In this stage of the analysis we assume that the decisions of the center country with respect to its level of external debt and reserves are exogenous variables for the periphery.

After substituting (5.3) in (5.4), one gets the revised probability for a local and globally transmitted crisis in a non-reserve currency country as

$$p_i^{LG} = \phi_i + \alpha_i \frac{B_i}{R_i} + \beta \frac{R_{ROW}}{R_C} \tag{5.5}$$

where $\beta = \lambda \alpha_C$ and $\phi_i = \phi_i^L + \lambda\left(\phi_C^L + \alpha_C \frac{B_C^{pr}}{R_C}\right)$. As a consequence, besides their crisis-preventing effect at the domestic level, reserves increase the likelihood of a global crisis.[13] Analytically, the level of external debt of the reserve country is a function of the demand for reserves by the rest of the world. The probability of a crisis in the center country is endogenous to the demand for reserves in the rest of the world.

The existing literature on the demand for reserves focuses on the benefits of reserves in the form of a lifejacket against crises. At the same time, it disregards the global effects of reserve accumulation. It does not take into account that exactly the desire for self-insurance might overturn the ship. The main arguments of this modified cost–benefit analysis are summarized in Figure 5.3.

5.3   The optimal amount of reserves

This section extends a base model of the demand for reserves by introducing the notion that reserve accumulation creates a negative externality and may cause systemic risk. While the model is rather simple, it provides sufficient leeway to make our case. The conclusions apply to a representative reserve-hoarding country. The basic structure follows the model introduced by Aizenman and Marion (2004) and its simplified version, which is provided by Cheung and Qian (2009). The comparison of the results with the benchmark model shows two effects: First, if the accumulation of reserves causes global crises, the optimal level of reserves is lower than in the benchmark

---

[12] Reinhart and Kaminsky (2008) and Reinhart and Rogoff (2008) document that crises spread globally when they emanate from financial center countries.

[13] This is an example of a fallacy of composition: Policies that enhance the stability of each individual country need not necessarily benefit the stability of the entire system (Morris and Shin, 2008).

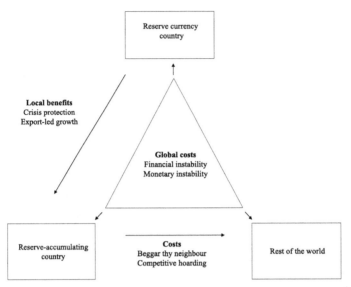

Figure 5.3 Cost–benefit analysis of reserve accumulation: A global view.

case, which disregards global crises. Second, the optimal amount of reserves is further reduced if the negative externality of reserve accumulation on other countries is internalized.

At this point it should be mentioned that the literature provides alternative approaches to determine the optimal amount of reserves. Examples are the cost–benefit approaches of Ben-Bassat and Gottlieb (1992) and Jeanne and Rancière (2011). All approaches share the characteristic that they focus on domestic variables and disregard interdependencies among countries' reserve policies.[14]

5.3.1 The benchmark model

We consider an extension of a standard model of a two-period economy, in which second period output is uncertain. The economy can intertemporally optimize its consumption path through borrowing and lending on the international capital market. In addition to the standard model there is a role for international reserves: They affect utility through an indirect transmission channel: Reserves determine the likelihood of a financial crisis and since a financial crisis depresses output, they indirectly influence income. Consumption smoothing via international debt has the negative side effect that international debt is positively related to the likelihood of a financial crisis. Hence, the level of foreign debt and the amount of reserves are the result of a joint decision.

---

[14] An exception is Cheung and Qian (2009) who analyze the Joneses effect, namely that countries reserve levels depend positively on the level of their peers.

As long as we consider a representative economy, the country index i is omitted. In the first period, the economy's output is Y_1 which is normalized to 1. The output of the second period is uncertain: Either a positive productivity shock increases output by an amount of δ or the economy suffers a financial crisis that depresses output by an amount of ϵ. The probability of a local financial crisis is given by p^L as defined by (5.1). Hence,

$$Y_2 = \begin{cases} 1 + \delta & \text{with probability} \quad 1 - p^L \\ 1 - \epsilon & \text{with probability} \quad p^L \end{cases} \qquad \delta, \epsilon > 0 \quad \text{and} \quad 0 < p^L < 1 \quad (5.6)$$

In the first period the economy allocates output (Y_1) among consumption (C_1), international borrowing (B) and international reserve accumulation (R):

$$C_1 = 1 + B - R \tag{5.7}$$

Since the economy may default in the second period, it faces a credit ceiling. The ceiling is determined by the incentive compatibility condition: Lenders will only provide credit up to an amount where the contractual repayment equals the expected cost of default. If the repayment were larger than the penalty, lenders would have an incentive to default. Let us assume that the international lender can confiscate a fraction of the output in period 2, given by θY_2 with $0 < \theta < 1$. Reserves, in turn, are beyond the reach of international creditors and can be used even after a country has defaulted. The repayment in period 2 is then given by

$$S = \text{MIN}\left[(1+r)B; \theta Y_2\right] \tag{5.8}$$

where MIN is the minimum operator. The country's interest rate for international borrowing (r) is determined so that the expected return on international credits equals their risk-free return:

$$E[S] = (1 + r^f)B \tag{5.9}$$

where r^f is the risk-free interest rate.[15] The credit ceiling $\bar{B}$ is hence given by the condition that the expected repayment equals the confiscated output when debt induces default both after positive and negative output shocks:

$$\bar{B} = \frac{(1 - p^L)\theta(1 + \delta) + p^L \theta(1 - \epsilon)}{1 + r^f} = \frac{\theta(1 + \delta) - p^L \theta(\delta + \epsilon)}{1 + r^f} \tag{5.10}$$

Assume that the economy does not default on its external debt obligations when it is hit by a positive productivity shock. The probability to default in the midst of a

---

[15] Here, we do not model the effects of reserve demand on the interest rate and risk-taking behavior in the reserve currency country. If a foreign central bank accumulates reserves and sterilizes the effect on the domestic monetary base, the accumulation of reserves constitutes a swap of domestic bonds for foreign bonds. Hence, the interest rate of reserve currency bonds falls because bonds are imperfect substitutes. This corresponds to the theoretical results of Korinek (2011) and Warnock and Cacdac Warnock (2009). Lower interest rates increase the credit ceiling $\bar{B}$, which again raises the probability of a currency crisis according to (5.1). As a consequence, the reserve accumulation might have an additional negative feedback effect. While we do not account for this effect in our analysis, it would only strengthen our argument for lowering the level of reserves.

financial crisis is given by q.[16] Furthermore, reserves earn an interest rate of r^f and accumulated reserves are spent in period 2 since this is the last period. The budget constraint of period 2 then reads as

$$C_2 = \begin{cases} C_{2,g} = 1 + \delta - (1+r)B + (1+r^f)R & \text{with probability} \quad 1 - p^L \\ C_{2,c} = 1 - \epsilon - (1+r)B + (1+r^f)R & \text{with probability} \quad p^L(1-q) \\ C_{2,c,d} = (1-\theta)(1-\epsilon) + (1+r^f)R & \text{with probability} \quad p^L q \end{cases}$$

(5.11)

where the indices g, c and d stand for the good state, crisis state and default, respectively.

In order to focus on a single first order condition, we assume in line with Aizenman and Marion (2004) that foreign debt reaches the credit ceiling, $B = \bar{B}$.[17] As a consequence, $B(1+r)|_{B=\bar{B}} = \theta(1+\delta)$. The expected utility is then given by

$$U(.)|_{B=\bar{B}} = (1 + \bar{B} - R)$$
$$+ \frac{1}{1+\rho}\left[(1-\theta)(1+\delta) + (1+r^f)R - p^L(1-q\theta)(\delta+\epsilon)\right] \quad (5.12)$$

where ρ is the individual discount rate. Government chooses the levels of foreign debt and reserves such that the expected utility is maximized given the budget constraints (5.7) and (5.11) and the probability of a financial crisis (5.1). The first order condition with respect to R then reads as:

$$1 - \frac{dB}{dR}\bigg|_{B=\bar{B}} = \frac{1}{1+\rho}\left[(1+r^f) - (1-q\theta)(\delta+\epsilon)\frac{dp^L}{dR}\right] \quad (5.13)$$

This equation can be interpreted as follows: The left-hand side represents the costs of a marginal unit of reserves which are given by the difference between the resources withdrawn from consumption and the additional external debt granted thanks to an increase of the credit ceiling. The right-hand side illustrates the benefits of a marginal unit of reserves, namely additional interest income and a reduced crisis probability. After calculating the partial derivatives and substituting them into (5.13), one obtains

$$\underbrace{\left[(1+r^f)R + \alpha\theta(\delta+\epsilon)\right]^2}_{A} =$$
$$\underbrace{\frac{(\delta+\epsilon)\left[(1+r^f)(1-q\theta) + \theta(1+\rho)\right]\left[\alpha\theta(1+\delta) - \alpha\theta\phi(\delta+\epsilon)\right]}{(\rho - r^f)}}_{D} \quad (5.14)$$

---

[16] It is assumed that q is not impacted by the level of reserves. If international creditors can confiscate reserves after default, higher reserves would raise the credit ceiling but not affect the probability of default (at the limit with $B = \bar{B}$). If reserves lower the probability of default for reasons not considered in the model, reserves had an additional benefit and their optimal level would be higher. This would increase the negative externality of reserves on other countries and strengthen our argument. The assumption that default occurs independently of the level of reserves might be a realistic assumption if one considers actual defaults like Greece 2011, where reserves were beyond the reach of international creditors.

[17] This is the case for a high discount rate ρ.

This equation can be solved for R. However, for the following sections this representation turns out to be convenient as a benchmark for comparisons. In subsequent sections, the left-hand side term is referred to as A, the right-hand side term as D. This equation shows that the optimal amount of reserves depends positively on the output cost of a financial crisis $(\delta + \epsilon)$ and negatively on the opportunity cost of reserves $(\rho - r^f)$.

5.3.2 Modeling the behavior of the reserve currency country

For simplicity we assume that the behavior of the reserve currency country can be described by the equations in the previous section. Its status as reserve currency provider may be grounded on a low crisis probability $\phi_C^L < \phi_i^L$ and a strong rule of law with high contract enforceability such that entire output may be confiscated in a default ($\theta_C = 1$). As a consequence of these better fundamentals, its credit ceiling is higher as in the other economies and it can borrow on international markets at the risk free interest rate r^f. Its crisis probability is given by (5.3).

Before we may conclude that the international demand for reserves increases the crisis propensity in the reserve currency country, two caveats have to be solved: (1) The formula for the credit ceiling, given by (5.10), equally applies to the reserve currency country. This ceiling corresponds to the maximum level of reserves, which the reserve currency country can provide to the rest of the world. If the worldwide demand for reserves exceeds the credit ceiling, a dilemma arises: Either the level of reserves in the rest of the world is sub-optimal or reserve-accumulating countries have to neglect the credit ceiling of the reserve provider.[18] (2) The reserve currency country might increase its reserve holdings so that the effect of an increase in external debt on the crisis probability is offset. While an accumulation of other reserve currencies is excluded by the assumption that the rest of the world acquires net reserves, the reserve currency country might increase its gold holdings.[19]

To explore the question whether the provision of reserves is restricted by the credit ceiling, we investigate how the ceiling may be raised. It can be shown that $\frac{d\bar{B}}{dR} > 1$. Hence, theoretically any demand for reserves can be satisfied if the reserve currency country invests part of the borrowed resources in reserve assets.

To answer the second question, we examine how changes in external debt affect the probability of a local crisis given that the center country optimizes its level of reserve hoardings. In contrast to reserve-accumulating countries we assume that the credit ceiling is not binding for the center country. That is, when the center country chooses its optimal level of reserves, it does not take into account that higher reserves

---

[18] In fact, there was a vivid debate in the 1960s and early 1970s whether there is a lack of international liquidity (for a literature survey see Williamson, 1973). To increase the supply of reserves, Special Drawing Rights (SDR) were created in 1969 by the IMF.

[19] In this case, the current account deficit does not reflect the net import of consumption goods, but net imports of gold.

raise the credit ceiling. The optimal level of reserves is then given by

$$R^* = \sqrt{\frac{\alpha \gamma B}{\rho - r^f}} \qquad (5.15)$$

where $\gamma = q + \epsilon + q\theta(1 - \epsilon) - q(1 + r)B$. After substituting (5.15) into the probability of a local crisis (equation (5.1)), the first derivative of the crisis probability with respect to B is given by

$$\frac{\partial p_L}{\partial B} = \frac{1}{2\gamma} \sqrt{\frac{(\rho - r^f)[\gamma + Bq(1 + r)]^2}{\alpha \gamma B}} \qquad (5.16)$$

For the economically relevant case where the time preference ρ is larger than the return of reserves r^f,[20] the crisis probability increases in the level of external debt. Hence, if the rest of the world increases its reserves, the reserve currency country has no incentive to catch up. That is, for the center country it is optimal to increase its own reserves underproportionally with respect to the amount of provided reserves. Consequently, the global accumulation of reserves increases the crisis probability in the center country.

In sum, the stronger the demand for reserve assets, the higher the crisis probability in the center country. One may argue that in a rational model of reserve accumulation, the rising default risk of the center country is reflected by an increase in the interest rate on reserves. Given this price signal, the accumulating countries demand even more reserves because their opportunity cost has fallen (decrease in $(r - r^f)$). As a consequence, the price mechanism does not work in this case and an endogenous response in r^f would even strengthen the negative externality argument of the model.

5.3.3 Optimal reserve level in the presence of local and global crises

Besides local crises, output may also be depressed by a global financial crisis. Whereas the probability of a local crisis depends on domestic fundamentals (as described by equation (5.1)), a global crisis is assumed to have its origin in the reserve currency country.

For the sake of simplicity it is assumed that there exist only two countries besides the reserve currency country.[21] These countries, home and foreign, are identical and denoted by H and F, respectively.

---

[20] This is equivalent to assuming that reserves have an opportunity cost ($\rho > r^f$), which is plausible for two main reasons: (1) If $r^f > \rho$, the optimal amount of reserves would tend to infinity. (2) For the center country, gold constitutes an important reserve asset. Besides valuation effects, $r^f = 0$ for gold.

[21] An extension that allows for more countries would only inflate the mathematical presentation, but not affect our basic results. Alternatively, if one relaxes the assumption of equal size, the foreign country may be regarded as the rest of the world except the reserve currency country.

The modified probability of a financial crisis in the home country, both a local and a global one based on (5.5) is given by:

$$p_H^{LG} = \phi_H + \alpha_H \frac{B_H}{R_H} + \beta(R_H + R_F) \tag{5.17}$$

where the change in reserves in the rest of the world is replaced by the reserve demand in our two reserve-accumulating countries ($R_{ROW} = R_H + R_F$) and the level of reserves in the reserve currency country is normalized to one.

This three-country-model may represent the current constellation with the US at the center and two periphery regions, namely the emerging markets as the reserve-accumulating countries (Home) and industrialized countries (Foreign), which maintain stable levels of reserves. In this interpretation, the reserve-accumulating emerging markets impose a negative externality on the industrialized countries because their behavior increases the probability of a global crisis.

The credit ceiling, the budget constraints (consumption equations), expected utility and the first order condition correspond to the respective equations of the benchmark case (Section 5.3.1) where p^L is replaced by p^{LG}. For simplicity, it is assumed that $\alpha_H = \alpha_F = \alpha$. The cost of a global crisis is equal to the cost of a local crisis, namely $(\delta + \epsilon)$. After computing the partial derivatives and substituting them into the first order condition, one obtains the expression for the optimal amount of reserves:

$$A = D + \frac{(\delta + \epsilon)}{(\rho - r^f)} \Big[\big[\beta(1 + r^f)R_H^2 + \alpha\beta\theta(\delta + \epsilon)(2R_H + R_F) \big]$$
$$\times \big[(1 + r^f)(q\theta - 1) - \theta(1 + \rho) \big] \Big] \tag{5.18}$$

where R is replaced by R_H in A and D. The terms after D on the right-hand side are called E. This quadratic expression in R_H might be solved for R_H. However, since we focus on qualitative effects, we compare this expression with equation (5.14) of the benchmark model. It turns out that the optimal amount of reserves is clearly lower when the probability of a global crisis is taken into account. It is the lower, (1) the larger the effect of reserve accumulation on the probability of a global crisis (large β) and (2) the stronger the mitigating effect of reserves on the probability of a local crisis (large α).[22] High costs of a crisis increase the reduction in the level of reserves. Finally, the more reserves the foreign country has accumulated (high R_F, which is taken as exogenous), the lower the optimal level of reserves in the home country. This is contradictory to empirical evidence, where competitive hoarding induces countries to increase their reserves if neighbors do so (see Cheung and Qian, 2009). Hence, from a perspective of systemic risk, countries' reserve policy is far from optimal.

---

[22] This result can be explained as follows: The larger α is, the stronger is the positive effect of higher reserves on the crisis probability in the center country. This effect overcompensates the negative impact of reserves on the probability of a domestic crisis.

5.3.4 Optimal reserve level in the presence of a global social planner

The analysis so far has focused on an individual country choosing the utility-maximizing level of reserves. If it accumulates reserves, it increases the probability of a global financial crisis. In contrast to the benchmark model, the monetary authority takes the negative effects of a global crisis on domestic income into account. However, it disregards that a global crisis also lowers income in other countries. In other words, when choosing its reserve level, a country neglects the negative externality its reserve accumulation imposes on other countries. This behavior is more probable if the number of reserve-accumulating countries is large. If there are only some large players they have an incentive to recognize the negative externality.

This section analyzes the solution of a global social planner that internalizes the negative externality.[23] Assume that the social planner maximizes the joint utility of both countries. Joint second period income is given by

$$
Y_{HF,2} = \begin{cases} 2(1+\delta) & \text{with probability} \quad 1 - p^{LG} \\ 2(1-\epsilon) & \text{with probability} \quad p^{LG} \end{cases} \tag{5.19}
$$

where the index HF (Home–Foreign) indicates that the sum of a variable over both countries is considered. Furthermore, $B_{HF} = 2B$. As a consequence, the joint credit ceiling of the two countries is given as $\bar{B}_{HF} = 2\bar{B}$ where $\bar{B}$ is defined by equation (5.10). As before, one obtains the expression for the optimal level of reserves after computing the partial derivatives and substituting them into the first order condition:

$$
A = D + E + \frac{(\delta + \epsilon)}{(\rho - r^f)} \beta R_H \big[(q\theta - 1) - \theta(1+\rho)\big]\big[(1 + r^f)R_H + \alpha\theta(\delta + \epsilon)\big] \tag{5.20}
$$

The term E quantifies the reduction in the level of reserves when an individual country's maximization problem accounts for the risks of a global crisis. In comparison to equation (5.18), the additional terms on the RHS measure how maximization by a social planner affects the optimal amount of reserves. Because all additional terms are negative, the amount of reserves, which a social planner chooses for each individual country, is clearly lower than what a domestic authority would accumulate. This reduction is positively affected by the costs of a crisis $(\delta + \epsilon)$ and by the risk-free interest rate (r^f). The larger the effect of reserve accumulation on the probability of a global crisis (large β) and the stronger the mitigating effect of reserves on the probability of a local crisis (large α), the stronger are the reserve reductions implemented by a social planner.

---

[23] The social planner coordinates the policies of both countries but does not take into account that alternative arrangements like reserve-pooling, mutual credit lines and swap lines might provide more efficient forms of insurance.

5.3.5 How can the socially optimal level of reserves be implemented?

As shown above, the socially optimal level of reserves is in general lower than the level of reserves individual countries hoard in the decentralized equilibrium. Welfare could be improved by taxing the hoarding of reserves. Since private domestic costs of reserves do not cover their social global costs, a tax might charge the difference. This Pigouvian tax induces individual countries to internalize the negative externality of their reserve accumulation. It corrects individual country behavior and leads to a globally efficient level of reserves.

We assume that a social planner – a global financial institution or the reserve currency country itself – taxes both the level of reserves and their interest earnings at a rate t. This policy modifies the budget constraint of period 2: In (5.11) the last term $(1 + r^f)R$ is multiplied by $(1 - t)$ for each state of the nature. The optimization of (5.12) under the modified set of budget constraints provides the first order condition for the optimal level of reserves:

$$A = \frac{\rho - r^f}{\rho - r^f + t(1+r)}D + E \tag{5.18'}$$

This expression corresponds to (5.18) where t and tr additionally appear in the denominator on the right-hand side. For $t > 0$, the level of reserves chosen by an optimizing country is lower than that without taxation. Since t has to be chosen such that the first order condition of an individual country equals the first order condition of a social planner (5.20) = (5.18'), the optimal tax rate is given by

$$t = \frac{(\delta + \epsilon)\beta R_H\big[(1 - q\theta) + \theta(1 + \rho)\big]\big[(1 + r^f)R_H + \alpha\theta(\delta + \epsilon)\big]}{D + \frac{(\delta+\epsilon)}{(\rho-r^f)}\beta R_H\big[(1 - q\theta) + \theta(1 + \rho)\big]\big[(1 + r^f)R_H + \alpha\theta(\delta + \epsilon)\big]}\frac{1}{1+r}$$

$$\tag{5.21}$$

As long as the assumptions of our model are satisfied – all parameters are positive – the optimal tax rate is larger than zero. The optimal allocation can be implemented with an appropriate tax on reserves, with tax revenue rebated as a lump sum transfer across countries or transferred to an international institution and used to grant liquidity to crisis-hit countries. The optimal tax rate is the higher, the stronger the relationship between reserve hoarding and the probability of a global crisis (large β). It is negatively associated with the opportunity costs of reserves defined as $(r - r^f)$ because opportunity costs and a tax may be considered as substitutes: Alike a tax, high opportunity costs discourage reserve hoardings. As a consequence the optimal tax rate increases in the risk-free interest rate r^f and decreases in the country's interest rate on foreign liabilities r. Moreover, the optimal tax increases in the level of reserves R_H, which, however, depends endogenously on the structural parameters of the economy. Our model also shows that the tax base should be rather the absolute level of reserves than reserves scaled by some domestic variable. In particular, it is irrelevant for the stability of the reserve currency country whether reserves are accumulated by a small or large country. The effect of accumulated reserves on the crisis probability depends on the level of reserves held by the center, which provides stabilizing collateral and is used as scaling variable in the behavioral equation for the crisis probability (see equation (5.3)).[24]

How could the Pigouvian tax be implemented? The reserve currency country might tax government bonds in the hands of foreign monetary authorities. Since the global demand for reserves increases the crisis probability in the center country, it might have an incentive to restrict the supply of reserve assets. In this case, however, the rest of the world would not be endowed with the reserves it demands. Since the demand for reserves is relatively inelastic with respect to their price, the demand–supply mechanism might not work properly. Alternatively, the accumulation of reserves might be taxed by an international financial institution. In this vein, Eichengreen (2009) proposes to levy a tax if reserves had been accumulated over the last three years and if the increase exceeded 3% of GDP.

Whereas our results indicate that the accumulation of reserves should be taxed, Aizenman (2011) comes to a seemingly opposing conclusion: It is socially desirable to subsidize reserve hoardings and to tax private borrowing. His argumentation is based on an overborrowing externality.[25] Although the results seem to be contradictory, they can be easily conciliated: Aizenman optimizes the level of foreign borrowing and reserve hoardings for a representative commercial bank. A central bank, however, is likely to internalize the overborrowing externality caused by individual borrowers. Therefore, the tax-cum-subsidy scheme of Aizenman is primarily a mechanism to guarantee that those who increase the need for reserves – namely domestic borrowers who benefit from lower interest rates abroad – also bear the costs their borrowing imposes on society as a whole.

Thus, from the perspective of an individual country, the level of reserves may well be optimal without subsidization.[26] The tax-cum-subsidy scheme may be combined with our policy of taxing reserve hoardings: At the national level, the overborrowing externality may be internalized by a monetary transfer from those who borrow internationally to the central bank. A global social planner, however, imposes a tax on central banks' reserve hoardings.

5.3.6   Robustness analysis

By considering some extensions to our model and relaxing restrictive assumptions, this section examines the robustness of our results.

---

[24] Alternative scaling variables might be the fiscal capacity or GDP of the center country (see Section 5.3.6).

[25] If (1) price-taking borrowers ignore their impact on the cost of a crisis and (2) the risk of liquidation of investment projects rises with the ratio of external borrowing to reserves, external borrowing imposes a negative externality. This externality implies that the marginal social benefit of borrowing is lower than the private benefit, whereas the marginal social benefit of hoarding reserves exceeds the private one. As a consequence, the optimal policy mix combines a tax on external borrowing with a subsidy on reserve hoardings.

[26] Within our model, this assumption implies that the central bank correctly estimates the costs of a crisis ($\delta + \epsilon$) and the effects of borrowing and reserves on the probability of a local crisis (α_i in equation (5.1)).

Output specification

The output function, formalized by (5.6), allows only for two states of nature, a positive productivity shock and an output-reducing financial crisis. This setting could be expanded by an intermediate state with stagnant output. Output in period 2 is then given by

$$Y_2 = \begin{cases} 1 + \eta & \text{with probability} \quad 1 - p^{LL} - s \\ 1 & \text{with probability} \quad s \\ 1 - \epsilon & \text{with probability} \quad p^{LL} \end{cases}$$

$$\eta, \epsilon > 0 \quad \text{and} \quad 0 < p^{LL} + s < 1 \tag{5.22}$$

where the positive productivity shock is now labeled η. A crisis occurs with probability p^{LL} and s denotes the probability of constant output.

Our analysis focuses on the bad state of nature: Without financial crises optimal reserve holdings would be zero. The benefits of reserves arise from their ability to reduce the probability and depth of a crisis. Without loss of generality, we can consider the cases of constant output and a positive productivity shock jointly. Expected output in period 2 in the absence of crises is given by

$$Y_2 = 1 + \eta(1 - s) \tag{5.23}$$

After setting $\delta = \eta(1 - s)$ and $p^L = p^{LL} + s$, we end up with (5.6). We conclude that our output function with two states of nature may be regarded as a simplification, which nests several substates of different positive productivity shocks and constant output.

Maturity structure of external debt

In our model a country determines the amount of external debt and reserve holdings in period 1 jointly. Both are held for one period. In period 2 a country defaults on its liabilities or repays them and reserves are consumed. We abstract from effects that might arise from the maturity structure of external debt.

The maturity structure of external assets and liabilities, however, might be pivotal for the probability of a financial crisis and the solvency of a country. We therefore examine how results are affected if we allow for different maturities.

With respect to reserves, we assume that they are held in short-term assets because reserves are by definition liquid assets readily available to central banks. This implies that official liabilities of the reserve currency country R_{ROW} are entirely short term. Regarding external debt of non-reserve countries, we allow for short-term liabilities with a maturity of one period and long-term liabilities characterized by a maturity of two periods. The determination of the optimal maturity structure of external debt is beyond the scope of this chapter (see, among others, Detragiache and Spilimbergo, 2004; Diamond, 1991; Rodrik and Velasco, 2000). For simplicity we assume that countries hold a share ω of total external debt in short-term liabilities (B^{ST}), hence $B^{ST} = \omega B$.

The share of short-term liabilities of the center country is larger than in other countries. We assume that alike in the rest of the world a share ω of total liabilities of private agents (B_C^{pr}) matures after one period, while official liabilities held as reserves in the rest of the world are entirely short-term. This is in line with the observation that the center country provides maturity transformation services to the rest of the world: It transform short-term external liabilities into long-term loans (e.g. Gourinchas and Rey, 2007).

The empirical literature concurs that short-term external debt, which is defined as debt with a remaining maturity of one year or less, is the key part of total external debt in determining crisis vulnerability.[27] Consequently, we replace B in (5.1) by $B^{ST} = \frac{(1+\omega)B}{2}$ taking into account that half of long-term debt has a remaining maturity of one year at the beginning of each period. Using (5.5), the probability of a local and global crisis is then governed by

$$p_i^{LG} = \phi_i + \alpha_i^{ST} \frac{B_i}{R_i} + \beta \frac{R_{ROW}}{R_C} \tag{5.24}$$

where $\alpha_i^{ST} = \frac{\alpha_i(1+\omega)}{2}$. Equation (5.24) shows that the probability of a crisis holds true to be a function of external debt relative to reserves, albeit their positive relationship is alleviated ($\alpha_i^{ST} < \alpha_i$). The spillover from the center country and the negative externality arising from other countries' reserve accumulation, as captured by the last term of (5.24), are not affected by the availability of two-period debt. In comparison to the benchmark model, the consideration of global crises still lowers the optimal amount of reserves, but the externality is smaller, which reduces the difference between benchmark and adjusted solution. In the same vein, a social planner chooses a lower level of reserves, but the difference between individual and centralized solution is smaller when only short-term debt induces crises. Consequently, the optimal tax rate on reserves remains positive but is lower.

Asymmetries between reserve-providing and reserve-accumulating countries

The benchmark model assumes that the crisis probability is governed by similar functional forms in reserve-accumulating and reserve-providing countries: The probability of a crisis depends on the ratio of external debt over reserves, while the impact coefficient α is country-specific. One might question whether this symmetric behavioral assumption is appropriate.

First, the reserve currency country is known to enjoy an exorbitant privilege. The major part of this privilege is due to an interest spread, which we model by the difference $(r - r^f) > 0$: The reserve currency country remunerates its liabilities – the reserve holdings in the rest of the world – at the rate r^f, which is lower than its return r on assets held abroad. In the steady-state equilibrium where B and R are given, the rest of the world has to run a surplus in the trade balance to finance the interest privilege of the reserve currency country. However, the privilege is independent of our assertion that the center country has to run a current account deficit when the rest of the world accumulates net reserves.

---

[27] Contributions to this literature include Chang and Velasco (2000), IMF (2000), Obstfeld (1996) and Radelet and Sachs (1998). This led to the Greenspan–Guidotti rule of thumb stating that reserves should cover entire short-term debt. Benmelech and Dvir (2013) challenge this view arguing that a high level of short-term debt is rather a symptom than a cause of crises.

Second, crisis vulnerability in the center might be governed by other factors than in the periphery. In contrast to the rest of the world, liabilities of the center country are denominated in its own currency. This rules out a crisis resulting from a devaluation combined with a currency mismatch in assets and liabilities. While external liabilities of non-reserve countries are collateralized by assets of the reserve currency country, the liabilities of the reserve country itself may be backed by different assets: (1) assets denominated in secondary reserve currencies, (2) gold, (3) reserve country GDP and/or (4) the fiscal capacity of the reserve providing country (see Farhi et al., 2011). Therefore, as an alternative specification, we replace R_C in (5.3) by Y_C. Hence, we end up with the modified probability of a crisis in the center as

$$p_C^L = \phi_C^L + \alpha_C \frac{B_C^{pr} + R_{ROW}}{Y_C} \tag{5.25}$$

The benchmark model assumes that the accumulation of net reserves in the periphery and the subsequent current account deficit in the center are entirely spent on consumption. In reality, however, capital derived from the sale of reserves could be invested. While investments in other reserve currency assets and gold are viable options, their supply probably comes short of the demand for the center's safe assets.[28] Alternatively, capital could be used for productive investment in the center country, which raises its output and fiscal capacity. Hence Y_C is a positive function of R_{ROW}. In particular, we assume that $Y_{C,2} = 1 + f(R_{ROW})$ in the absence of shocks and $f' > 0$.

In the limiting case, output growth from investment thanks to reserve income ($f(R_{ROW})$) and R_{ROW} are such that $\frac{B_C^{pr}}{Y_C} = \frac{B_C^{pr} + R_{ROW}}{Y_C(R_{ROW})}$. Then reserve accumulation does not affect the probability of a global crisis. The optimal amount of reserves degenerates to (5.14). If, however, output growth is lower, the marginal effect of reserve accumulation on the crisis probability in the center is still positive, but smaller. Since the demand for reserve assets lowers r^f in the reserve currency country, optimizing agents increase current consumption as a result of intertemporal substitution. Hence, it is reasonable to assume that only a fraction of reserve income will be invested. A discussion of this point in greater depth may be found in Appendix 5.A.

In our symmetric specification center and periphery both hold reserves and incur external liabilities. Their net foreign asset position $(R - B)$, however, is not specified ex-ante. Reserve holdings may be financed through current account surpluses or foreign borrowing. Everything being equal, the lower costs of foreign borrowing for the center raise its foreign debt and lower its net foreign asset position. This is especially true if reserves are not held in foreign assets, but in gold or domestic real investment goods. Hence, our model is consistent with the empirical fact that the US as center is a large debtor country and the periphery a net creditor.

---

[28] World gold production evaluated at prices in the year of extraction between 1900 and 2010 accounts for 11.7% of the increase in globally held foreign exchange reserves over the same period. See also Obstfeld (2014).

Specification of crisis probability

Equation (5.1) imposes a linear relation between the ratio of external debt over reserves and the probability of a domestic crisis while a non-linear approach might be more appropriate. The empirical literature finds that this relationship is characterized by nonlinearities and threshold effects. We therefore examine how a non-linear relationship, which is specified in the following equation, affects our results:

$$p_i^L = \phi_i + \alpha_{1,i}\frac{B_i}{R_i} + \alpha_{2,i}\left(\frac{B_i}{R_i}\right)^2 \tag{5.26}$$

In line with empirical findings we assume that the insurance effect of reserves is larger at high levels of debt, that is $\alpha_{2,i} > 0$. The marginal effect of reserves rises in $\frac{B_i}{R_i}$.

The basic implications of our model are robust to this variation, although their magnitude changes. We can distinguish two cases: For $\alpha < \alpha_1 + 2\alpha_2\frac{B}{R}$, the global externality of reserve hoardings is larger than in the model with a linear relation between $\frac{B}{R}$ and crises. This further lowers the optimal level of reserves and increases the optimal tax rate. In the other case, our results are still valid but lower in magnitude.

Volume effects

In the extended model allowing for external debt of different maturities, reserve accumulation raises systemic risk even in the limiting case, in which the center country's net foreign asset position is independent of the amount of provided reserves. That is, the crisis probability rises with the volume of provided reserves even if capital inflows due to reserve accumulation are re-invested abroad (balanced financial account).

The reason for the increased crisis probability is a maturity mismatch. Center liabilities are short-term while its assets are long-term. A sudden sale of reserves might cause an illiquidity and subsequent insolvency of the center country. That is, as long as the center does not invest its reserve income in foreign short-term assets, any increase in global reserves raises the probability of a crisis emanating from the center. This link between reserves and a crisis in the center suffices to produce the negative externality of reserve accumulation, which lowers the socially optimal amount of global reserves. Hence, the consideration of "volume effects" reinforces our argument.

5.4   Quantitative implications of the model – a calibration analysis

To explore the quantitative implications of our model we proceed by a calibration analysis. We first present a base-case calibration and then conduct some sensitivity analysis. Table 5.1 lists the 11 structural parameters of our economy, their benchmark value and their value range used in the sensitivity analysis.

In our benchmark scenario we set the risk-free interest rate r^f equal to 3%, which lies between the parameters chosen by Bianchi et al. (2013) and Jeanne and

Table 5.1 **Calibration parameters**

Parameter	Benchmark value	Range of variation	Source
Risk-free rate	$r^f = 0.03$	$[0.02, 0.04]$	
Risk premium	$r - r^f = 0.015$		Jeanne and Rancière (2011)
Discount rate	$\rho = 0.042$		Korinek and Servén (2016), Prescott (1986)
Output loss	$\epsilon = 0.1$	$[0.05, 0.3]$	
Potential output growth	$\delta = 0.033$		Jeanne and Rancière (2011)
Pledgeable output	$\theta = 0.5$	$[0.25, 0.75]$	Devereux and Yetman (2010)
Default probability	$q = 0.5$		
Crisis probability	$\phi = 0.1$	$[0.05, 0.15]$	
Transmission coefficient	$\lambda = 0.3$	$[0.1, 0.5]$	
Marginal effect (B/R)	$\alpha = 0.007$	$[0.0005, 0.02]$	
Marginal effect (B/R) in center country	$\alpha_C = 0.002$	$[0.001, 0.003]$	

Rancière (2011), who set r^f equal to 1% and 5%, respectively. The country's interest rate for international borrowing r equals the risk-free interest rate plus a risk premium. Empirical studies concur that the risk premium of emerging market bonds is relatively small and lies between 0 and 1.5% (see Broner et al., 2013; Klingen et al., 2004). Following Jeanne and Rancière (2011) we set the risk premium equal to 1.5%. In practice, opportunity costs of reserves also include a term premium because B is rather long term compared to R. Although this is not modeled in our one-period setting, we account for it through higher risk premia in the sensitivity analysis. Following the literature we assume a time-preference factor of 0.96. Since the time-preference factor equals $\frac{1}{1+\rho}$ in our specification, it follows that the individual time-preference rate ρ is 0.042.

We account for the observed variation of crisis-induced output costs by a large parameter range in our sensitivity analysis, where output costs are assumed to lie between 5% and 30% of GDP. The benchmark sets $\epsilon = 0.1$. Without claiming completeness, Table 5.2 provides a list of recent estimates of the output cost of different types of crises.

We follow Jeanne and Rancière (2011) and set the growth rate of potential output equal to 3.3%. Half of output is pledgeable ($\theta = 0.5$) and the default probability conditional on a crisis is set to 50%. To simplify the exposition, the level of reserves in the center country R_C was normalized to one in the model. In the calibration analysis we assume that the center country behaves like an average industrialized country and set $R_C = 0.1$.

Table 5.2 Output cost of crises (in % of GDP)

Source	Banking crisis	Currency crisis	Debt crisis	Sudden stop	Financial crisis
Bordo et al. (2001)	6.2	5.9			8.3/18.6
Cecchetti et al. (2009)	9.2				
Cerra and Chaman Saxena (2008)	7.7	4			10
De Paoli et al. (2011)			0.5–2.5		12–13
Furceri and Zdzienicka (2012a)			10		
Gourinchas and Obstfeld (2012)	5.2[a]				
Gourinchas and Obstfeld (2012)	8.5[b]				
Hutchison (2003)		2[c]			
Hutchison and Noy (2002)		5–8[a]		13–15[a]	
IMF (2009b)	10	3		10	
Jeanne and Rancière (2011)			27		
Kapp and Vega (2012)	18	15			9–15
Reinhart and Rogoff (2009)	9.3				

Notes: Indices denote the nature of the country sample: [a]advanced economies, [b]emerging markets, [c]developing and emerging economies.

Concerning the unconditional probability of a financial crisis we assume that the average country is hit by a banking, currency or debt crisis or a combination of them (twin crisis) every ten years, that is, $\phi = 0.1$ in the benchmark regression (for estimates of the unconditional probability of different types of financial crises see Bordo et al., 2001, Gourinchas and Obstfeld, 2012, and Jeanne and Rancière, 2011).

Spillovers with respect to economic activity from core to periphery countries play a crucial role in our model because they induce the negative externality of reserve accumulation. We base our calibration of these spillovers on the work of Vitek (2012) who measures international business cycle comovement in the face of macroeconomic and financial shocks. Financial shocks that raise the US output gap by 1% increase the output gap in the periphery by more than 0.25%. Macroeconomic shocks have a quantitatively smaller impact ranging from 0.025 to 0.25%. Helbling et al. (2007) examine the global impact of US downturns. The transmission coefficient, defined as the domestic fall in output relative to the decrease in the US, is 0.5 for other industrialized countries and Latin American countries, 0.36 for emerging Asia and almost one for emerging Europe and CIS countries. We set the transmission coefficient λ equal to 0.3, but allow in the sensitivity analysis for a large window ranging between 0.1 and 0.5.

At the core of our model is the relationship between the level of external debt relative to reserves and the probability of a domestic financial crisis. We estimate these effects by a multivariate probit panel regression analysis. Following the literature of early warning signals for financial crises, we regress a crisis dummy variable on a set of potential indicators. In particular, we consider banking, currency and sovereign debt crises as dependent variables. Financial crises are defined as the occurrence of at least one of these crises. The choice of indicator variables follows the literature on early warning indicators (e.g. Bussière and Fratzscher, 2006; Frankel and Saravelos, 2012). Besides external debt relative to reserves we include GDP, the current account balance (relative to GDP), a measure of real exchange rate overvaluation and domestic credit growth as a measure of the vulnerability of the financial sector.

In line with our model where reserves reduce the probability of an output loss independently of the type of crisis, we focus on the effect of reserves on the probability of financial crises. Results are presented in Table 5.3. Details on the data set, a description of the estimation approach and results for specific types of crises (banking, currency and sovereign debt crises, respectively) may be found in Appendix 5.B. We report the estimated coefficients for all covariates and the marginal effect of external debt over reserves evaluated at the means of the covariates. Besides the full sample we also present results for subsamples of industrialized, emerging and developing countries.

The following findings may be highlighted: The lower the ratio of external debt to reserves, the lower the probability of a financial crisis. This effect is significant across all regressions independently of the specification and country subsample. The marginal effect of (B/R) varies between 0.019 in emerging markets and 0.0005 in de-

Table 5.3 Determinants of financial crises

	Full sample		Industrialized countries		Emerging markets		Developing countries	
	(1)	(2)	(3)	(4)	(5)	(6)	(7)	(8)
(B/R)	0.0028***	0.0021**	0.0093*	0.0091*	0.0532***	0.0644***	0.0021***	0.0015*
	(3.46)	(2.56)	(1.68)	(1.66)	(5.30)	(2.77)	(2.70)	(1.81)
GDP growth		−0.9925*		1.2129		−1.2498		−1.6683**
		(−1.95)		(1.02)		(−0.79)		(−2.46)
Growth in REER		0.0809		1.2348		−0.0828		0.1593
		(0.19)		(0.51)		(−0.05)		(0.34)
Current account balance, growth (relative to GDP)		0.0017		−0.0068		0.0265		−0.0340
		(0.12)		(−0.32)		(1.01)		(−0.94)
Domestic credit, growth rate (relative to GDP)		0.6117*		0.5858		1.2305		0.5894
		(1.76)		(0.62)		(1.05)		(1.47)
Marginal effect of (B/R)	0.0009***	0.0006**	0.0022*	0.0022*	0.0177***	0.0186***	0.0007***	0.0005*
	(3.44)	(2.55)	(1.66)	(1.66)	(5.15)	(2.77)	(2.69)	(1.80)
Observations	2018	1030	615	459	559	173	881	398
Number of countries	63	45	20	18	17	8	27	19
Pseudo R^2	0.01	0.01	0.01	0.02	0.05	0.08	0.01	0.03
$p >$ chi2	0.00	0.01	0.09	0.23	0.00	0.02	0.01	0.02

Notes: z-Statistics are reported in parentheses. The symbols *, **, and *** denote statistical significance at the 10%, 5%, and 1% levels, respectively. The marginal effect of (B/R) is evaluated at the means of the covariates.

veloping countries. Taking the average effect across the three country subsamples,[29] we set α equal to 0.007 and perform robustness checks allowing for lower and higher values. To be more precise, we set the lower bound equal to the marginal effect for developing countries and choose the upper bound equal to the marginal effect for emerging market countries.[30] While for each individual country the marginal effect of (B/R) reflects the effectiveness of reserve accumulation for crisis prevention, the same marginal effect in the center country determines the extent to which global reserve accumulation destabilizes the center. Since the center country is a financially highly developed nation, we proxy its marginal effect of (B/R) by the marginal effect obtained in the sample of industrialized countries and set α_C equal to 0.002 (see also equation (5.3)).

In our benchmark calibration (see Table 5.4), the optimal level of reserves equals 25.6% relative to GDP in the standard model, which ignores systemic risk creation. This number is surprisingly consistent with the actual level of reserves, whose mean across 156 countries amounted to 23.5% in 2010 (with median of 18.8%). If the country takes into account that its reserve accumulation raises the probability of a global crisis, the optimal level of reserves falls to 17.5%. An optimizing social planner, who internalizes the negative externality of reserve accumulation on the rest of the world, chooses reserves equal to 14.1% of GDP. This shows that the systemic risk factor highlighted in this chapter is economically significant. Its consideration lowers the optimal amount of reserves by 45%. To implement the socially optimal solution in a decentralized economy, reserves have to be taxed by a rate equal to 1.3%.

Our sensitivity analysis shows that the optimal amount of reserves varies with the chosen parameters. It lies between 6.9% and 62.5%. The qualitative result that global crises and a social planner both reduce the optimal amount of reserves is confirmed across all specifications. Quantitatively, these effects reduce the optimal amount of reserves by 24.6 to 73.9%. Across the 15 specifications of our sensitivity analysis the consideration of systemic risk creation reduces the optimal amount of reserves on average by 44.9% and the average tax rate equals 1.3%.

Larger expected output losses go hand in hand with a higher level of optimal reserves. If a large share of output can be confiscated by external creditors, the optimal amount of reserves is higher. Since default is an ineffective instrument to smooth consumption, reserves assume this role. As expected, the choice of the unconditional crisis probability has only minor effects on the optimal reserve level because in our model the marginal effect of reserves is independent of the unconditional crisis probability. The strength of spillover effects does not affect the optimal level of reserves in the base-case because this specification ignores crisis spillovers. However, the larger the correlation in countries' output, the larger the reductions in the optimal level of reserves when these spillovers are accounted for. The marginal effect of external debt

---

[29] Instead of using the coefficient obtained from the full sample, we prefer to weight the three country groups equally by taking the average coefficient. This better reflects the share of our country groups in global output and reserves.

[30] Later on, we provide results that differentiate between industrialized, emerging and developing countries. For each country group we set α equal to its group-specific value.

Table 5.4 **Calibration results: Full sample**

Specification	Optimal reserves (in % GDP)			Tax rate (in %)
	Benchmark	Global crisis	Social planner	
Standard	25.6	17.5	14.1	1.3
Varying risk-free interest rate				
$r^f = 0.02$	19.0	14.9	12.7	1.3
$r^f = 0.04$	62.5	22.3	16.3	1.3
Varying output loss				
$\epsilon = 0.05$	17.4	14.1	12.2	0.6
$\epsilon = 0.3$	34.3	19.5	15.1	2.4
Varying pledgeable output				
$\theta = 0.25$	17.2	12.1	9.8	1.2
$\theta = 0.75$	32.9	21.9	17.5	1.4
Varying crisis probability				
$\phi = 0.05$	25.8	17.6	14.2	1.3
$\phi = 0.15$	25.5	17.4	14.1	1.3
Varying transmission coefficient				
$\lambda = 0.1$	25.6	21.8	19.3	0.4
$\lambda = 0.5$	25.6	15.0	11.7	2.2
Varying marginal effect of (B/R)				
$\alpha = 0.0005$	6.9	4.7	3.8	1.3
$\alpha = 0.02$	43.3	29.5	23.8	1.3
Varying marginal effect of (B/R) in center country				
$\alpha_C = 0.001$	26.5	20.4	17.5	0.7
$\alpha_C = 0.003$	26.5	15.5	12.2	2.0

Note: Since $Y_1 = 1$, the calibrated values of R equal the ratio of reserves over GDP.

relative to reserves on the crisis probability significantly affects the optimal reserve level. The larger reserves' negative effect on the crisis probability, the higher their optimal level. For the marginal effect of (B/R) in the center country, the reverse is true: The larger this effect, the lower the optimal level of reserves in the periphery.

The benchmark calibration and sensitivity analysis presented in Table 5.4 use an average value for the effect of (B/R) on the crisis probability in individual countries, namely $\alpha = 0.007$. Our regression analysis, however, provides group-specific estimates of α for industrialized, emerging and developing countries, respectively. Hence, we are able to distinguish between these groups when calibrating the optimal level of reserves.

In these group-specific calibrations we set the marginal effect of (B/R) equal to its value estimated within the respective group in regressions including the full set of covariates, that is $\alpha_{IND} = 0.0022$ in industrialized countries, $\alpha_{EME} = 0.0186$ in emerging markets and $\alpha_{DEV} = 0.0005$ in developing countries. The borders of the value range for the sensitivity analysis are calculated as $\alpha_i +/-$ standard deviation of α_i where $i = IND, EME, DEV$. The marginal effect in the center country, α_C, is independent of the chosen subsample and set equal to 0.002 as in the full sample. The results are reported in Tables 5.5–5.7.

The optimal amount of reserves relative to GDP in industrialized countries is substantially lower than in the full sample. It amounts to 14.4% in the standard specification and falls to 7.9% after considering systemic risk creation. The tax rate to implement the socially optimal solution equals 1.3% just as in the full sample. Depending on parameter values, the optimal level of reserves relative to GDP ranges between 9.2 and 35.0% in the benchmark model and between 5.1 and 10.8% when the negative externality of reserve accumulation is internalized. The finding that reserves over GDP are lower in industrialized countries is consistent with actual behavior: The mean of reserves over GDP in industrialized countries was 11.2% in 2010 in our sample (with median 6.2%).

Emerging markets are characterized by larger optimal reserve holdings: In the standard specification reserves over GDP equal 41.7% and amount to 23.0% when determined by a social planner. The tax rate of 1.3% equals that in industrialized countries. Concerning actual behavior, the recent behavior of reserve accumulation was driven by emerging markets. However, their ratios of reserves to GDP are not exceptionally high. In 2010, their mean was 25.3% with a median of 19.9%.

According to our calibration, developing countries figure the lowest optimal ratio of reserves over GDP. It equals 6.9% in the standard specification and falls to 3.8% when systemic risk is accounted for. A tax rate of 1.3% may implement the socially optimal solution. This finding contrasts with observed data for developing countries: As a group, their reserves over GDP equal 25.4% on average (median of 19.9%) and are not significantly lower than in the full sample.

The calibration suggests the following results for the benchmark specification: The larger the return on reserves and the bigger the crisis-induced output losses, the larger is the optimal level of reserves. If a large share of output can be confiscated by foreign creditors, the optimal level of reserves is high. This holds because reserves ensure a minimum level of second period consumption after default given that they are beyond the reach of foreigners by assumption. The smaller the crisis-reducing effect of reserves, the lower the optimal level of reserves. Since crisis transmission is ignored in the benchmark calibration, the marginal effect of (B/R) in the center country does not affect optimal reserves in the periphery.

The consideration of systemic risk lowers the optimal amount of reserves across all specifications and country groups. This effect is especially strong in the following cases: First, when the optimal level of reserves is high in the benchmark model, sys-

Table 5.5 **Calibration results: Industrial countries ($\alpha = 0.0022$)**

Specification	Optimal reserves (in % GDP)			Tax rate (in %)
	Benchmark	Global crisis	Social planner	
Standard	14.4	9.8	7.9	1.3
Varying risk-free interest rate				
$r^f = 0.02$	10.7	8.4	7.1	1.3
$r^f = 0.04$	35.0	12.5	9.1	1.3
Varying output loss				
$\epsilon = 0.05$	9.7	7.9	6.8	0.6
$\epsilon = 0.3$	19.3	11.0	8.5	2.4
Varying pledgeable output				
$\theta = 0.25$	9.6	6.8	5.5	1.2
$\theta = 0.75$	18.5	12.3	9.8	1.4
Varying crisis probability				
$\phi = 0.05$	14.5	9.9	8.0	1.3
$\phi = 0.15$	14.3	9.8	7.9	1.3
Varying transmission coefficient				
$\lambda = 0.1$	14.4	12.2	10.8	0.4
$\lambda = 0.5$	14.4	8.4	6.5	2.2
Varying marginal effect of (B/R)				
$\alpha = 0.0009$	9.2	6.3	5.1	1.3
$\alpha = 0.0036$	18.4	12.6	10.1	1.3
Varying marginal effect of (B/R) in center country				
$\alpha_C = 0.001$	14.4	11.5	9.8	0.7
$\alpha_C = 0.003$	14.4	8.7	6.8	2.0

Note: Since $Y_1 = 1$, the calibrated values of R equal the ratio of reserves over GDP.

temic risk lowers the optimal amount of reserves considerably because higher reserve levels are associated with a larger negative externality. This effect arises when reserve hoardings are an attractive investment due to a high return on reserves (large r^f), when the output loss of a crisis is large or when the marginal effect of (B/R) on the probability of a domestic crisis is strong. Second, the decrease in the optimal level of reserves after the consideration of systemic risk is large when a crisis in the center has

Table **5.6** **Calibration results: Emerging markets ($\alpha = 0.0186$)**

Specification	Optimal reserves (in % GDP)			Tax rate (in %)
	Benchmark	Global crisis	Social planner	
Standard	41.7	28.5	23.0	1.3
Varying risk-free interest rate				
$r^f = 0.02$	31.0	24.3	20.6	1.3
$r^f = 0.04$	101.7	36.3	26.5	1.3
Varying output loss				
$\epsilon = 0.05$	28.3	22.9	19.8	0.6
$\epsilon = 0.3$	55.8	31.8	24.5	2.3
Varying pledgeable output				
$\theta = 0.25$	28.0	19.6	16.0	1.2
$\theta = 0.75$	53.6	35.6	28.6	1.4
Varying crisis probability				
$\phi = 0.05$	41.9	28.6	23.1	1.3
$\phi = 0.15$	41.5	28.4	22.9	1.3
Varying transmission coefficient				
$\lambda = 0.1$	41.7	35.5	31.4	0.4
$\lambda = 0.5$	41.7	24.5	19.0	2.2
Varying marginal effect of (B/R)				
$\alpha = 0.0119$	33.4	22.8	18.4	1.3
$\alpha = 0.0253$	48.6	33.2	26.8	1.3
Varying marginal effect of (B/R) in center country				
$\alpha_C = 0.001$	41.7	33.3	28.5	0.7
$\alpha_C = 0.003$	41.7	25.3	19.8	1.9

Note: Since $Y_1 = 1$, the calibrated values of R equal the ratio of reserves over GDP.

strong effects on output in the periphery. This especially holds for large output costs of crises and a strong transmission from the center to the periphery. Third, the negative effect on optimal reserves is the stronger, the larger the effect of reserves on the crisis probability in the center, namely the larger α_C.

The tax rate that induces the socially optimal level of reserves equals 1.3% in the standard specification across all four country groups. Its average value across different

Table 5.7 **Calibration results: Developing countries ($\alpha = 0.0005$)**

Specification	Optimal reserves (in % GDP)			Tax rate (in %)
	Benchmark	Global crisis	Social planner	
Standard	6.9	4.7	3.8	1.3
Varying risk-free interest rate				
$r^f = 0.02$	5.1	4.0	3.4	1.3
$r^f = 0.04$	16.7	6.0	4.4	1.3
Varying output loss				
$\epsilon = 0.05$	4.6	3.8	3.3	0.6
$\epsilon = 0.3$	9.2	5.2	4.0	2.4
Varying pledgeable output				
$\theta = 0.25$	4.6	3.2	2.6	1.2
$\theta = 0.75$	8.8	5.9	4.7	1.5
Varying crisis probability				
$\phi = 0.05$	6.9	4.7	3.8	1.3
$\phi = 0.15$	6.8	4.7	3.8	1.3
Varying transmission coefficient				
$\lambda = 0.1$	6.9	5.8	5.2	0.4
$\lambda = 0.5$	6.9	4.0	3.1	2.2
Varying marginal effect of (B/R)				
$\alpha = 0.0002$	4.3	3.0	2.4	1.3
$\alpha = 0.0008$	8.7	5.9	4.8	1.3
Varying marginal effect of (B/R) in center country				
$\alpha_C = 0.001$	6.9	5.5	4.7	0.7
$\alpha_C = 0.003$	6.9	4.2	3.3	2.0

Note: Since $Y_1 = 1$, the calibrated values of R equal the ratio of reserves over GDP.

specifications also amounts to 1.3%. Since both the level of reserves and its return are taxed, a tax rate of 1.3% reduces the return on reserves in the benchmark specification from $r^f = 3.0\%$ to less than 1.7%.

In sum, the calibration analysis shows two effects: First, our simple model matches the observed level of reserves quite well. Second, the consideration of systemic risk almost halves the optimal reserve level.

5.5   Conclusions

This chapter has put central banks' accumulation of international reserves in new context: The policy of reserve accumulation as a form of self-insurance, which has gained popularity since the East Asian financial crisis, might rather cause than prevent financial crises. The empirical evidence suggests that the global financial crisis of 2008–10 is an example of a global crisis that is a by-product of central banks' appetite for reserves. However, as we have shown, this correlation is not coincidental. On the contrary, if the reserve currency fulfills the double role of global store of value and national medium of exchange, the accumulation of reserves increases the vulnerability of the reserve currency country. There exist externalities that suggest that it might be optimal to tax the accumulation of reserves in a second-best world.

These considerations are integrated in a model of the optimal demand for reserves. The resulting demand for reserves is lower than in the benchmark case, which disregards the relationship between reserve accumulation and global crises. First, if countries take into account that their reserve accumulation increases the probability of a global financial crisis, their optimal demand for reserves will be lower. Second, if a supranational authority determines the optimal level of reserves for each country, it internalizes the negative externality and further reduces its demand for reserves. Both effects have not been analyzed in a model of the optimal demand for reserves so far.

The calibrated model shows that the optimal amount of reserves relative to GDP equals 25.6% in the standard model without spillovers. The consideration of systemic risk lowers this number to 17.5%. It amounts to 14.1% after negative externalities have been accounted for. A macroprudential tax might induce the socially optimal level of reserves in a decentralized world. According to our calibration the optimal tax rate equals 1.3% in the benchmark case. The negative externality reinforces the case for supranational reserve pooling since the internalization of the social externality is more probable for larger players.[31]

This re-opens the discussion on the adequate level of international reserves. Arguments in favor of lower reserves point usually to the fiscal opportunity costs of reserves. They disregard that as long as a national currency serves as fiduciary reserves central banks buy a product that – besides being expensive – may not hold its promise. The question whether the medicine is worse than the disease is warranted.

Appendix 5.A   Uses of reserve income: Investment vs. consumption

The critical question here is whether the effect – global reserve accumulation increases the crisis probability in the center – is still economically significant after the possibil-

---

[31] In other words, social relative to private costs decrease in the share of one reserve pool in global reserves.

ity of productive investment has been accounted for. I address this question first on theoretical grounds, then on empirical ones.

As shown in the theoretical section, if reserves raise the center's output via increased investment and if output is the correct measure that backs the real value of the center's liabilities,[32] then the marginal effect of global reserve accumulation on the probability of a financial crisis is lower. In the limiting case, when output growth from investment thanks to reserve income ($f(R_{ROW})$) and R_{ROW} are such that $\frac{B_C^{pr}}{Y_C} = \frac{B_C^{pr}+R_{ROW}}{Y_C(R_{ROW})}$, crisis probability in the center is independent of the demand and provision of reserves. However, as the following considerations show, it might be fair to assume that income from the provision of reserves is only partly invested in productive uses.

There are several reasons one might think of: First, it is questionable whether the center offers enough efficient productive uses to absorb reserve income. One has to remember that capital inflows are not attracted by high yields. They are rather the result of a search for safety, which is linked to habit and persistence.

Second, it has been widely recognized that the demand for reserves in the rest of the world lowers US interest rates (see, among others, Warnock and Cacdac Warnock, 2009 and Krishnamurthy and Vissing-Jorgensen, 2012). As an equilibrium outcome, optimizing agents (private households as well as government) lower savings and increase consumption. That is, reserve income is partly consumed. Figure 5.A.1 shows the declining US saving rate (gross saving as a percentage of GDP) together with the demand for US assets by foreign official entities (relative to GDP). The decline in US saving starts in the early 1980s when also the demand for reserves rises as a consequence of the first systemic crisis of the international monetary system, the Latin American debt crisis, since the demise of the Bretton Woods system. While it would be premature to draw conclusions from this bivariate relationship, it suggests that in the US the increasing demand for reserves has not been saved and invested. External savings rather substituted for domestic ones.

Third, in more general terms, if external liabilities were invested efficiently in productive uses, external indebtedness of countries should not be a reason for concern. The empirical literature, however, finds that high external debt is an early warning indicator for financial crises. This points to an additional argument: Besides the ability to pay, the willingness to pay matters. In sum, if reserve income does not unfold sufficient increases in output, our negative externality of reserve accumulation is present even though reserves are partly invested and increase output.

---

[32] In case of a financial crisis and default in the center, the periphery may confiscate the center's output. However, along the lines of equation (5.8) it might be more realistic to assume that the periphery can confiscate only a fraction of the center's output, that is, confiscable output is given by θY with $0 < \theta < 1$. While the center might be able to pay, it might not be willing to do so. This lowers the ability of the periphery to enforce its claims.

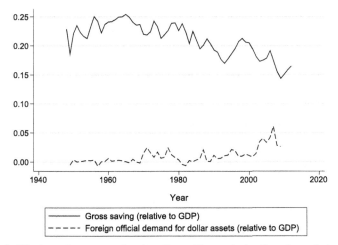

Figure 5.A.1 US: domestic vs. external saving. *Notes:* The graph visualizes the evolution of US gross saving (private and government saving) relative to GDP. The second line shows the demand for dollar assets by foreign official institutions relative to GDP. The demand for dollar assets is calculated as the change in globally held foreign exchange reserves denominated in US dollar.
Data sources: Gross saving: US Department of Commerce: Bureau of Economic Analysis; international reserves: IMF (2013); currency composition of official foreign exchange reserves: IMF Annual Reports and COFER database.

Let us now turn to the question whether our empirical results are compatible with the fact that reserve income may increase output. We find in the probit analysis that (*B/R*) raises the probability of a financial crisis. This effect also holds after controlling for GDP growth. GDP growth itself does not significantly affect the crisis probability. We can therefore conclude that, while there might exist a feedback between reserves and output, (*B/R*) significantly increases the crisis probability independently of the evolution of output. From this it follows that higher global reserves, which increase B_C, raise the crisis probability in the center.

To test whether our empirical finding of a positive relationship between (*B/R*) and the probability of a financial crisis is robust to an alternative scaling by GDP, we replace (*B/R*) by the ratio of *B* to *GDP*. Results for the relevant sample of industrialized countries are presented in Table 5.A.1. It applies the probit analysis with the same set of control variables as in Table 5.3. While the marginal effect of (*B/GDP*) is insignificant in specifications (1) and (2), the effect becomes significant in all specifications after controlling for the growth in REER. I conclude that (*B/GDP*) positively affects the probability of a financial crisis although this effect is not robust across all specifications. Hence, as long as the feedback between reserve income and GDP is sufficiently low and the ratio (*B/GDP*) increases, reserve provision by industrialized countries increases their crisis probability.

Table 5.A.1 **Determinants of financial crises: Industrialized countries (external debt scaled by GDP)**

	(1)	(2)	(3)	(4)	(5)
(B/GDP)	0.2757	0.2986	0.4060*	0.3894*	0.3795*
	(1.29)	(1.39)	(1.90)	(1.85)	(1.84)
GDP growth		1.0451	0.6161	0.9119	1.0242
		(1.44)	(0.56)	(0.81)	(0.90)
Growth in REER			2.5004	2.0888	1.5472
			(1.06)	(0.88)	(0.64)
Current account balance, growth (relative to GDP)				−0.0059	−0.0072
				(−0.28)	(−0.33)
Domestic credit, growth rate (relative to GDP)					0.6730
					(0.78)
Marginal effect of (B/GDP)	0.0686	0.0752	0.0983*	0.0962*	0.0947*
	(1.28)	(1.37)	(1.89)	(1.85)	(1.84)
Observations	624	612	509	492	481
Number of countries	21	21	20	19	19
Pseudo R^2	0.00	0.01	0.01	0.02	0.02
$p >$ chi2	0.20	0.18	0.08	0.15	0.23

Notes: Probit panel regression including random country effects. z-Statistics are reported in parentheses. The symbols *, ** and *** denote statistical significance at the 10%, 5%, and 1% levels, respectively. The marginal effect of (B/GDP) is evaluated at the means of the covariates.

Appendix 5.B   Probit analysis of financial crises

Data

Our data set covers a maximum of 64 countries, among them 20 industrialized, 17 emerging and 27 developing countries. It contains annual data from 1970 to 2010. Since some data are not available for the whole period, the data set is unbalanced. Table 5.B.1 provides details on variable definitions and sources.

Estimation

We perform a multivariate probit panel regression analysis including random country effects. Following the literature on early warning signals for financial crises, we regress a dummy variable for crisis (I) on a set of potential indicators (x). The probability of a crisis is a non-linear function of the indicators and given by

$$Pr\left(I_{i,t}^{crisis} = 1\right) = Pr\left(I_{i,t}^{*} > 0\right) = \Phi(ax_{i,t} + c_i) \tag{5.B.1}$$

where Φ is the standard normal cumulative distribution function, I^* an unobservable latent variable and c_i a random country effect. I takes on the value one in years when a crisis has been identified. In order to concentrate on the onset of crises, the two years that follow a banking, currency or sovereign debt crisis are discarded in the regression analysis. The covariates (x) are lagged to mitigate endogeneity issues. More precisely,

Table 5.B.1 Variable definitions and sources

Variable	Definition and source
Dependent variables	
Currency crisis	Dummy variable that takes on the value one when the annual depreciation rate with respect to the dollar or other relevant anchor currencies equals or exceeds 15%. *Source:* Reinhart and Rogoff (2011).
Sovereign debt crisis	Dummy variable equals one in years where an external debt crisis (sovereign default, failure of payments) and/or domestic debt crisis (freezing and/or forced currency conversion of deposits) is identified. *Source:* Reinhart and Rogoff (2011).
Banking crisis	Dummy variable takes on the value one when an important financial institution is merged, closed or taken over by the public sector or if the same happens to at least one financial institution after a bank run. *Source:* Reinhart and Rogoff (2011).
Financial crisis	A financial crisis is defined as the occurrence of a currency crisis, sovereign debt crisis or banking crisis or a combination of them.
Independent variables	
External debt relative to reserves (B/R)	External debt is measured as total foreign liabilities minus total foreign assets. This concept of net external debt is consistent with our theoretical model. *Source:* Lane and Milesi-Ferretti (2007) and update. Reserves are defined as total official reserve assets. *Source:* IMF (2011a).
Nominal GDP	The analysis uses the growth rate of nominal GDP. *Source:* World Bank (2011).
Growth in REER	Growth rate of the real effective exchange rate is calculated over the preceding three years based on an REER index. An increase corresponds to an appreciation of the domestic currency. *Source:* World Bank (2011).
Current account balance	Balance of the current account relative to GDP. The analysis uses the growth rate of this variable. *Source:* World Bank (2011).
Domestic credit	Domestic credit provided by the banking sector (relative to GDP). Analysis uses the growth rate of this variable. *Source:* World Bank (2011).
Government debt	Total (domestic plus external) gross central government debt relative to GDP (in %). *Source:* Reinhart and Rogoff (2011).

since crises rather result from persistent, long-term developments than cyclical deviations, we average all covariates over the preceding three years.[33] In particular, we include the following independent variables: The level of net external debt relative to total reserves, denoted by (B/R), is our variable of interest. The growth rate of nominal GDP is expected to affect the crisis probability negatively. Boom periods with high economic growth are characterized by a low incidence of crises. The behavior of REER is measured as the growth rate of an index of the real effective exchange rate. An appreciating real exchange rate (equivalent to an increase in the index) is expected to increase the probability of a crisis because it might lead to exchange rate overvaluation. The average growth rate of the current account balance relative to GDP over the preceding three years accounts for potential balance-of-payments problems: The lower this growth rate, the higher the probability of a financial crisis. The expansion of domestic credit relative to GDP has been identified as an important predictor for financial crises (see Jordà et al., 2013; Schularick and Taylor, 2012). We therefore include the growth rate of domestic credit, averaged over the preceding three years, as an explanatory variable. The regressions for sovereign debt crises additionally include the level of government debt relative to GDP.

The partial effect of a change in one variable on the crisis probability is not constant, but depends on the value of the other variables. Therefore, marginal effects are provided for our variable of interest (B/R). These show the impact of a one-unit change in the regressor on the probability of a crisis evaluated at the mean of the data.

Results

Section 5.4 of the main text provides estimation results for the determinants of financial crises (see Table 5.3). Financial crises are defined as the occurrence of a banking, currency and/or sovereign debt crisis. The dependent variable takes on the value one if the onset of at least one type of crisis can be identified in a given year. Here we report the results for specific types of crises.

The role of external debt over reserves on the way to currency crises seems to be restricted to emerging markets, where higher reserves reduce the probability of a crisis (see Table 5.B.2). In the sub-samples of industrialized and developing countries (B/R) does not significantly affect the incidence of currency crises. While in emerging markets the growth in REER seems to be an important driver of crises, high growth of GDP lowers the probability of a currency crisis in developing countries.

With respect to crises in the banking sector (Table 5.B.3), crisis incidence in industrial countries and emerging markets increases the level of external debt over reserves. In the full sample the growth in REER is positively associated with crises. While this effect seems to be primarily present in developing countries, banking crises in emerging markets are positively associated with decreasing current account balances.

The specifications for sovereign debt crises (see Table 5.B.4) include the level of sovereign debt relative to GDP averaged over the three preceding years as an additional covariate. Because of a low number of crisis events in industrialized countries,

---

[33] To increase the number of observations we rely on the average value of external debt over reserves over the preceding two periods only when the third lag is not available.

Table 5.B.2 Determinants of currency crises

	Full sample		Industrialized countries		Emerging markets		Developing countries	
	(1)	(2)	(3)	(4)	(5)	(6)	(7)	(8)
(B/R)	0.0021*	0.0009	−0.0049	−0.0017	0.0722***	0.1141***	0.0018	0.0009
	(1.87)	(0.84)	(−0.57)	(−0.20)	(4.70)	(3.06)	(1.54)	(0.75)
GDP growth		−0.8021		0.1246		3.4956		−2.4894**
		(−1.08)		(0.08)		(1.42)		(−2.42)
Growth in REER		−1.6164		4.3077		−6.2909**		−2.0058
		(−1.64)		(1.38)		(−2.05)		(−1.63)
Current account balance growth (relative to GDP)		−0.0267		−0.0330		0.0852		−0.0725
		(−1.10)		(−1.15)		(1.14)		(−1.01)
Domestic credit, growth rate (relative to GDP)		0.6933		−0.5330		1.6599		1.0491
		(1.34)		(−0.40)		(1.13)		(1.58)
Marginal effect of (B/R)	0.0005*	0.0002	−0.0009	−0.0003	0.0210***	0.0237***	0.0004	0.00002
	(1.68)	(0.84)	(−0.57)	(−0.20)	(4.20)	(3.05)	(1.53)	(0.75)
Observations	1564	814	491	376	397	133	693	305
Number of countries	63	45	20	18	17	8	27	19
Pseudo R^2	0.00	0.02	0.00	0.02	0.06	0.13	0.00	0.07
$p >$ chi2	0.06	0.06	0.57	0.45	0.00	0.03	0.12	0.00

Notes: z-Statistics are reported in parentheses. The symbols *, **, and *** denote statistical significance at the 10%, 5%, and 1% levels, respectively. The marginal effect of (B/R) is evaluated at the means of the covariates.

Table 5.B.3 **Determinants of banking crises**

	Full sample		Industrialized countries		Emerging markets		Developing countries	
	(1)	(2)	(3)	(4)	(5)	(6)	(7)	(8)
(B/R)	0.0017*	0.0014	0.0225***	0.0195***	0.0118	0.0562*	0.0015	0.0009
	(1.90)	(1.51)	(2.96)	(2.62)	(1.07)	(1.93)	(1.49)	(0.93)
GDP growth		−0.8020		1.8417		1.0233		−1.9870*
		(−1.13)		(1.21)		(0.48)		(−1.87)
Growth in REER		1.3004*		−3.1186		1.6280		1.9223*
		(1.88)		(−1.01)		(0.77)		(1.84)
Current account balance, growth (relative to GDP)		−0.0213		0.0180		−0.1448*		−0.0884
		(−1.05)		(0.57)		(−1.81)		(−1.48)
Domestic credit, growth rate (relative to GDP)		0.6252		1.5324		0.6796		0.3838
		(1.26)		(1.35)		(0.47)		(0.59)
Marginal effect of (B/R)	0.0003**	0.0003	0.0032***	0.0195***	0.0024	0.0123*	0.0002	0.0002
	(1.89)	(1.51)	(2.89)	(2.62)	(1.07)	(1.94)	(1.50)	(0.93)
Observations	1724	857	538	392	459	135	756	330
Number of countries	63	45	20	18	17	8	27	19
Pseudo R^2	0.00	0.02	0.03	0.05	0.00	0.10	0.00	0.07
$p > chi2$	0.06	0.06	0.00	0.07	0.28	0.20	0.14	0.07

Notes: z-Statistics are reported in parentheses. The symbols *, **, and *** denote statistical significance at the 10%, 5%, and 1% levels, respectively. The marginal effect of (B/R) is evaluated at the means of the covariates.

Table 5.B.4 Determinants of sovereign debt crises

	Full sample		Emerging markets		Developing countries	
	(1)	(2)	(3)	(4)	(5)	(6)
(B/R)	0.0102***	0.0075	0.1280***	0.3131***	0.0068***	0.0027
	(3.37)	(0.85)	(6.18)	(2.91)	(2.60)	(0.59)
GDP growth		−0.8860		1.3707		−0.6348
		(−0.72)		(0.33)		(−0.43)
Growth in REER		−5.6293***		−6.0275		−5.1462***
		(−3.98)		(−1.10)		(−3.41)
Current account balance, growth (relative to GDP)		0.0425		0.0998		0.0394
		(1.34)		(1.64)		(0.53)
Domestic credit, growth rate (relative to GDP)		−0.1929		−0.0465		0.0900
		(−0.23)		(−0.02)		(0.09)
Government debt (relative to GDP)		0.0154***		0.0118		0.0132***
		(3.93)		(1.08)		(2.99)
Marginal effect of (B/R)	0.0012***	0.0003	0.0128***	0.0063	0.0018**	0.0027
	(2.68)	(0.75)	(2.94)	(0.76)	(2.48)	(0.59)
Observations	1712	841	485	143	654	242
Number of countries	63	43	17	8	27	17
Pseudo R^2	0.02	0.17	0.51	0.02	0.02	0.16
$p >$ chi2	0.00	0.00	0.00	0.07	0.01	0.00

Notes: z-Statistics are reported in parentheses. The symbols *, **, and *** denote statistical significance at the 10%, 5%, and 1% levels, respectively. The marginal effect of (B/R) is evaluated at the means of the covariates.

this subsample cannot be analyzed individually. External debt over reserves positively affects the crisis incidence across all samples in the bivariate regressions; this effect, however, vanishes when other covariates are included. A depreciation of the real effective exchange rate and high levels of government debt turn out to be important determinants of sovereign debt crises.

Independently of the type of crisis, the explanatory power of our set of covariates is low as indicated by small values of R^2. That is, we can neither explain nor predict the occurrence of crises. For our purpose, however, it suffices that we identify reserves as an instrument that significantly affects the probability of crises.

Global Aspects of Central Bank Policies

Contents

6.1 Reform of the international monetary system in light of our findings 161
Lowering the demand for reserves 162
Diversification of reserves among various currencies 163
Provision of a supranational reserve asset 164
Domestic distortions 164
6.2 Global liquidity and central bank cooperation 164
6.2.1 Global liquidity spillovers 164
6.2.2 The political economy of central bank cooperation 165
Central bank cooperation in reserve policies 167
6.3 The Target system in the Euro area 168
6.4 Outlook 171

This concluding chapter relates our findings to various aspects of global central banking: First, we provide suggestions for a reform of the international monetary system in order to reduce the instabilities highlighted in this book. Second, we explain how financial integration and global liquidity spillovers have changed central bank cooperation. Finally, by describing the interbank payment system of the European Union (Target) we show that Target balances may be considered as a substitute for reserves; alike reserves they contribute to balance-of-payments imbalances.

6.1 Reform of the international monetary system in light of our findings

One challenge in economics is to assess the consequences of policies: While interest often focuses on a bivariate causal relationship, changes in one variable may cause a variety of effects: They may affect a number of other variables leading to manifold outcomes including unexpected consequences, namely beneficial windfalls or effects that are opposed to original intentions. There might be feedback effects and external effects that have to be taken into account. Finally, when policies affect incentives, economic agents change their behavior and the Lucas critique applies (Lucas, 1976).

This book attempts to shed light on the unintended global effects of central banks' reserve policies. In particular, we measure empirically the economic impact of central bank policies, namely the effect of official capital flows resulting from exchange market interventions. While the existing literature usually focuses on the effects of reserve policies on domestic variables, their global effects and externalities take center stage

Global Imbalances, Financial Crises, and Central Bank Policies
Copyright © 2016 Elsevier Inc. All rights reserved.

in our analysis. We show that global reserve accumulation lowers both the current account balance and the public budget balance of the center country of the international monetary system.

This finding provides a new interpretation of the twin deficit hypothesis. While we do not find a causal relationship between current account and public budget balances, we show that a third factor, namely reserve currency status, is responsible for their co-movement. The accumulation of net dollar reserves in the rest of the world lowers the current account balance of the reserve currency country. Since reserves are predominantly invested in Treasury bonds, the same transaction also lowers the government budget balance.

These lower balances might destabilize the financial system of the center country in the long run. Chapter 5 integrates these findings in a model of the optimal demand for reserves and shows that the optimal reserve level is significantly lower when negative externalities are accounted for.

What are the implications of this analysis for a possible reform of the international monetary system? Policies intended to lower the global demand for reserves would reduce the privilege of the reserve currency country and weaken the negative effects on its balances.

Besides taxing the accumulation of reserves, which has been proposed in Chapter 5, there exist several alternative policy options to reduce the probability of global crises emanating from countries' desire for reserves. A first approach could aim at lowering the demand for reserves. This option comes closest to the solution a social planner would implement in our model. Second, since instabilities stem from the fact that a national currency serves as reserve currency, the introduction of a supranational reserve asset alleviates the problem. Third, given that the reserve demand is linked to the external indebtedness of private agents, who disregard the social costs of their borrowing decisions, a removal of these domestic distortions might reduce the demand for reserves. Finally, cooperation between central banks reduces the demand for reserves. We discuss these options in the following subsections.

Lowering the demand for reserves

Besides lowering the demand for reserves by raising their costs (taxation), one might prefer to rely on market-based instruments: The provision of substitutes for reserves should reduce their demand.

Credible mechanisms of crisis management might be a substitute. To this end, the IMF has adjusted its lending facilities with the intention of creating a global financial safety net: It redefined its Flexible Credit Line (FCL) making it more generous and introduced the Precautionary Credit Line (PCL) aiming to provide crisis prevention for countries that do not meet the high standards of sound policies as required for the FCL. Despite increased transparency and access, those safety nets are only imperfect substitutes for reserves because there will always be selectivity and conditionality in the access to international liquidity.

The pooling of reserves provides another means of lowering the worldwide demand for reserves. Besides economies of scale, regional reserve pools prevent inefficient competitive hoarding games. First steps in this direction are the Chiang Mai Initiative in Asia and the Latin American Reserve Fund (FLAR).

Diversification of reserves among various currencies

Alternatively, one might encourage the diversification of reserves into various competing reserve currencies. The present system is characterized by the dominant role of the US dollar. This dominance, which emerged endogenously, implies that the quantitative effects of rising global reserves on the US current account and public budget balances are significant. If world reserves are no longer concentrated in the currency of a single country, the negative effects on the reserve currency country are spread between several countries. This statement is corroborated by our regression results for secondary reserve currency countries: Effects on these countries are often insignificant.

In this regard, the Chinese policy of Renminbi internationalization[1] might not only be in the Chinese interest (see Cheung et al., 2011), but also beneficial from a global perspective. Since 2008, China has put forward a number of initiatives to promote the international role of the Renminbi. Noteworthy are the following projects: In 2009 a pilot scheme was launched that allowed selected firms to settle trade between five Chinese cities and Asian partner countries in Renminbi. Controls on FDI and portfolio investment flows have been relaxed. Next, the development of an offshore market in Hong Kong for Renminbi-denominated bonds was fostered; while the largest share of Renminbi bonds is issued by firms from China, international firms have also made use of this new instrument. Finally, the Executive Board of the IMF accepted the Chinese request and decided to include the Renminbi as fifth currency in the SDR basket beginning in October 2016.[2] Since this internationalization strategy helps to reduce the Chinese currency mismatch between assets and liabilities – its assets are predominantly denominated in foreign currency while liabilities are held in Renminbi, it lowers the Chinese exposure to exchange rate risk and thereby contributes to a stabilizing role of China in the world economy. As a side effect of deeper and more liquid domestic financial markets, these steps might contribute to a growing role of the Renminbi in central banks' international reserves.

However, a multicurrency reserve currency system might also create instabilities: Substitution among reserve currencies increases the volatility of exchange rates (see Canzoneri et al., 2013 for an analysis of the effects of a sudden sale of reserve assets on fundamentals and potential policy responses). Monetary history has shown that except for periods of transition the financial system has been based on a single dominant reserve currency.

---

[1] There are various aspects that make a currency international including its use in trade settlement, for investment, as denomination in bond issuances on international markets and as a reserve currency at central banks.

[2] For studies on the Renminbi internationalization strategy see, among others, Chen and Cheung (2011), Eichengreen (2011) and Eichengreen and Kawai (2014).

Provision of a supranational reserve asset

Systematic problems might be mitigated by international financial institutions that are endowed to create outside liquidity in a crisis. However, any lender of last resort creates moral hazard problems if support is expected. The IMF might be endowed with additional financial resources to be able to credibly assist countries during crises. This might be accomplished by the creation of new SDRs. In fact, SDRs were created in 1969 as a response to the lack of safe reserve assets under the Bretton Woods system of fixed exchange rates. To separate the creation of SDRs from political pressures, their increase could be automatized with SDRs increasing with worldwide real output growth.[3] However, the use of SDRs as reserve assets also contains pitfalls: SDRs are only backed by the credibility and liquidity of the IMF. A national currency, however, is at least backed by GDP of the issuing country.

Domestic distortions

The discussion of policies that lower the demand for reserves has shown that, while desirable, their implementation in a decentralized world is a delicate endeavor. Individual countries are autonomous in their reserve policies and due to political economy considerations might prefer to continue their policy of reserve hoarding in a second-best world.

We have justified the taxation of reserve hoardings by the presence of policy distortions and market failures. An alternative might be to address the distortions that cause excessive private borrowing and lending directly along the lines described in Aizenman and Turnovsky (2002). Excessive borrowing may be derived in a financial amplification framework in the spirit of Bernanke and Gertler (1989) and Kiyotaki and Moore (1997), where external finance is collateral constrained. If individual agents sell assets, this reduces the price of the collateral. Hence, capital outflows in a crisis are magnified because financial constraints become binding as asset prices and aggregate demand fall. A social planner that reduces the level of debt would also mitigate the negative amplification effects during crises. It might be easier to resolve these externalities at the domestic level than those arising at the global level. Lower levels of external debt might then lower the demand for reserves and hence mitigate the negative externality of reserve accumulation.

6.2   Global liquidity and central bank cooperation

6.2.1   Global liquidity spillovers

Liquidity may be defined as "ease of financing"; global liquidity then refers to the ease of financing in the global financial system (see Caruana, 2014). It is driven by market participants' attitudes toward risk, by their willingness to extend credit and central

---

[3] See IMF (2011b) and Obstfeld (2011c) for proposals concerning the future of SDRs.

bank actions. It affects monetary and financial stability as well as the real economy. It is often mentioned as a possible cause of capital inflows, exchange rate appreciations and global imbalances. Global liquidity is more fragile than domestic one because it is often characterized by currency transformation, the involvement of multiple regulatory institutions and a lack of global collateral.

The rise of the term global liquidity goes hand in hand with financial integration: Financial integration defined as both capital mobility and market participants' access to external financial resources is the precondition for global liquidity being a meaningful concept. Only if capital is globally mobile, global conditions determine local financing conditions. This, however, implies that the leeway of the domestic central bank is limited.

Passari and Rey (2015) identify a global financial cycle in capital flows, credit growth and asset prices. Monetary policy in the center country is one of its determinants. With free capital mobility it constrains national monetary policy regardless of the exchange rate system. This reduces the macroeconomic trilemma, which states that an independent monetary policy, fixed exchange rates and capital mobility are mutually inconsistent, to a dilemma: In order to regain monetary policy autonomy, central banks have to restrict capital mobility (see Rey, 2015).

As Landau (2013) emphasizes global liquidity is created by both private agents and official entities. If reserve accumulation goes hand in hand with an increase in the supply of assets of the reserve currency country, it creates liquidity. From the viewpoint of the accumulating country additional liquidity is generated as long as it is not fully sterilized. In particular, the IMF (2010b) finds a strong transmission from global liquidity expansion to asset prices, which works through the accumulation of reserves. Moreover, if the resulting monetary expansion is not fully sterilized and exceeds the growth of money demand, the accumulation of reserves might result in inflationary pressures according to the quantity theory of money.

These considerations show that central banks' reserve accumulation may create spillovers in addition to the externalities examined in the previous chapters. This calls for cooperative central banking across borders, whose past and prospects are addressed briefly in the following section.

6.2.2 The political economy of central bank cooperation

Central banks are national institutions, whose mandate focuses on national variables like inflation and economic growth. As such cooperation is only indicated when it is in the national interest.

At the beginning of central banking cooperation took place on an ad-hoc basis, especially in the face of banking crises (i.e. Baring crisis in 1890 and the 1907 financial crisis). In 1930, when the Bank for International Settlements (BIS) was founded, central bank cooperation was institutionalized. Under the Bretton Woods system of fixed exchange rates, central banks cooperated to keep exchange rates stable despite increasing capital mobility and divergent monetary policies. While the breakdown of the Bretton Woods system and the transition to flexible exchange rate regimes reduced the need for cooperation, increasing real and financial integration as well as the internationalization of banking implied that countries have become more inter-dependent. This gave new impetus to central bank cooperation because capital flow surges, crisis contagion and spillovers threaten financial stability, which moved to the forefront of central bank concerns. Recently the global financial crisis has highlighted both global interdependencies and central bank flexibility: Major central banks estab-lished currency swap lines to limit spillover effects and contain repercussions on other markets.[4]

To the extent that the global financial crisis has widened the spectrum of central bank functions – moving from the traditional goal of price stability to the broader objectives of macroeconomic and financial stability, it also opened up the fields for central bank cooperation. The crisis itself has shown how financial instabilities spread around the globe. This has demonstrated that financial stability requires macropruden-tial tools at the domestic level (i.e. countercyclical capital adequacy requirements) to be complemented by international coordination.

As Morris and Shin (2008) point out ensuring the soundness of each individual financial institution does not imply the soundness of the entire system. This insight may be transferred to the relationship between the soundness of individual countries' financial system and the global monetary system. Macroprudential policies in each in-dividual country are a precondition for global stability; however, stability also requires the containment of systemic risks at the global level. This calls for the cooperation be-tween central banks, supervisory agencies and supranational institutions like the IMF.

Even if the pursuit of financial stability and macroprudential surveillance is dele-gated to another national institution (e.g. macroprudential supervisory board, systemic risk board) the central bank has to be involved in the decision process given that there may be trade-offs between monetary policy and macroprudential measures. The dis-cussion of global spillovers has made clear that cooperation is also indicated at the international and supranational level. Examples are the Financial Sector Assessment Program (FSAP) of IMF and World Bank (established in 1999) and the European Sys-temic Risk Board (ESRB) of the European Union (founded in 2010 as a response to the crisis).

While this book focuses on the externality of reserve accumulation to justify cen-tral bank cooperation, the scope of spillovers is much wider and calls for cooperation in monetary policy in general. Financial integration implies that the stocks of cross-border assets and liabilities that respond to changes in monetary conditions have grown enormously. Global capital flows and the global financial cycle may be shaped by monetary policy in major economies. Unconventional monetary policies like quan-titative easing have been found to affect capital flows to emerging markets and their exchange rates considerably (see, among others, Bhattarai et al., 2015 and Tillmann, 2014). Major central banks tended to focus on the domestic consequences of the global crisis; this initialized a debate on *currency wars* and *competitive devaluations* (see Frankel, forthcoming).

---

[4] In October 2008 the US Federal Reserve opened swap lines amounting to US$30 billion to Brazil, Ko-rea, Mexico and Singapore. The People's Bank of China (PBC) provided bilateral swap lines, among other countries, to Hong Kong, Indonesia and Malaysia during the crisis. These swap lines were ad-hoc measures, only provided to selected countries and of short-term or unknown duration.

Central bank cooperation in reserve policies

Might independent central banks be willing to cooperate in order to stabilize the international financial system? Important lessons might be drawn from two historical episodes, when major central banks agreed to coordinate their reserve policies in order to preserve the stability of the monetary system.

One example is the Gold Pool, which was established in 1961 by the United States and seven European countries under the gold–dollar standard of the Bretton Woods system. The arrangement aimed at stabilizing the price of gold in terms of dollars to prevent a depletion of US gold reserves. Analogously to the current issue of reserve accumulation, it is an example where individual and collective interests of central banks differ. Arbitrage transactions by individual central banks were individually rational, but collectively undesirable: They reduced US gold reserves and questioned the US commitment to exchange gold for dollars at the fixed price. The Gold Pool intended to prevent this depletion of US gold reserves by driving the market price to the official price. This cooperation worked as long as the market price fell below the official price and the Pool was a net buyer of gold. However, when the market price rose and the Pool sold gold for dollars, the arrangement collapsed. Individual central banks left the pool or engaged in offsetting transactions – they bought gold when the pool sold gold.[5]

A second example of central bank coordination in reserve policies is the Central Bank Gold Agreement. A number of central banks – especially in industrial countries – aim for getting rid of their large reserve holdings in the form of gold. Knowing that a simultaneous sale of gold decreases its price, they agreed to coordinate their sales of gold. The first Central Bank Gold Agreement was signed in 1999 by 14 European central banks for the purpose of limiting the amount of gold to be sold in the following 5 years. The signatories roughly made up 50% of worldwide official gold holdings. This agreement was renewed in 2004, 2009 and 2014. Although the accumulation of foreign exchange has similar price effects – it lowers the interest rate in the reserve currency country and thereby decreases the return on reserve assets – central banks do not coordinate their reserve policies when it comes to foreign exchange accumulation.[6]

Cooperation might be intensified in the future. The extension of swap lines between central banks, pioneered during the financial crisis of 2008–10, might become a standardized instrument to tackle future global crises (see Aizenman et al., 2011). Swap lines may be considered as a form of borrowed reserves. As part of the internationalization of its currency, China has signed bilateral swap agreements with more than 20 partner countries since 2008, including Asian countries in the framework of the Chiang Mai Initiative, industrialized countries like the EU, the UK and Australia and other emerging markets like Argentina, Brazil and Turkey.

[5] For a detailed description of the Gold Pool refer to Eichengreen (2007), Chapter 2.

[6] There exists, however, an 'automatic stabilizer effect': Since the massive accumulation of reserves reduces the interest rate paid on reserves, it increases reserves' opportunity costs defined as the difference between the domestic cost of capital and the return on reserves. As a consequence, theory predicts that this slows down the accumulation of reserves.

6.3   The Target system in the Euro area

A book on current account imbalances, crises and the global aspects of central bank policies would be incomplete without making reference to the Target system of the European Union and its relation to intra-European imbalances. Target is a unique example of how official capital flows sustain current account imbalances in a monetary union. Moreover, we will show that Target balances may be considered as a substitute for reserves because they fulfill the same tasks as reserves outside a monetary union. While this section focuses on aspects related to our book, we refrain from describing the mechanism of the Target system in detail and do not provide an interpretation of Target balances. These issues may be found in the brilliant book of Hans-Werner Sinn (Sinn, 2014), who in early 2011 brought the issue of rising Target balances to public attention.

Target (Trans-European Automated Real-Time Gross Settlement Express Transfer System) is the interbank payment system for the real-time processing of cross-border transfers throughout the European Union. It is owned and operated by the Eurosystem (European Central Bank and national central banks of the members of the Euro area). Target2, the second generation of the Target system, was implemented in 2007.

Figure 6.1 shows stylized central bank balance sheets for a monetary union with Target system: Central bank assets consist of domestic bonds or refinancing credit (B) and international reserves (R) whereas currency in circulation (M) and reserve accounts of commercial banks (D) figure on the liability side. Central banks operating within the Target system may also accumulate Target assets (TA) and incur Target liabilities (TL). In the consolidated balance sheet of the currency union Target balances have to cancel out by construction.

To illustrate the mechanism of the Target system, we shortly describe how a cross-border transaction works through the system: Imagine that person A in country A

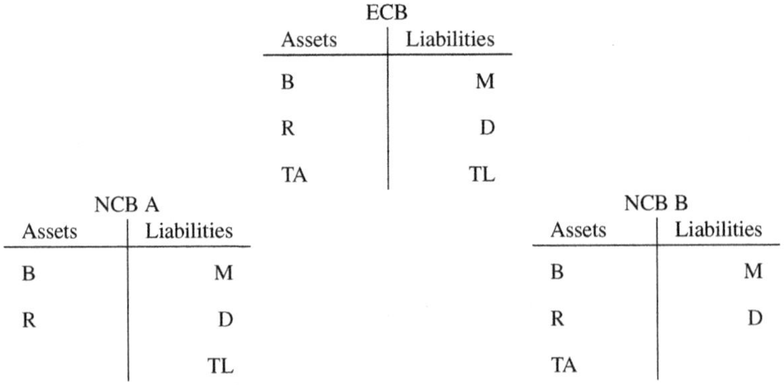

Figure 6.1 Central bank balance sheets in Target system. *Notes:* The figure shows stylized balance sheets for the European Central Bank (ECB) and two national central banks (NCB A and NCB B). Central bank assets consist of domestic bonds or refinancing credit (B) and international reserves (R) whereas currency in circulation (M) and reserve accounts of commercial banks (D) figure on the liability side. National central banks may accumulate Target assets (TA) and incur Target liabilities (TL).

Mr. A

Assets	Liabilities
B	$FW\downarrow$
$D^{bs}\downarrow$	
M	

Bank A

Assets	Liabilities
B	$D^{bs}\downarrow$
$D^{cb}\downarrow$	

NCB A

Assets	Liabilities
B	M
R	$D^{cb}\downarrow$
	$TL\uparrow$

Mr. B

Assets	Liabilities
B	$FW\uparrow$
$D^{bs}\uparrow$	
M	

Bank B

Assets	Liabilities
B	$D^{bs}\uparrow$
$D^{cb}\uparrow$	

NCB B

Assets	Liabilities
B	M
R	$D^{cb}\uparrow$
$TA\uparrow$	

Figure 6.2 Accounting entries of a cross-border transaction. *Notation:* D^{bs} = private deposits in banking system; D^{cb} = deposits of commercial banks on the reserve account at the central bank; TA = Target assets; TL = Target liabilities; FW = financial wealth.

imports a good from country B. In order to pay the good, the buyer transfers money from his account with commercial bank A to the account of the supplier at commercial bank B. To be more precise, the commercial bank of the buyer reduces its liabilities to the buyer (charges the amount to his account) and reduces its assets because it asks central bank A to deduct the amount from its reserve account. Central bank A then instructs central bank B to transfer the money to the commercial bank B of the supplier. As a consequence, assets of this commercial bank increase in its reserve account with central bank B. At the same time, its liabilities increase because it credits the amount to the account of the supplier. These transactions are visualized in Figure 6.2. The example assumes that commercial bank A's reserve account exceeds the minimum reserve requirement such that reserves do not have to be restocked in response to this transfer.

Of special interest is how the transaction between both central banks is settled: In the case of two independent central banks without Target-like agreement, the transaction includes a transfer of assets from central bank A to central bank B. Typically reserves are sold. Under the Target system, however, there is no transfer of assets between both central banks: Central bank A incurs Target liabilities with respect to central bank B, which accumulates Target assets.[7]

Target assets can be considered as a form of credit: Whereas normally balance of payments imbalances have to be financed by the sale of reserves, under Target national central banks accumulating Target assets provide a credit to the country that incurs Target liabilities. The special feature of the Target system is that the credit

---

[7] In practice, all central bank transactions go through the ECB. Therefore, assets and liabilities are officially held with the European System of Central Banks (ESCB).

is extended automatically without individual approval of the creditor central bank. Moreover, Target balances are not limited by an upper bound.

As long as real and financial flows are balanced, Target is only an accounting system. If, however, current and capital account do not sum up to zero, Target assets and liabilities arise. That is, Target balances arise in the face of net cross-border capital flows. These might be the result of a current account deficit that is not financed by private capital inflows or capital flight, that is, an unbalanced capital account. Both transactions imply that home agents exchange domestic central bank money for foreign one. Westermann (2014) shows that the increase in Target balances may be rather described as a flight from low quality assets than as a flight of deposits.

In case of a current account deficit, the transfer is used to pay the foreign provider of goods and services. In the case of capital flight, the home agent invests money in the foreign country or repays the foreign investor who withdraws its money from the domestic economy. The main difference between both transactions is that in the first case foreign agents hold additional bonds, while in the second the international investment position of private agents in the home country increases.

We now focus on the effects of net cross-border capital flows on central bank balance sheets. In order to highlight the particularities of a currency union with Target system, we start with the case of two independent central banks that supply their own money. Assume that country A and country B use different currencies as means of payment.[8] A cross-border financial transfer from country A to country B has the following implications: NCB_A loses reserves, which lowers central bank money: Either it debits commercial banks' reserve account by the value of the provided reserves or the amount of currency in circulation is reduced if reserves are provided in exchange for cash. In sum, the balance sheet of NCB_A is contracted. Sterilization via the provision of refinancing credit allows NCB_A to restore the balance sheet total and to keep the amount of central bank money constant. The balance sheet of NCB_B is affected by opposed transactions: The net inflow of money increases its reserves and its liabilities to the banking sector. The increase in central bank money can be sterilized through a reduction in refinancing credit.

Note that for both NCBs the transaction changes the supply of central bank money in the first place. Sterilization implies that the balance sheet total remains constant and the transactions materialize as an accounting exchange on the asset side. The maximum amount of sterilization, however, is limited: When NCB_B's assets are entirely held in the form of foreign exchange, further inflows of reserves cannot be sterilized. Comparably, the external resources of NCB_A are limited. When NCB_A has lost all reserves, assets consist solely of domestic bonds and cross-border payments can no longer be financed.

In a currency union with Target system the same net capital flows affect central bank balance sheets in the following way: Since we only consider transactions within the currency union, the aggregate balance sheet of the system of central banks remains unchanged. NCB_A increases refinancing credit and accumulates liabilities with

---

[8] Assume that the reserve asset, which is used for international transactions, is provided by a third country or a supranational agency.

respect to the foreign central bank (Target liabilities increase).[9] Note that the Target position basically assumes the function played by reserves of an individual central bank operating outside a currency union with Target system: While an independent central bank runs down its reserves to finance a balance of payments deficit, a national central bank operating in a currency union accumulates liabilities toward other member central banks. NCB_B registers opposing effects: Its refinancing credit decreases while its Target assets increase.

However, analogously to the case of independent central banks, the capacity to sterilize within a currency union is limited. Sterilization implies that domestic assets decrease in the country with capital inflows. When domestic bonds of NCB_B reach zero, Target balances reach their upper limit and further capital inflows cannot be sterilized. The increase in reserves is replaced by an increase in claims toward the other central bank. In other words, while outside a currency union assets are transferred between central banks, within a union this transaction is replaced by a claim on the assets of the other central bank.[10]

In sum, the Target system has two main implications that are related to our analysis: First, Target balances are the result of official capital flows. Central banks of deficit countries create additional central bank money that flows to surplus countries (see Sinn and Wollmershäuser, 2012). Target balances sustain balance of payments imbalances just as reserves finance a balance of payments deficit. As such they are another example of the relationship between official capital and imbalances. Second, while it seems problematic that there is no upper limit on Target balances, in the short run they help to smooth adjustment processes to external and internal shocks. As a substitute for reserves, the existence of a Target system is expected to lower the demand for international reserves.

There exists also an analogy with central bank swap lines, which have been institutionalized during the recent financial crisis. While a swap line allows the central bank to transfer money without making recurrence to its stock of reserves, Target liabilities allow money transactions without transfer of securities. As such, Target assets can be interpreted as a swap line provided to the central bank that incurs Target liabilities.

6.4 Outlook

The intention of this book was to highlight the global dimension of central bank actions, in particular of their reserve policies. Domestic reserve policies are shown to contribute to global imbalances. They affect fundamentals – the current account balance and the public budget balance – of reserve-providing countries. Finally, they might contribute to systemic risk and lay the ground for a global financial crisis.

---

[9] Provided that the commercial bank does not hold excess reserves on its reserve account with NCB_A, it has to provide collateral to NCB_A to finance the transaction. This increases refinancing credit of NCB_A.

[10] While the described system of target claims and liabilities corresponds to the practice in the Eurosystem, net capital flows within the Federal Reserve System induce de facto movements of bonds between districts' Federal Reserve Banks. Liabilities are settled once a year by the transfer of gold certificates.

Given that the existing literature on reserve hoardings mostly takes a domestic view by emphasizing the benefits of reserves as a buffer against external shocks, this book has widened this perspective by incorporating the international spillovers of reserve policies in the analysis. This re-opens the debate on the optimal amount of reserves. The structure of the international monetary system plays a fundamental role: As long as national assets of particular countries constitute the dominant global reserve assets, the system is characterized by a dichotomy between countries of the center and the periphery. They depend on each other: While the periphery trusts in the liquidity of the reserve assets and their stable purchasing power, the center's financial system may be destabilized if the periphery suddenly sells its reserve assets.

This study, however, does not aim at providing ideas for a reform of the international monetary system in the first place. These are expressed in a series of recent papers (see Alessandrini and Fratianni, 2009; Eichengreen, 2009; Farhi et al., 2011; Mateos y Lago et al., 2009). The provided empirical facts rather emphasize the relevance of these papers and might enliven the urgent debate about the future of the international monetary system.

The book's focus on official capital emphasizes that global capital markets are not only driven by private capital but also by official institutions' investment decisions. Depending on time period and specific country, official capital in the form of international reserves and development aid has played an important role both in smoothing adjustment processes and in creating risks. The literature on official capital has emerged only recently and there are many open questions: How do private and official capital flows differ in determining consumption and growth volatility? Should the definition of financial integration discriminate between private and official capital stocks? Do official capital flows crowd in or crowd out private capital? These are only examples of questions that may be addressed by future research. While I hope that this book is interesting in itself, it also intends to foster future research on these issues.

Bibliography

Accominotti, Olivier, 2009. The sterling trap: foreign reserves management at the Bank of France, 1928–1936. European Review of Economic History 13, 349–376.

Accominotti, Olivier, Flandreau, Marc, Rezzik, Riad, 2011. The spread of empire: Clio and the measurement of colonial borrowing costs. The Economic History Review 64 (2), 385–407.

Aizenman, Joshua, 2010. On the causes of global imbalances and their persistence: myths, facts and conjectures. In: Claessens, Stijn, Evenett, Simon J., Hoekman, Bernard (Eds.), Rebalancing the Global Economy: A Primer for Policymaking. CEPR, London.

Aizenman, Joshua, 2011. Hoarding international reserves versus a Pigovian tax-cum-subsidy scheme: reflections on the deleveraging crisis of 2008–2009, and a cost benefit analysis. Journal of Economic Dynamics and Control 35 (9), 1502–1513.

Aizenman, Joshua, Edwards, Sebastian, Riera-Crichton, Daniel, 2012. Adjustment patterns to commodity terms of trade shocks: the role of exchange rate and international reserves policies. Journal of International Money and Finance 31 (8), 1990–2016.

Aizenman, Joshua, Jinjarak, Yothin, 2009. The USA as the 'demander of last resort' and the implications for China's current account. Pacific Economic Review 14 (3), 426–442.

Aizenman, Joshua, Jinjarak, Yothin, Park, Donghyun, 2011. International reserves and swap lines: substitutes or complements? International Review of Economics & Finance 20 (1), 5–18.

Aizenman, Joshua, Lee, Jaewoo, 2007. International reserves: precautionary versus mercantilist views, theory and evidence. Open Economies Review 18 (2), 191–214.

Aizenman, Joshua, Marion, Nancy, 2004. International reserve holdings with sovereign risk and costly tax collection. The Economic Journal 114, 569–591.

Aizenman, Joshua, Marion, Nancy, 2011. Using inflation to erode the US public debt. Journal of Macroeconomics 33 (4), 524–541.

Aizenman, Joshua, Turnovsky, Stephen J., 2002. Reserve requirements on sovereign debt in the presence of moral hazard – on debtors or creditors? The Economic Journal 112, 107–132.

Alberola, Enrique, Erce, Aitor, Serena, José María, 2012. International reserves and gross capital flows. Dynamics during financial stress. Banco de España Working Paper 1211.

Alesina, Alberto, Tabellini, Guido, 1990. A positive theory of fiscal deficits and government debt. The Review of Economic Studies 57 (3), 403–414.

Alessandrini, Pietro, Fratianni, Michele, 2009. Resurrecting Keynes to stabilize the International Monetary System. Open Economies Review 20, 339–358.

Alfaro, Laura, Kalemli-Ozcan, Sebnem, Volosovych, Vadym, 2014. Sovereigns, upstream capital flows, and global imbalances. Journal of the European Economic Association 12 (5), 1240–1284.

Aliber, Robert Z., 1964. The costs and benefits of the U.S. role as a reserve currency country. The Quarterly Journal of Economics 78 (3), 442–456.

Armingeon, Klaus, Weisstanner, David, Engler, Sarah, Potolidis, Panajotis, Gerber, Marlène, Leimgruber, Philipp, 2011. Comparative political data set 1960–2009. Institute of Political Science, University of Bern.

Bacchetta, Philippe, Benhima, Kenza, 2015. The demand for liquid assets, corporate saving, and global imbalances. Journal of the European Economic Association 13 (6), 1101–1135.

Balakrishnan, Ravi, Bayoumi, Tamim, Tulin, Volodymyr, 2009. Rhyme or reason: what explains the easy financing of the U.S. current account deficit? IMF Staff Papers 56 (2), 410–445.

Bank of England, 2012. Statistical Interactive Database.

Barro, Robert J., 1979. On the determination of the public debt. Journal of Political Economy 87 (5), 940–971.

Barro, Robert J., 1986. U.S. deficits since World War I. Scandinavian Journal of Economics 88 (1), 195–222.

Barro, Robert J., 1987. Government spending, interest rates, prices, and budget deficits in the United Kingdom, 1701–1918. Journal of Monetary Economics 20 (2), 221–247.

Bayoumi, Tamim, Saborowski, Christian, 2014. Accounting for reserves. Journal of International Money and Finance 41, 1–29.

Becerra, Oscar, Cavallo, Eduardo, Scartascini, Carlos, 2012. The politics of financial development: the role of interest groups and government capabilities. Journal of Banking & Finance 36 (3), 626–643.

Belke, Ansgar, Gros, Daniel, 2010. Global liquidity, world savings glut and global policy coordination. DIW Discussion Paper No. 973.

Belke, Ansgar, Schnabl, Gunther, 2013. Four generations of global imbalances. Review of International Economics 21, 1–5.

Beltran, Daniel O., Kretchmer, Maxwell, Marquez, Jaime, Thomas, Charles P., 2013. Foreign holdings of U.S. Treasuries and U.S. Treasury yields. Journal of International Money and Finance 32, 1120–1143.

Ben-Bassat, Avraham, Gottlieb, Daniel, 1992. Optimal international reserves and sovereign risk. Journal of International Economics 33, 345–362.

Benigno, Gianluca, Fornaro, Luca, 2012. Reserve accumulation, growth and financial crises. CEP Discussion Paper dp1161. Centre for Economic Performance, LSE.

Benmelech, Efraim, Dvir, Eyal, 2013. Does short-term debt increase vulnerability to crisis? Evidence from the East Asian financial crisis. Journal of International Economics 89 (2), 485–494.

Bernanke, Ben, Gertler, Mark L., 1989. Agency costs, net worth, and business fluctuations. The American Economic Review 79 (1), 14–31.

Bhattarai, Saroj, Chatterjee, Arpita, Park, Woong Yong, 2015. Effects of US quantitative easing on emerging market economies. Globalization and Monetary Policy Institute Working Paper 255. Federal Reserve Bank of Dallas.

Bianchi, Javier, Hatchondo, Juan Carlos, Martinez, Leonardo, 2013. International reserves and rollover risk. IMF Working Paper 13/33.

Bird, Graham, Mandilaras, Alex, 2011. Once bitten: the effect of IMF programs on subsequent reserve behaviour. Review of Development Economics 15, 264–278.

Blanchard, Olivier, Giavazzi, Francesco, Sa, Filipa, 2005. International investors, the U.S. current account, and the dollar. Brookings Papers on Economic Activity 2005 (1), 1–49.

Blanchard, Olivier, Milesi-Ferretti, Gian Maria, 2010. Global imbalances: in midstream? In: Blanchard, Olivier, SaKong, Il (Eds.), Reconstructing the World Economy. International Monetary Fund, Washington.

Bloomfield, Arthur I., 1963. Short-term capital movements under the pre-1914 gold standard. Princeton Studies in International Finance No. 11. Princeton University.

Bohn, Henning, 1995. The sustainability of budget deficits in a stochastic economy. Journal of Money, Credit, and Banking 27 (1), 257–271.

Bohn, Henning, 1998. The behavior of U.S. public debt and deficits. The Quarterly Journal of Economics 113 (3), 949–963.

Bohn, Henning, 2005. The sustainability of fiscal policy in the United States. CESifo Working Paper No. 1446.

Bohn, Henning, 2011. The economic consequences of rising U.S. government debt: privileges at risk. FinanzArchiv: Public Finance Analysis 67 (3), 282–302.

Bordo, Michael, Eichengreen, Barry, 2001. The rise and fall of a barbarous relic: the role of gold in the international monetary system. In: Calvo, Guillermo, Dornbusch, Rüdiger, Obstfeld, Maurice (Eds.), Money, Capital Mobility, and Trade: Essays in Honor of Robert A. Mundell. MIT Press.

Bordo, Michael, Eichengreen, Barry, Klingebiel, Daniela, Martinez-Peria, Maria Soledad, 2001. Is the crisis problem growing more severe? Economic Policy 16 (32), 51–82.

Bracke, Thierry, Bussière, Matthieu, Fidora, Michael, Straub, Roland, 2008. A framework for assessing global imbalances. Occasional Paper Series 78. European Central Bank.

Branson, William H., 1977. Asset markets and relative prices in exchange rate determination. Sozialwissenschaftliche Annalen 1, 69–89.

Broner, Fernando A., Lorenzoni, Guido, Schmukler, Sergio L., 2013. Why do emerging economies borrow short term? Journal of the European Economic Association 11, 67–100.

Bulow, Jeremy, Rogoff, Kenneth, 1989. A constant recontracting model of sovereign debt. Journal of Political Economy 97 (1), 155–178.

Bussière, Matthieu, Fratzscher, Marcel, 2006. Towards a new early warning system of financial crises. Journal of International Money and Finance 25, 953–973.

Caballero, Ricardo, Farhi, Emmanuel, 2013. A model of the safe asset mechanism (SAM): safety traps and economic policy. Mimeo.

Caballero, Ricardo, Farhi, Emmanuel, Gourinchas, Pierre-Olivier, 2008. An equilibrium model of global imbalances and low interest rates. The American Economic Review 98 (1), 358–393.

Caballero, Ricardo, Krishnamurthy, Arvind, 2009. Global imbalances and financial fragility. The American Economic Review 99 (2), 584–588.

Calvo, Guillermo A., Leiderman, Leonardo, Reinhart, Carmen M., 1994. The capital inflows problem: concepts and issues. Contemporary Economic Policy 12, 54–66.

Canzoneri, Matthew, Cumby, Robert E., Diba, Behzad, Lopez-Salido, David, 2013. Key currency status: an exorbitant privilege and an extraordinary risk. Journal of International Money and Finance 37, 371–393.

Caruana, Jaime, 2014. Global liquidity: where it stands, and why it matters. IMFS Distinguished Lecture at Goethe University, Frankfurt, March 5.

Cecchetti, Stephen G., Kohler, Marion, Upper, Christian, 2009. Financial crises and economic activity. NBER Working Paper 15379.

Cerra, Valerie, Chaman Saxena, Sweta, 2008. Growth dynamics: the myth of economic recovery. The American Economic Review 98 (1), 439–457.

Chang, Roberto, Velasco, Andrés, 2000. Banks, debt maturity and financial crises. Journal of International Economics 51, 169–194.

Chen, Xiaoli, Cheung, Yin-Wong, 2011. Renminbi going global. China & World Economy 19 (2), 1–18.

Cheung, Yin-Wong, Ma, Guonan, McCauley, Robert N., 2011. Renminbising China's foreign assets. Pacific Economic Review 16 (1), 1–17.

Cheung, Yin-Wong, Qian, Xingwang, 2009. Hoarding of international reserves: Mrs. Machlup's wardrobe and the Joneses. Review of International Economics 17 (4), 824–843.

Chinn, Menzie D., Eichengreen, Barry, Ito, Hiro, 2014. A forensic analysis of global imbalances. Oxford Economic Papers 66 (2), 465–490.

Chinn, Menzie, Frankel, Jeffrey, 2007. Will the Euro eventually surpass the Dollar as leading international reserve currency? In: Clarida, Richard (Ed.), G7 Current Account Imbalances: Sustainability and Adjustment. University of Chicago Press, Chicago, pp. 285–323.

Chinn, Menzie, Frankel, Jeffrey, 2008. Why the Euro will rival the Dollar. International Finance 11 (1), 49–73.

Chinn, Menzie D., Ito, Hiro, 2006. What matters for financial development? Capital controls, institutions, and interactions. Journal of Development Economics 81 (1), 163–192.

Chinn, Menzie D., Ito, Hiro, 2007. Current account balances, financial development and institutions: assaying the world "saving glut". Journal of International Money and Finance 26, 546–569.

Chinn, Menzie D., Prasad, Eswar S., 2003. Medium-term determinants of current accounts in industrial and developing countries: an empirical exploration. Journal of International Economics 59, 47–76.

Comin, Diego A., Hobijn, Bart, 2009. The CHAT dataset. NBER Working Paper No. 15319.

Daniel, Betty C., 2001. A fiscal theory of currency crises. International Economic Review 42 (4), 969–988.

De Gregorio, José, Lee, Jong-Wha, 2004. Growth and adjustment in East Asia and Latin America. Economía 5 (1), 69–115.

De Haan, Jakob, Sturm, Jan-Egbert, 1997. Political and economic determinants of OECD budget deficits and government expenditures: a reinvestigation. European Journal of Political Economy 13, 739–750.

De Haan, Jakob, Sturm, Jan-Egbert, Beekhuis, Geert, 1999. The weak government thesis: some new evidence. Public Choice 101, 163–176.

De Paoli, Bianca, Hoggarth, Glenn, Saporta, Victoria, 2011. Costs of sovereign default. In: Kolb, Robert W. (Ed.), Sovereign Debt: From Safety to Default. Wiley, Hoboken, NJ.

De Santis, Roberto A., Luehrmann, Melanie, 2009. On the determinants of net international portfolio flows: a global perspective. Journal of International Money and Finance 28, 880–901.

Despres, Emile, Kindleberger, Charles P., Salant, Walter S., 1966. The dollar and world liquidity: a minority view. Brookings Institution Reprint 115.

Detragiache, Enrica, Spilimbergo, Antonio, 2004. Empirical models of short-term debt and crises: do they test the creditor run hypothesis? European Economic Review 48, 379–389.

Devereux, Michael D., Yetman, James, 2010. Leverage constraints and the international transmission of shocks. Journal of Money, Credit, and Banking 42 (s1), 71–105.

Diamond, Douglas W., 1991. Debt maturity structure and liquidity risk. The Quarterly Journal of Economics 106 (3), 709–737.

Dooley, Michael P., Folkerts-Landau, David, Garber, Peter, 2003. An essay on the revived Bretton Woods system. NBER Working Paper No. 9971.

Dooley, Michael, Folkerts-Landau, David, Garber, Peter M., 2004. The revived Bretton Woods system: the effects of periphery intervention and reserve management on interest rates and exchange rates in center countries. NBER Working Paper No. 10332.

Dreher, Axel, 2006. Does globalization affect growth? Evidence from a new index of globalization. Applied Economics 38 (10), 1091–1110.

Eaton, Jonathan, Gersovitz, Mark, 1981. Debt with potential repudiation: theoretical and empirical analysis. The Review of Economic Studies 48 (2), 289–309.

Eichengreen, Barry, 2007. Global Imbalances and the Lessons of Bretton Woods. MIT Press, Cambridge, MA.

Eichengreen, Barry, 2009. Out of the box thoughts about the international financial architecture. IMF Working Paper 09/116.

Eichengreen, Barry, 2011. The renminbi as an international currency. Journal of Policy Modeling 33 (5), 723–730.

Eichengreen, Barry, Flandreau, Marc, 2009. The rise and fall of the dollar (or when did the dollar replace sterling as the leading reserve currency?). European Review of Economic History 13, 377–411.

Eichengreen, Barry, Gullapalli, Rachita, Panizza, Ugo, 2011. Capital account liberalization, financial development and industry growth: a synthetic view. Journal of International Money and Finance 30 (6), 1090–1106.

Eichengreen, Barry, Kawai, Masahiro, 2014. Issues for Renminbi internationalization: an overview. ADBI Working Paper 454. Asian Development Bank Institute.

Eichengreen, Barry, Rose, Andrew, Wyplosz, Charles, 1996. Contagious currency crises: first tests. Scandinavian Journal of Economics 98 (4), 463–484.

Farhi, Emmanuel, Gourinchas, Pierre-Olivier, Rey, Hélène, 2011. Reforming the international monetary system. CEPR eReport.

Faruqee, Hamid, Lee, Jaewoo, 2009. Global dispersion of current accounts: is the universe expanding? IMF Staff Papers 56 (3), 574–595.

Favilukis, Jack, Ludvigson, Sydney C., Van Nieuwerburgh, Stijn, 2012. Foreign ownership of U.S. safe assets: good or bad? Mimeo.

Federal Reserve System, 1936. Federal Reserve Bulletin. July.

Federal Reserve System, 1948. Federal Reserve Bulletin. January.

Feldstein, Martin, 1999. Self-protection for emerging market economies. NBER Working Paper No. 6907.

Feldstein, Martin, Horioka, Charles, 1980. Domestic saving and international capital flows. The Economic Journal 90, 14–29.

Ferguson, Niall, Schularick, Moritz, 2011. The end of chimerica. International Finance 14 (1), 1–26.

Fernández, Andrés, Rebucci, Alessandro, Uribe, Martín, 2015. Are capital controls counter-cyclical? Journal of Monetary Economics 76, 1–14.

Flood, Robert P., Garber, Peter M., 1984. Collapsing exchange rate regimes: some linear examples. Journal of International Economics 17, 1–13.

Focarelli, Dario, Pozzolo, Alberto F., 2001. The patterns of cross-border bank mergers and shareholdings in OECD countries. Journal of Banking & Finance 25, 2305–2337.

Frankel, Jeffrey A., forthcoming. International coordination. In: Glick, Reuven, Spiegel, Mark M. (Eds.), Policy Challenges in a Diverging Global Economy. Federal Reserve Bank of San Francisco.

Frankel, Jeffrey A., Saravelos, George, 2012. Are leading indicators of financial crises useful for assessing country vulnerability? Evidence from the 2008–09 global crisis. Journal of International Economics 87 (2), 216–231.

Fratzscher, Marcel, 2009. What explains global exchange rate movements during the financial crisis? Journal of International Money and Finance 28, 1390–1407.

Friedrich, Christian, Schnabel, Isabel, Zettelmeyer, Jeromin, 2013. Financial integration and growth – why is emerging Europe different? Journal of International Economics 89 (2), 522–538.

Furceri, Davide, Zdzienicka, Aleksandra, 2012a. How costly are debt crises? Journal of International Money and Finance 31 (4), 726–742.

Furceri, Davide, Zdzienicka, Aleksandra, 2012b. Financial integration and fiscal policy. Open Economies Review 23 (5), 805–822.

Gagnon, Joseph E., 2012. Global imbalances and foreign asset expansion by developing-economy central banks. In: Bank for International Settlements (Ed.), Are Central Bank Balance Sheets in Asia Too Large? In: BIS Papers, vol. 66, pp. 168–185.

Gagnon, Joseph, 2013. The elephant hiding in the room: currency intervention and trade imbalances. Peterson Institute for International Economics, Working Paper 13-2.

Gemmill, Robert F., 1961. Interest rates and foreign dollar balances. The Journal of Finance 16 (3), 363–376.

Ghosh, Indradeep, 2011. Imperfect asset substitutability and current account dynamics. Review of Development Economics 15 (1), 66–77.

Gourinchas, Pierre-Olivier, Jeanne, Olivier, 2012. Global safe assets. Mimeo.

Gourinchas, Pierre-Olivier, Obstfeld, Maurice, 2012. Stories of the twentieth century for the twenty-first. American Economic Journal: Macroeconomics 4 (1), 226–265.

Gourinchas, Pierre-Oliver, Rey, Hélène, 2007. From world banker to world venture capitalist: US external adjustment and the exorbitant privilege. In: Clarida, Richard (Ed.), G-7 Current Account Imbalances: Sustainability and Adjustment. University of Chicago Press, Chicago.

Gourinchas, Pierre-Olivier, Rey, Hélène, Govillot, Nicolas, 2010. Exorbitant privilege and exorbitant duty. IMES Discussion Paper Series 10-E-20. Bank of Japan.

Grilli, Vittorio, Masciandaro, Donato, Tabellini, Guido, 1991. Political and monetary institutions and public financial policies in the industrial countries. Economic Policy 6 (13), 341–392.

Grossman, Herschel I., Van Huyck, John B., 1988. Sovereign debt as a contingent claim: excusable default, repudiation, and reputation. The American Economic Review 78 (5), 1088–1097.

Group of Ten, 1965. Report of the study group on the creation of reserve assets (Ossola Report).

Gruber, Joseph W., Kamin, Steven B., 2007. Explaining the global pattern of current account imbalances. Journal of International Money and Finance 26, 500–522.

Habib, Maurizio M., Stracca, Livio, 2012. Getting beyond carry trade: what makes a safe haven currency? Journal of International Economics 87 (1), 50–64.

Hall, Robert E., 2009. Reconciling cyclical movements in the marginal value of time and the marginal product of labor. Journal of Political Economy 117 (2), 281–323.

Helbling, Thomas, Berezin, Peter, Kose, Ayhan, Kumhof, Michael, Laxton, Doug, Spatafora, Nikola, 2007. Decoupling the train? Spillovers and cycles in the global economy. In: World Economic Outlook. International Monetary Fund. Chapter 4, April.

Heller, Heinz R., 1966. Optimal international reserves. The Economic Journal 76, 296–311.

Henderson, Dale W., Rogoff, Kenneth, 1982. Negative net foreign asset positions and stability in a world portfolio balance model. Journal of International Economics 13, 85–104.

Hutchison, Michael M., 2003. A cure worse than the disease? Currency crises and the output costs of IMF-supported stabilization programs. In: Dooley, Michael P., Frankel, Jeffrey A. (Eds.), Managing Currency Crises in Emerging Markets. University of Chicago Press.

Hutchison, Michael M., Noy, Ilan, 2002. Output costs of currency and balance of payments crises in emerging markets. Comparative Economic Studies 44 (2–3), 27–44.

IMF, 2000. Debt- and reserve-related indicators of external vulnerability. Prepared by the Policy Development and Review Department in consultation with other departments.

IMF, 2009a. World Economic Outlook: Crisis and Recovery. April.

IMF, 2009b. What's the damage? Medium-term output dynamics after financial crises. In: World Economic Outlook. Chapter 4, October.

IMF, 2009c. Balance of Payments and International Investment Position Manual, sixth edition. BPM6, Washington, DC.

IMF, 2010a. Reserve accumulation and international monetary stability. Paper prepared by the Strategy, Policy and Review Department.

IMF, 2010b. Global liquidity expansion: effects on "receiving" economies and policy response options. In: Global Financial Stability Report. World Economic and Financial Surveys, Washington. April.

IMF, 2011a. International Financial Statistics. Online database.

IMF, 2011b. Enhancing international monetary stability – a role for the SDR? Paper prepared by the Strategy, Policy, and Review Department.

IMF, 2012. Global Financial Stability Report. Chapter 3, April.

IMF, 2013. International Financial Statistics. Online database.

Irwin, Douglas A., 2012. The French gold sink and the great deflation. Cato Papers on Public Policy 2 (2012-13), 3–41.

Jeanne, Olivier, 2007. International reserves in emerging market countries: too much of a good thing? Brookings Papers on Economic Activity 38 (1), 1–80.

Jeanne, Olivier, Rancière, Romain, 2011. The optimal level of international reserves for emerging market countries: a new formula and some applications. The Economic Journal 121, 905–930.

Jordà, Òscar, Schularick, Moritz, Taylor, Alan M., 2013. When credit bites back. Journal of Money, Credit, and Banking 45 (s2), 3–28.

Joyce, Joseph P., Noy, Ilan, 2008. The IMF and the liberalization of capital flows. Review of International Economics 16 (3), 413–430.

Kapp, Daniel, Vega, Marco, 2012. The real output costs of financial crisis: a loss distribution approach. Working Paper 2012-013. Banco Central de Reserva del Perú.

Kenen, Peter B., 1960. International liquidity and the balance of payments of a reserve-currency country. The Quarterly Journal of Economics 74 (4), 572–586.

Kim, Soyoung, Roubini, Nouriel, 2008. Twin deficit or twin divergence? Fiscal policy, current account, and real exchange rate in the U.S. Journal of International Economics 74 (2), 362–383.

Kindleberger, Charles P., 1969. Europe and the Dollar, 2. pr. MIT Press, Cambridge, MA.

Kitchen, John, Chinn, Menzie, 2011. Financing U.S. debt: is there enough money in the world – and at what cost? International Finance 14, 373–413.

Kiyotaki, Nobuhiro, Moore, John H., 1997. Credit cycles. Journal of Political Economy 105 (2), 211–248.

Klingen, Christoph, Weder, Beatrice, Zettelmeyer, Jeromin, 2004. How private creditors fared in emerging debt markets, 1970–2000. IMF Working Paper 04/13.

Korinek, Anton, 2011. Hot money and serial financial crises. IMF Economic Review 59 (2), 306–339.

Korinek, Anton, Servén, Luis, 2016. Undervaluation through foreign reserve accumulation: static losses, dynamic gains. Journal of International Money and Finance 64, 104–136.

Kose, M. Ayhan, Otrok, Christopher, Whiteman, Charles H., 2003. International business cycles: world, region, and country-specific factors. The American Economic Review 93 (4), 1216–1239.

Kose, M. Ayhan, Prasad, Eswar S., Rogoff, Kenneth, Wie, Shang-Jin, 2009a. Financial globalization: a reappraisal. IMF Staff Papers 56 (1), 8–62.

Kose, M. Ayhan, Prasad, Eswar, Terrones, Marco E., 2009b. Does openness to international financial flows raise productivity growth? Journal of International Money and Finance 28 (4), 554–580.

Kouri, Pentti J.K., 1983. The balance of payments and the foreign exchange market: a dynamic partial equilibrium model. In: Bhandari, Jagdeep S., Putnam, Bluford H. (Eds.), Economic Interdependence and Flexible Exchange Rates. MIT Press, Cambridge, MA.

Krishnamurthy, Arvind, Vissing-Jorgensen, Annette, 2012. The aggregate demand for treasury debt. Journal of Political Economy 120 (2), 233–267.

Krugman, Paul R., 1979. A model of balance-of-payments crises. Journal of Money, Credit, and Banking 11 (3), 311–325.

Landau, Jean-Pierre, 2013. Global liquidity: public and private. In: Proceedings – Economic Policy Symposium – Jackson Hole. Federal Reserve Bank of Kansas City.

Lane, Philip, Milesi-Ferretti, Gian Maria, 2003. International financial integration. IMF Staff Papers 50, 82–113.

Lane, Philip, Milesi-Ferretti, Gian Maria, 2007. The external wealth of nations mark II: revised and extended estimates of foreign assets and liabilities, 1970–2004. Journal of International Economics 73 (2), 223–250.

Lane, Philip, Milesi-Ferretti, Gian Maria, 2011. The cross-country incidence of the global crisis. IMF Economic Review 59 (1), 77–110.

Laubach, Thomas, 2009. New evidence on the interest rate effects of budget deficits and debt. Journal of the European Economic Association 7 (4), 858–885.

League of Nations, 1925. Memorandum on Currency and Central Banks, 1913–1924, vol. 1. Geneva.

Li, Jie, Rajan, Ramkishen S., 2009. Can high reserves offset weak fundamentals? A simple model of precautionary demand for reserves. Economia Internazionale (International Economics) LIX, 317–328.

Lindert, Peter H., 1967. Key currencies and gold exchange standard, 1900–1913. Dissertation. Cornell University.

Lindert, Peter H., 1969. Key currencies and gold 1900–1913. Princeton Studies in International Finance No. 24. Princeton University.

Lucas, Robert E., 1976. Econometric policy evaluation: a critique. Carnegie–Rochester Conference Series on Public Policy 1, 19–46.

Maggiori, Matteo, 2013. Financial intermediation, international risk sharing, and reserve currencies. Mimeo. New York University.

Marshall, Monty G., Jaggers, Keith, 2011. Polity IV project: political regime characteristics and transitions, 1800–2010. Available at: http://www.systemicpeace.org/polity/polity4.htm.

Mateos y Lago, Isabelle, Duttagupta, Rupa, Goyal, Rishi, 2009. The debate on the International Monetary System. IMF Staff Position Note 09/26.

Meissner, Christopher C., 2010. Surplus reversals in large nations: the cases of France and Great Britain in the interwar period. In: Claessens, Stijn, Evenett, Simon J., Hoekman, Bernard (Eds.), Rebalancing the Global Economy: A Primer for Policymaking. CEPR, London.

Mendoza, Enrique G., Quadrini, Vincenzo, Ríos-Rull, José-Víctor, 2009. Financial integration, financial development, and global imbalances. Journal of Political Economy 117 (3), 371–416.

Mitchell, Brian, 2007. International Historical Statistics (Europe 1750–2005). Palgrave.

Mlynarski, Feliks, 1929. Gold and Central Banks. Macmillan, New York.

Morris, Stephen, Shin, Hyun Song, 2008. Financial regulation in a system context. Brookings Papers on Economic Activity, 229–261.

Nurske, Ragnar, 1944. International Currency Experience: Lessons of the Interwar Period. League of Nations, Geneva.

Obstfeld, Maurice, 1996. Models of currency crises with self-fulfilling features. European Economic Review 40, 1037–1047.

Obstfeld, Maurice, 2009. International finance and growth in developing countries: what have we learned? IMF Staff Papers 56 (1), 63–111.

Obstfeld, Maurice, 2011a. International liquidity: the fiscal dimension. NBER Working Paper No. 17379.

Obstfeld, Maurice, 2011b. The international monetary system: living with asymmetry. CEPR Discussion Paper No. DP8703.

Obstfeld, Maurice, 2011c. The SDR as an international reserve asset: what future? International Growth Center, Rapid Response 11/0885. London School of Economics.

Obstfeld, Maurice, 2014. The international monetary system: living with asymmetry. NBER Chapters. In: Feenstra, Robert C., Taylor, Alan M. (Eds.), Globalization in an Age of Crisis: Multilateral Economic Cooperation in the Twenty-First Century. University of Chicago Press.

Obstfeld, Maurice, Rogoff, Kenneth, 2010. Global imbalances and the financial crisis: products of common causes. In: Asia Economic Policy Conference Volume: Asia and the Global Financial Crisis. Federal Reserve Bank of San Francisco, pp. 131–172.

Obstfeld, Maurice, Shambaugh, Jay C., Taylor, Alan M., 2009. Financial instability, reserves, and central bank swap lines in the panic of 2008. The American Economic Review 99 (2), 480–486.

Obstfeld, Maurice, Shambaugh, Jay C., Taylor, Alan M., 2010. Financial stability, the trilemma, and international reserves. American Economic Journal: Macroeconomics 2 (2), 57–94.

Obstfeld, Maurice, Taylor, Alan M., 2003. Globalization and capital markets. In: Bordo, Michael D., Taylor, Alan M., Williamson, Jeffrey G. (Eds.), Globalization in Historical Perspective. University of Chicago Press.

Officer, Lawrence H., Willett, Thomas D., 1969. Reserve-asset preferences and the confidence problem in the crisis zone. The Quarterly Journal of Economics 83 (4), 688–695.

Øksendal, Lars Fredrik, 2008. Monetary policy under the gold standard – examining the case of Norway, 1893–1914. Norges Bank Working Paper 2008/14.

Papaioannou, Elias, Portes, Richard, Siourounis, Gregorios, 2006. Optimal currency shares in international reserves: the impact of the euro and the prospects for the dollar. Journal of the Japanese and International Economies 20, 508–547.

Passari, Evgenia, Rey, Hélène, 2015. Financial flows and the international monetary system. The Economic Journal 125 (584), 675–698.

Portes, Richard, 2009. Global imbalances. In: Dewatripont, Mathias, Freixas, Xavier, Portes, Richard (Eds.), Macroeconomic Stability and Financial Regulation: Key Issues for the G20. CEPR, London.

Prades, Elvira, Rabitsch, Katrin, 2012. Capital liberalization and the US external imbalance. Journal of International Economics 87 (1), 36–49.

Prasad, Eswar S., 2011. Role reversal in global finance. NBER Working Paper No. 17497.

Prasad, Eswar S., Rogoff, Kenneth, Wei, Shang-Jin, Kose, M. Ayhan, 2007. Financial globalization, growth and volatility in developing countries. In: Harrison, Ann (Ed.), Globalization and Poverty. National Bureau of Economic Research, Inc.

Prescott, Edward C., 1986. Theory ahead of business cycle measurement. Carnegie–Rochester Conference Series on Public Policy 25, 11–44.

Radelet, Steven, Sachs, Jeffrey D., 1998. The East Asian financial crisis: diagnosis, remedies, prospects. Brookings Papers on Economic Activity 1, 1–90.

Rancière, Romain, Tornell, Aaron, Westermann, Frank, 2008. Systemic crises and growth. The Quarterly Journal of Economics 123 (1), 359–406.

Reinhart, Carmen, Kaminsky, Graciela, 2008. The center and the periphery: the globalization of financial turmoil. In: Flows, Crisis, and Stabilization: Essays in Honor of Guillermo A. Calvo, pp. 171–216.

Reinhart, Carmen M., Rogoff, Kenneth S., 2008. This time is different: a panoramic view of eight centuries of financial crises. NBER Working Paper No. 13882.

Reinhart, Carmen M., Rogoff, Kenneth S., 2009. The aftermath of financial crises. The American Economic Review 99 (2), 466–472.

Reinhart, Carmen M., Rogoff, Kenneth S., 2011. From financial crash to debt crisis. The American Economic Review 101 (5), 1676–1706.

Reinhart, Carmen M., Rogoff, Kenneth S., Savastano, Miguel A., 2003. Debt intolerance. Brookings Papers on Economic Activity 2003 (1), 1–62.

Rey, Hélène, 2015. Dilemma not trilemma: the global financial cycle and monetary policy independence. NBER Working Paper 21162.

Rodrik, Dani, Velasco, Andrés, 2000. Short-term capital flows. In: Pleskovic, Boris, Stiglitz, Joseph E. (Eds.), Proceedings of the Annual World Bank Conference on Development Economics 1999. The World Bank, Washington, DC.

Roubini, Nouriel, Sachs, Jeffrey D., 1989a. Political and economic determinants of budget deficits in the industrial democracies. European Economic Review 33 (5), 903–933.

Roubini, Nouriel, Sachs, Jeffrey D., 1989b. Government spending and budget deficits in the industrial countries. Economic Policy 8, 99–132.

Sá, Filipa, Viani, Francesca, 2013. Shifts in portfolio preferences of international investors: an application to sovereign wealth funds. Review of International Economics 21, 868–885.

Schenk, Catherine, 2011. The retirement of sterling as a reserve currency after 1945: lessons for the US dollar? Mimeo.

Schindler, Martin, 2009. Measuring financial integration: a new data set. IMF Staff Papers 56 (1), 222–238.

Schnabl, Gunther, Freitag, Stephan, 2012. Reverse causality in global and intra-European imbalances. Review of International Economics 20 (4), 674–690.

Schularick, Moritz, Taylor, Alan M., 2012. Credit booms gone bust: monetary policy, leverage cycles, and financial crises, 1870–2008. American Economic Review 102 (2), 1029–1061.

Sinn, Hans-Werner, 2014. The Euro Trap. On Bursting Bubbles, Budgets, and Beliefs. Oxford University Press.

Sinn, Hans-Werner, Wollmershäuser, Timo, 2012. Target loans, current account balances and capital flows: the ECB's rescue facility. International Tax and Public Finance 19 (4), 468–508.

Song, Zhang, Storesletten, Kjetil, Zilibotti, Fabrizio, 2011. Growing like China. The American Economic Review 101, 202–241.

Spiegel, Mark M., 2009. Financial globalization and monetary policy discipline: a survey with new evidence from financial remoteness. IMF Staff Papers 56 (1), 198–221.

Staiger, Douglas, Stock, James H., 1997. Instrumental variables regression with weak instruments. Econometrica 65 (3), 557–586.

Steiner, Andreas, 2013. A tale of two deficits: public budget balance of reserve currency countries. Institute of Empirical Economic Research Working Paper No. 97. University of Osnabrück.

Steiner, Andreas, 2014a. Current account balance and dollar standard: exploring the linkages. Journal of International Money and Finance 41, 65–94.

Steiner, Andreas, 2014b. Reserve accumulation and financial crises: from individual protection to systemic risk? European Economic Review 70, 126–144.

Tavlas, George S., 1997. The international use of the US dollar: an Optimum Currency Area perspective. World Economy 20, 709–747.

Taylor, Alan M., 2013. The future of international liquidity and the role of China. Journal of Applied Corporate Finance 25, 86–94.

Tillmann, Peter, 2014. Unconventional monetary policy shocks and the spillovers to emerging markets. HKIMR Working Paper No. 18/2014.

Triffin, Robert, 1960. Gold and the Dollar Crisis. Yale University Press.

Troutman, Mark D., 2010. Dominance shifts and international currency leadership: past patterns and future prospects. Dissertation. Department of Economics, George Mason University, Fairfax, VA.

Tujula, Mika, Wolswijk, Guido, 2007. Budget balances in OECD countries: what makes them change? Empirica 34 (1), 1–14.

U.S. Census Bureau, 2003. Statistical abstract of the United States: 2003 (No. HS-3). Population by age: 1900 to 2002. Available at: http://www.census.gov/statab/hist/HS-03.pdf.

Vitek, Francis, 2012. Policy analysis and forecasting in the world economy: a panel unobserved components approach. IMF Working Paper 12/149.

Warnock, Francis E., 2010. How dangerous is U.S. government debt? The risks of a sudden spike in U.S. interest rates. Capital Flows Quarterly, 2010 Q2. Council on Foreign Relations.

Warnock, Francis E., Cacdac Warnock, Veronica, 2009. International capital flows and U.S. interest rates. Journal of International Money and Finance 28, 903–919.

Westermann, Frank, 2014. Discussion of "TARGET2 and central bank balance sheets". Economic Policy 29 (77), 117–125.

Williamson, John, 1973. Surveys in applied economics: international liquidity. The Economic Journal 83, 685–746.

Woo, Jaejoon, 2003. Economic, political, and institutional determinants of public deficits. Journal of Public Economics 87, 387–426.

World Bank, 2010. World Development Indicators.

World Bank, 2011. World Development Indicators.

World Bank, 2012. World Development Indicators.

World Bank, 2013. World Development Indicators.

Index

A

Accumulated reserves, 30, 130, 135
Accumulation
  of debt, 28
  of foreign reserves, 120
  of net reserve assets, 33
  of reserve currency bonds, 90
  of various currencies reserves, 28, 76, 131, 162
Asset prices, 33, 82, 164, 165
Assets
  central bank reserve, 74
  dollar reserve, 57, 94
  domestic, 13, 32
  dominant global reserve, 172
  important reserve, 79, 132
  net foreign, 11, 39
  reserve-currency, 90
  safe, 31, 74, 109
  supranational reserve, 162, 164
  total, 22, 23, 36, 155
Average capital flows, 16

B

Balance of payments, 13, 33, 60, 61, 123
Balance sheet, 36, 62, 170
  crises, 122
Banking crises, 8, 123, 155, 156, 165
Bonds
  domestic, 129, 168, 170, 171
  foreign reserve, 73
  reserve-currency, 45, 51
Borrower, 13, 32, 84, 136
British Pound, 41, 57
Budget balance, 44, 104
Budget constraints, 83, 133
Buffer stocks, 32, 33

C

Capital, 15, 23, 61, 165
  inflows, 13, 48
  outflows, 13, 48, 164

Capital controls, 1, 48, 53, 64
Capital flight, 53, 125, 170
Capital flows, 1, 2, 12, 13, 30, 49
Cash, 62, 63, 109, 170
Central bank
  assets, 168
  balance sheets, 170
  cooperation, 164
  functions, 166
Central Bank Gold Agreement, 167
Central bank intervention, 32, 121
Central bank money, 170, 171
Central bank swap lines, 171
Central bank transactions, 61, 169
Central banks
  domestic, 165
  global, 120
  independent, 167, 169–171
  major, 166, 167
  national, 168, 171
Civil liberties, 48, 49, 53, 64, 110
Claims, 19, 23, 24, 152, 171
Collateral, 72, 125, 164, 171
Commercial banks, 62, 168–171
Confidence, 60, 78, 125
  loss of, 108, 109, 125
Consumption, 152
Convertibility, 75, 77, 79
Cooperation, 162, 165–167
Counterbalancing operations, 33, 62
Countries
  advanced, 40, 108, 122
  average deficit, 7
  average surplus, 7
  capital-poor, 40
  capital-receiving, 1
  capital-rich, 28
  developing, 145
  dominant center, 61
  emerging, 1, 23, 85, 107, 143
  financial center, 127
  indebted, 23, 88
  key currency, 29, 31

Countries (*cont.*)
  non-accumulating, 3, 121
  non-reserve currency, 55, 62, 127
  oil-exporting, 6, 40, 49
  peer, 89
  periphery, 30, 123, 143
  representative reserve-hoarding, 127
  reserve-accumulating, 28, 131
Creation of new SDRs, 164
Creation of the Euro, 79
Creation of the Federal Reserve System, 77
Credit ceiling, 82, 126, 129, 133
Creditor, 11, 12, 19
  international, 129, 130
Creditor countries, 23, 28, 88
Credits, 38, 129, 169
  domestic, 156
  refinancing, 168, 170, 171
Crises, 1, 55, 121, 123, 166, 168
  domestic, 122
  sovereign, 8, 122
Crisis
  global, 120, 132, 138, 151, 166
  prevention, 120, 145, 162
  probability, 125, 132, 140, 145
  zone, 60, 125
Currency, 28, 143, 154, 163
  crises, 8, 122, 129
  gold-convertible, 75, 77
  shares, 85
  structure, 11
  union, 170

D
De jure openness, 9, 64
Debt, 32, 82, 84, 108, 126
Decreasing global reserve levels, 55, 130
Deficit countries, 38, 171
Deficit/surplus of consolidated central
    government, 63, 109
Deficits
  balanced, 77
  public, 39, 74
Democracy, 100, 110
Depletion of US gold reserves, 167
Deposits, 8, 11
Devaluation, 77–79, 82, 139
Developing countries, 10, 24, 44, 143
Development aid, 12–14, 16, 19, 23, 172

Development Assistance Committee (DAC),
  12
Diversification of reserves, 163
Dollar
  assets, 45, 77, 78, 81, 86
  dominance, 3, 78, 81, 96, 103, 108
  exchange reserves, 72
  reserves, 3, 28, 30, 38, 77, 96
Domestic economies, 13, 120
Domestic reserve accumulation, 53
Domestic reserve policies, 171
Dual reserve currency system, 76
Dutch Guilder, 57

E
East Asian financial crisis, 15, 19, 85, 120,
  151
Economic shocks, 84
Emerging markets, 23, 45, 60, 90, 147
Equilibrium, 31, 32, 34, 36, 37, 58, 73
Euro, 55, 57, 61, 79, 90
Euro area, 168
Euro reserves, 57
European Central Bank (ECB), 110, 168
European central banks, 78, 167
European System of Central Banks (ESCB),
  169
European Systemic Risk Board (ESRB), 166
European Union, 161, 166, 168
Exchange, 36, 170
Exchange rate, 36, 45, 51, 155, 164
Exchange reserves, 51, 58, 76–79, 86, 112
Exports, 40
External debt, 137, 156, 160
External liabilities, 40, 139, 152
External savings, 152
External shocks, 40, 88, 96, 103, 110

F
Federal Reserve Banks, 171
Federal Reserve System, 75, 77, 171
Financial center status, 48
Financial centers, 28, 48, 53, 89, 96
Financial crisis
  Asian, 1
  domestic, 122, 143
  global, 7, 13, 19, 108, 121, 132, 151
  local, 125, 129
Financial development, 31, 49, 82
Financial globalization, 1, 9

Financial integration, 9, 89, 161, 165, 166
Financial liberalization, 1
Financial markets, 31, 38, 40, 57, 92, 104, 108
Financial openness, 1, 9, 25, 120
Financial Sector Assessment Program (FSAP), 166
Financial shocks, 143
Financial stability, 110, 121, 123, 165, 166
Financial system, 3, 60, 90, 119, 162
Fiscal balances, 3, 10, 73, 74, 92, 96
Fiscal capacity, 60, 125, 136, 139
Fiscal deficits, 72, 73
Flexible Credit Line (FCL), 162
Foreign asset position, 5, 11, 53, 60, 74, 120
Foreign assets (FA), 11, 19, 79, 139
Foreign capital, 19
Foreign central banks, 32, 61, 94
    finance, 107
Foreign direct investment (FDI), 11, 13, 163
Foreign exchange, 41, 51, 72, 75, 170
    reserves, 13, 28, 32, 40, 44, 74, 75, 85
Foreign goods, 34
Foreign liabilities (FL), 22, 37, 60, 64, 111, 120, 125
Foreign monetary assets, 61, 62
Foreign official institutions, 42, 51, 58, 80, 87, 94, 107, 120, 153
Foreign sovereigns, 78
Foreigners, 10, 13, 16, 62, 74, 78
French Franc, 41, 57, 77, 96, 108
FSAP (Financial Sector Assessment Program), 166
Fuel exports, 40, 49, 64

G
GDP growth, 40, 87, 153
German Mark, 41, 55, 57, 79, 108
German public budget balance, 104
Global deficit, 38, 124
Global foreign exchange holdings, 40, 76
Global imbalances, 2, 5, 30, 120
Global liquidity spillovers, 161, 164
Global reserves, 140, 163
Gold assets, 29
Gold Pool, 167
Gold reserves, 75
Gold-exchange, 75
Government bonds, 72, 79, 103

Government budget balance, 39, 44, 63
Government debt, 72, 84, 88, 96, 104
Government securities, 72, 74
Government spending, 84
Governments, 61, 74, 87
Gross national income (GNI), 12
Growth rate, 65, 84, 88, 110
    nominal GDP, 83, 155, 156

H
Historical data, 74, 85, 88, 107, 110, 111
Home bonds, 73

I
Imbalances, 5, 28, 168
    intra-European, 168
IMF, 1, 13, 33, 51, 72, 120, 163, 164, 166
Imports, 2, 40, 64, 110
Income effect, 84
Indebtedness, 2, 19, 120, 152, 162
Index
    Chinn–Ito, 9, 48
    civil liberties measures personal freedom, 48
    democracy, 89
    Edwards, 9
    Schindler, 10
    the real effective exchange rate, 156
Individual countries hoard, 135
Industrial countries, 10, 13, 23, 49
Industrialized countries, 19, 44, 85, 107, 133, 167
Inflation, 2, 60, 87, 108
Instabilities, 78, 119, 126, 163
Instrumental variables approach, 45, 49
Insurance, 28, 32, 123
Interest rates, 32, 33, 80, 88, 90, 96, 104, 126, 141
International monetary system, 28, 60, 75, 152, 161, 172
    reform, 161, 172
International reserves, 2, 13, 72, 85, 119, 122, 151
Investment, 5, 11, 39, 40, 151
Investors, 11, 31, 35, 36, 60, 103

J
Japanese Yen, 41, 78, 86

K

Key currencies, 3, 28, 31, 86

L

Latin American Reserve Fund, 163
Least Developed Countries (LDCs), 12
Lenders, 8, 82, 126, 129, 164
Liabilities, 11, 23, 24, 28, 62, 137, 170
Liquidity, 164, 165
Loans, 11, 32
  outstanding development, 24

M

Marginal effect, 139, 140
Marginal social benefit, 136
Market capitalization, 49, 89
Market price, 51, 167
Markets
  large stock, 49, 89
  world capital, 1
Maturity, 11, 137
Military expenditures, 88, 96, 103, 110
Minimum reserve requirement, 169
Monetary policies, 30, 126, 165, 166
Monetary union, 168
Money, 63, 75, 110, 165
Multilateral institutions, 12

N

National central banks (NCB), 168
National currencies, 29, 59, 61, 72, 108, 151,
  162, 164
National institutions, 165, 166
Negative effects, 45, 134, 146
Negative externality, 121, 127, 130
Net capital flows, 15, 170
Net of repayments, 12
Net reserves, 120, 124, 125, 131, 138, 139
Netherlands Guilder, 41, 86
Nominal GDP, 15, 22, 63, 83, 155, 156
Non-high income countries, 15

O

Official agencies, 12
Official capital flows, 7, 12, 39
Official development aid (ODA), 12
Official entities, 12, 45, 165
Openness, 23, 75

Outlier, 30, 55, 57, 100
Output costs, 122, 131, 141
Output growth, 139, 164
Overborrowing externalities, 136

P

Payments, 8, 37, 155, 170
  deficit, 79, 171
  imbalances, 169
Periphery, 75
Pigouvian tax, 135, 136
Policies
  active central bank, 53
  fiscal, 73
Political factors, 73
Population, 39, 63, 64, 109
Portfolio balance model, 3, 33
Positive productivity shock, 129
Precautionary Credit Line (PCL), 162
Present consumption, 84
Price
  collateral, 164
  debt, 126
  foreign goods, 34
  gold, 78, 167
  government bonds, 73
  loans, 32
Private agents, 23, 29
Private capital, 30
Private financial openness, 23
Private investors, 11, 35, 36, 48
Probability
  of a crisis, 138, 154
  of a currency crisis, 129, 156
  of a domestic financial crisis, 143
  of a financial crisis, 121
  of a global crisis, 133
  of a global financial crisis, 134
  of a local crisis, 132
  of a local financial crisis, 125, 129
  of a sovereign debt crisis, 108
  of an output loss, 143
Public balances, 96
Public budget balance, 73, 92, 94
Public budget deficits, 88, 103
Public debt, 74, 108
Public finance, 3, 73
Purchase, 13, 103, 104

R

Ratio of reserves, 77
Real GDP, 45, 72, 92, 96, 109
Regressions, 39, 46, 49, 55, 88, 104, 107, 156
Relative income, 44, 49, 57, 64, 88
Renminbi, 61, 79, 163
  reserve assets, 79
Repayments, 12, 129
Reserve accumulation, 2, 32, 51, 53, 59, 78,
    120, 129, 136, 151, 165
  global, 2, 3, 30, 59, 132, 151
  massive, 77, 167
Reserve asset composition, 79
Reserve asset preferences, 78
Reserve assets, 32, 34, 36, 39
  German, 55
  US, 30, 42, 51
Reserve changes, 39, 53, 134
  annual, 86
Reserve composition, 40, 41, 124
Reserve country, 55, 104, 126, 127, 139
Reserve country GDP, 139
Reserve currencies, 32, 60, 75, 86, 103, 108,
    162, 163
  dominant, 76, 96, 108
  global, 61, 76, 108
  important, 76–78
  major, 28, 41, 76, 86
  potential, 79
  secondary, 51, 55, 57, 94, 103, 108, 139
  single dominant, 163
  world's, 123
Reserve currency assets, 40, 139
Reserve currency bonds, 32, 89, 90, 129
Reserve currency countries, 30, 55, 57, 62,
    65, 72, 74, 78, 80, 120, 121, 123, 131,
    136, 138
Reserve currency countries outliers, 100
Reserve currency provider, 2, 30, 31, 33, 36,
    61, 74, 131
Reserve currency status, 31, 33, 59, 61, 80,
    83–85, 100, 103, 107
Reserve flows, 10, 19
Reserve hoardings, 32, 123, 136, 164
  taxing, 136
Reserve holdings, 12, 36, 62, 77, 119, 121,
    137, 138, 147
Reserve income, 151
Reserve level, 132

Reserve liabilities, 60
Reserve policies, 2, 8, 12, 30, 86, 167
Reserve pool, 162
Reserve position, 13, 62, 72
Reserve preference shock, 37
Reserve provider, 123, 131
Reserve sales, 55, 85
Reserve status, 33
  shock, 36
  US, 37
Reserve stocks, 13, 85
Reserve-providing countries, 39, 72, 80, 83
Reserves
  aggregate, 85
  confiscate, 130
  dollar, 28, 78, 96, 162
  excess, 171
  fiduciary, 151
  first, 77
  foreign, 35, 44, 73, 120
  franc, 94
  hoarding, 136
  mark, 94, 96
  mitigating effect of, 133, 134
  optimal, 127, 132
  sizable dollar, 76
  world, 85
  worldwide, 77
  worldwide level of, 40, 124
Reserves finance, 171
Return, 12, 32, 34, 82, 126, 132, 138, 147
Ricardian equivalence, 39, 44, 84
Risk premium, 141
Robustness, 41, 46, 48, 66, 107, 112, 136,
    145

S

Sales, 13, 41, 51
Saving, 5, 39, 153
Schindler index, 10
Short-term debt, 11, 138
Social planner, 126, 134, 135
Socially optimal solution, 4, 145, 147
Sovereign debt, 2, 3, 9, 73, 83, 84, 108, 156
Sovereign debt crises, 8, 108, 123, 143,
    154–156, 160
Special drawing rights (SDRs), 13, 72, 131,
    164
Speculative attacks, 122

Spillovers, 138, 143, 145, 151, 165, 166
Stability
  of each individual country, 127
  of exchange rates, 77
  of the entire system, 127
  of the monetary system, 167
  of the reserve currency, 108, 135
Sterling
  area, 78, 79
  dominance, 60, 75, 81, 94, 100, 104
  global reserves, 94, 96, 104
  pound, 57, 60, 75–79, 86, 94, 103
  reserves, 77, 78, 85, 86, 90, 103
Stocks, 5, 9, 11, 12, 22, 34, 62, 166
Substitute, 58, 73, 77, 81, 135, 161, 162, 168,
  171
Surplus, 6, 38, 48, 53, 59, 77, 138
Surplus countries, 30, 38, 171
Sustainability, 5, 108
Swap lines, 134, 167
Swiss Franc, 41, 86
Systemic risk, 2, 127, 140, 148
Systemic risk creation, 121, 145, 147

T
Target assets (TA), 168–171
Target balances, 161, 168, 170, 171
Target liabilities (TL), 168, 169, 171
Target system, 168–171
Tax, 63, 87, 96, 135, 151
Tax rate, 73, 135, 138, 140
Trade, 2, 28, 30, 40, 75, 88, 119, 163
Trade balance, 77, 138
Trade imbalances, 77
Trade openness, 40, 45, 46, 49, 51, 88, 110

Trade surplus, 34, 35, 37
Transfer
  of gold certificates, 171
  of know-how, 11
  of money, 63, 169, 170
  of securities, 171
  of wealth, 123
Treasuries, 32, 41, 78, 80, 82
Trend GDP, 16
Triffin dilemma, 3, 29, 37, 59, 61

U
UK GDP, 90, 94, 96
Unemployment, 88, 90, 96, 108
US assets, 30, 36, 59, 78
US dollars, 8, 42, 64, 78, 109, 163
US Federal Reserve, 166
US GDP, 28, 30, 41, 60, 76, 90, 94
US gold reserves, 78, 167

V
Valuation effects, 5, 6, 11, 132
Volume effects, 140

W
Wars, 73, 88, 92, 100, 103
Wealth, 32, 34, 123
World Bank classification, 12, 16
World GDP, 6, 15
World gold production, 139
World interest rate, 58, 90, 104
World policy rate, 92, 94
Worldwide level of real reserves, 120
Worldwide official gold holdings, 167

Printed in the United States
By Bookmasters